THE ECONOMICS OF CRIME AND PUNISHMENT

A conference sponsored by
American Enterprise Institute
for Public Policy Research

American Enterprise Institute for Public Policy Research
Washington, D. C.

ISBN 0-8447-2041-0 (Paper)
ISBN 0-8447-2042-9 (Cloth)
Library of Congress Catalog Card Number L.C. 73-86979

Printed in the United States of America

THE ECONOMICS OF
CRIME AND PUNISHMENT

MAJOR CONTRIBUTORS

Annelise Anderson
The Hoover Institution on War, Revolution and Peace, Stanford University

William C. Bailey
Professor, Department of Sociology, The Cleveland State University

Dagobert L. Brito
Professor, Department of Economics, University of Wisconsin at Madison

James M. Buchanan
Professor, Department of Economics
Virginia Polytechnic Institute and State University

William E. Cobb
Director, Research Division, West Virginia Tax Department

John Ll. J. Edwards
Professor, Department of Sociology, University of Toronto

Jack P. Gibbs
Professor, Department of Sociology, University of Texas at Austin

J. Patrick Gunning, Jr.
Professor, Center for Study of Public Choice
Virginia Polytechnic Institute and State University

Paul B. Horton
Professor, Department of Sociology, Western Michigan University

Francis A. J. Ianni
Professor, Department of Sociology, Columbia University

Thomas R. Ireland
Professor, Department of Economics, University of Wisconsin at Milwaukee

Benjamin Klein
National Bureau of Economic Research, New York

Gregory Krohm
Professor, Center for Study of Public Choice
Virginia Polytechnic Institute and State University

William M. Landes
National Bureau of Economic Research, New York

Charles H. Logan
Professor, Department of Sociology, University of Connecticut

Llad Phillips
Professor, Department of Economics
University of California at Santa Barbara

Simon Rottenberg
Dean, College of Business, University of Massachusetts

Paul H. Rubin
Professor, Department of Economics, University of Georgia

Jan Štěpán
Research Librarian, Harvard Law School Library

Charles R. Tittle
Professor, Department of Sociology, Florida Atlantic University

Serapio R. Zalba
Professor, Department of Sociology, The Cleveland State University

CONTENTS

PART THREE: ORGANIZED CRIME

PART FOUR: FOREIGN CRIMINAL PROCEDURE

PREFACE

This volume is the result of a conference held in July 1972 at the American Enterprise Institute in Washington, D. C. The conference was jointly sponsored by the Center for Study of Public Choice at the Virginia Polytechnic Institute and State University at Blacksburg, Virginia and by the American Enterprise Institute. It grew out of a research project on crime conducted by the Center for Study of Public Choice and funded by the National Science Foundation. This project was part of the recent invasion of the field of law by economists. This "economic imperialism," in our opinion, is one of the more promising developments in the study of crime.

Briefly, economists tend to believe that crime, far from being the result of sickness or mental disorder, in most cases is simply a business oriented economic activity which is undertaken for much the same reasons as other types of economic activity. To reduce the frequency of crime, economists generally recommend we raise the costs of crime. It would be difficult to find a more revolutionary departure from the conventional wisdom. On the other hand, the work of the economists, which, in addition to that done at V.P.I., involves such men as Gary Becker, George Stigler, Michael Ehrlich, and William Landes, has been of such a high quality that it is very hard to find a spokesman for the prevailing orthodoxy. Thus, the proceedings of this conference, although presenting a good deal of research work done from the economic standpoint, are relatively weak in presenting what is still the dominant view among criminologists. We regret this weakness, but our efforts to find criminologists to discuss these diverging views of the crime problem with economists were to no avail. This unanticipated and striking silence may be the most important aspect of this conference.

DAVID MEISELMAN and GORDON TULLOCK,
Center for Study of Public Choice,
Virginia Polytechnic Institute
and State University

INTRODUCTION

Simon Rottenberg

In the summer of 1972, the American Enterprise Institute for Public Policy Research and the Reston Economics Program of the Virginia Polytechnic Institute and State University assembled in Washington, D. C., a conference on the economics of crime and punishment. This volume contains the papers prepared for that conference, and the comments of discussants of those papers.

The conference participants were largely drawn from institutions of higher learning and most were economists, although other disciplines of the social sciences and legal scholarship were also represented.

The conference sought to examine the uses of economics, and the limits on those uses, in the treatment of crime and crime prevention systems. Confronting points of view were aggressively represented, discussion was hard and sharp, and no quarter was given. Participants were required to offer logical and empirical defenses for their positions. Some differences were reconciled and some were clarified. And all of it was done in an ambience of intellectual good faith.

Economics has been conventionally defined as a discipline that studies the allocation of scarce means among alternative ends. The same idea has been more recently and more comprehensively expressed by saying that it is the study of the principles of constrained choice.

It is because resources are scarce that choice is constrained. When resources are put to some given use, other possible uses to which they might have been put are foregone. Therefore, every choice, once made, is costly, and the cost consists in those foregone uses. Any resource which is not scarce is "free"; there is no cost associated with any use of it and the calculus of choice does not arise with respect to its use.

Economics has something to say about any institution that is required to make choices, although usually it deals with the choice problems of "households," including individuals, firms, and agencies of the public sector. Although it treats maximizing choice principles for individual persons and firms, it really has not very much to say about individual choice. This is not to say that the understanding of individual behavior is uninteresting, but only that it is the proper object of study of other disciplines. The treatment of individuals by economics is, however, only an analytical and didactic device, employed as a building block in the construction

1

of predictive and explanatory statements about the choices of aggregates of individuals.

Economics is a positive discipline. It will permit statements to be made about the consequences of phenomenological or policy changes, but it cannot rank-order phenomena and policies in some preference sense. It is indifferent about ends. The discipline is technique in the purest sense. If objectives sought to be achieved are defined for the economist, and if he is told those objectives, including the avoidance of cost, he can enumerate strategies in their appropriate rank-order, but he cannot specify desired ends. He can say whether a choice will produce gains that exceed or fall short of cost, as society values gains and the resources employed to produce them; but he cannot say that it is wrong for an individual to attach different values to gains and resources so that outcomes that are socially not worthwhile may be worthwhile for an individual.

This is not to say that economists make only purely positivist statements. They do not; they often indicate which ends they do and do not prefer. But this is only because they are citizens as well as economists and, like all citizens, they have their own preferences. *Their* preferences among ends have, however, no special merit. There is nothing in their training qua economists which gives them special qualification in the ordering of ends.

Economics employs the conventional methods of the sciences. It postulates a rather small set of assumptions. This set is called a theory, and it generates what are sometimes called hypotheses, sometimes implications, and sometimes predictions or explanations. These are always statements about the real world. They are "operational" statements, if they can be rejected by finding them to be inconsistent with what is observed in the real world.

Because the initial set of postulates has a small number of members, and the real world is complex and, therefore, is descriptively replicated by a model with many variables, economics is an abstract discipline. It is precisely because it is abstract that it has power; a small set of assumptions is discovered to permit the generation of a large number of statements about the world and about highly diverse aspects of it. Besides, the assumptions of economic theory are not intended to describe the world; they are intended as analytical instruments to generate testable implications. It is the consistency of those implications with experience, and not the descriptive accuracy and completeness of the assumptions, that is the appropriate test of the merit of the theory.

Economics has been defined as the study of the principles of constrained choice. The exercise of choice is, of course, the same as the execution of behavior. To choose is to act. Economics may be said to be, therefore, the study of behavior subject to constraint.

This rather lengthy introduction to the nature of economics as a discipline of study, and to the tasks properly defined for those who are its practitioners will, perhaps, make more understandable the papers written by economists that appear

2

in this volume. It may also clarify and place in their proper perspective some of the comments of those of other disciplines that also appear here.

Among the postulates of economics—indeed, perhaps the most important postulate—is the assumption that man behaves rationally in making choices. Behavior is rational when the acts of given men are consistent with one another, and when they tend to achieve the constrained maximization of some desired quantity. That quantity may be utility or income. Behaving rationally implies that, in making choices, account is taken of expected gains and of expected costs, and that choices are made that are, on net balance, more gainful than any other in the opportunity set open to the relevant individual.

The first two parts of the conference—on the motives of criminals, and on deterrence of criminal behavior—were devoted to a discussion of the rationality of criminal behavior. The economists assumed that persons, when settling upon whether they would engage in criminal careers or undertake specific criminal acts, were governed by the same principles as those that applied when people make legal occupational choices; that is, they assumed that criminals do not choose by random methods nor seek to diminish their well-being but, rather, they seek to enhance their welfare. In other words, they are not driven to act as they do; the option sets they confront have more than a single member and they choose among alternatives.

Since they choose in conditions of uncertainty and ignorance, criminals might be mistaken in the alternatives they choose even in an ex ante sense. If they had been better informed of the true magnitudes of the values of the variables that are relevant to their decisions, they might have chosen other alternatives, but the choice process would be rational, nonetheless. Or their choice might be correct ex ante but wrong ex post. There is a distribution of gains from criminal activity which can be estimated by taking account of the outcomes of crimes that have occurred in the past. There is a certain probability that a criminal venture will be successful. There are foregone opportunity costs associated with doing crime, costs of the tools of the trade, a certain probability of failure, by which is meant a certain probability that the criminal will be found out, charged and convicted, and there are the costs of a sense of guilt, of a conscience stricken at having transgressed social norms of correct conduct.

The probability of failure is partially dependent upon the particular set of skills in the execution of criminal activity that is possessed by the relevant person engaged in choosing among his options. If failure occurs, punishment costs of some expected magnitude, which are also estimated by extrapolation of past experience, are imposed upon the failed criminal. These punishment costs include a smaller lifetime income stream in legal occupations after conviction. Thus, taking all of these quantities into account, a person might correctly opt to engage in a criminal career or a criminal act, but he might be one of those who fails. The economist would say that he behaved rationally and was engaged in a risky activity.

In the eyes of an economist, such an occupational choice would not be any more irrational, or incorrect, than to accept employment painting steeples, although some steeple painters suffer broken backs, or to open a shoe store, though some shoe stores become bankrupt.

It is not meaningful, however, to test whether this assumption of rational criminal behavior is consistent with what is observed in the world, just as it is not meaningful to put any assumption of theory to the consistency test. What *is* meaningful is to see whether, from this assumption—whether or not it is realistic—behavioral implications can be derived, whether the number of implications is many or few, whether those implications are important or trivial, and whether the *implications* are consistent with observed behavior in the world. Thus, while the direct examination of what moves persons to act in ways that are proscribed by the law, and the direct examination of whether, in making choices, persons take into account the expected costs of punishment, are interesting exercises from the vantage points of other disciplines, they are not interesting from the standpoint of testing the goodness and the power of economics. One can assume any set of motivating forces; there are many such sets that can be constructed by processes of intellectual reflection. From each such set can be extracted a set of predictive statements about what one would expect to find in the world. It is the consistency with experience of the implied expectations extracted from the maximizing, rational-behavioral postulate that is the appropriate test of the power of economics as a social scientific discipline when employed for the analysis of criminal activity by aggregates of individuals.

One example may illustrate the fruitfulness of this postulate in the sense that it permits the articulation of an implication found to be confirmed by an experience that others believe to be surprising or, at the least, to be consistent with the postulate of irrationality of those engaged in crime. It has been noticed that, at least in the United States, recidivism rates are very high. A large fraction of convicted persons and imprisoned persons return to careers in crime upon their release. A large fraction of those in prison have been in prison before for earlier offenses. Lay persons sometimes find this phenomenon beyond comprehension. Having committed an offense, been convicted and imprisoned, they reason, any rational person should come to learn that crime does not pay. Convicted persons should, upon release, be expected to engage in only legal work. Ensuing offenses should be expected to be found to be done more than proportionately by those not previously convicted and less than proportionately by those previously convicted. When it is observed that this expectation is not borne out by experience, lay persons conclude that criminals behave irrationally.

The economist, on the other hand, turns the layman's reasoning on its back. He reasons that, if a person takes account of all probabilistic gains and all probabilistic costs, and rationally concludes that it is worthwhile for him to engage in an illegal act before a first conviction, and if nothing transpires in the world to alter the probability numbers or the magnitudes of gains and costs, then he must rationally conclude that it is worthwhile for him to commit a second offense. This is especially true if, when in prison, he has acquired, by association with other criminals, skills and information that alter the calculus of choice in ways that reduce the probability of conviction the second time around, and if the fact of a first conviction diminishes the quality of legal opportunities open to him upon release. Since those changes might well have occurred, they reinforce the criminal choice outcome that would have been expected even in the absence of those changes. Thus, high recidivism rates are discovered to be consistent with a rational-behavioral postulate and not with an irrational-behavioral postulate. What had been surprising becomes sensibly to be expected.

The third part of the conference was devoted to a discussion of the behavior of organized crime, by which is roughly meant the behavior of "firms" organized to engage in criminal enterprise. The papers in this section also embody the rational-behavioral assumption.

One of them presents the view that any firm, including any criminal firm, will, if it achieves monopoly power and if it rationally seeks to maximize its net revenue, sell its services at a higher price and sell fewer services than will a firm in a competitive industry. Only in this way can it convert to income—the economists say only in this way can it acquire rents—its monopoly position in markets. Since criminal firms produce socially and legally defined undesired commodities ("bads" or discommodities), monopoly in criminal industries is to be socially preferred to competition. By thus organizing markets for the production of criminal goods and services, society will consume a smaller quantity of discommodities than would be true if these industries were competitively organized. This inferentially suggests that the social purpose would be served by the allocation of police and prosecutorial resources in such a way as to reinforce monopoly in these industries. This can be done by an appropriate allocation of the resources of the criminal justice system. Explicitly, they could do so by imposing higher costs upon those seeking to break the monopolies of organized crime by seeking to enter criminal industries in which organized crime firms are incumbents. Implicitly, they could do so by giving more proportional attention than now to competitive criminal activities and less proportional attention than now to monopolized criminal activities. Another paper in the same section attends to the question of the kinds of criminal activities that can be expected to be engaged in by organized criminal firms, if these firms are rational maximizers.

The main papers of the fourth part of the conference were produced by legal scholars. They are in the nature of inputs of information which can be grist for the economists' mills. They describe European Continental and English criminal justice procedural and organizational systems, and suggest ways in which arrangements in Europe differ from those in the United States. The economists' comments on these papers examine the behavioral implications of the differences in procedures, behavioral tests of whether procedural differences are real or only apparent, behavioral tests for the priority rank-ordering of different procedural rules and organizational arrangements, and certain assumptions about the objectives sought to be served by the administration of criminal justice. These economists' comments, too, are derived from the postulate of rational maximization.

There are other facets of the economist's professional outlook and method that affect his treatment of crime and punishment, and which were touched upon in the conference, either in papers, commentaries, or in the discussions of the conference participants. Practitioners of the discipline have a strong faith in the capacity to measure, at least roughly and sometimes through the media of proxies, phenomena that are often thought not to be susceptible to measurement, either because they have amorphous properties or because the data required for mensuration do not exist. Thus, this volume contains materials that discuss the return to investment in criminal careers in theft, and the value of the loss of freedom when imprisoned.

There is a sharp awareness among economists of the existence of uncertainty in the world. Where there is not certainty, there are probability distributions of outcomes; both gains and costs have "expected" values which are the products of probability numbers and certain value magnitudes. The influences of the two multiplied quantities are sometimes decomposed, and there are separate references to the differential effects upon criminal behavior of changes in the probability that the criminal will be convicted, and changes in the magnitudes of punishments inflicted upon convicted criminals. This is suggestive in the contrivance of policy for the allocation of criminal justice resources between police and court systems, on the one side, and penal systems on the other.

There is a consciousness among economists of opportunity costs—of opportunities foregone, given scarcity, when resources are put to particular uses. Thus, time, having alternative uses, is lost to legal occupations when it is used in illegal ventures, and it is seen that the probability that people will act illegally will be a partial negative function of their legal earnings opportunities. The higher the remuneration in legal activities, other things being equal, the smaller the incentive provided by illegal gain of given expected magnitudes to engage in criminal work. On the same principle, it would be expected that an increase in the cost of doing some particular kind of criminal business will tend to move criminals to the execution of other kinds of crime.

Economists reason that the present is preferred to the future, that people will pay something for the right to bring consumption forward in time, and will have to be paid for postponing consumption. Therefore, both gains and costs occurring in the future have a smaller present value than their nominal values at the times when they occur. The process of converting from nominal to present values is called "discounting" and the rates at which discounting is done will affect the present values of given future gain and cost streams. The calculation of the

6

present value of a prison term is, thus, based on the application of a discount rate. The last month of a five-year prison term will carry less weight than the last month of a three-year term in the choice calculus of an incipient criminal. Addicts have high discount rates (they cannot wait), and it is this that explains why quick-return criminal income-generating activities will be preferred by them to legal earnings opportunities in which the return to effort and skill may be higher but the payoff is lagged. The conference discussion dealt with these questions.

Economists give attention to marginal effects. Theoretically derived implications will often be found to be consistent with experience even if only marginal responsive behavioral adjustment occurs. An increase in the cost of criminal activity will often be found to diminish the quantity of crime done, even if criminal activity is eschewed only at the margin by those who are just at the edge of turning to legal alternatives. Therefore, the implication will turn out to be not disproved by observed evidence, even if the criminal community is nonhomogeneous and there are many within it who are behaviorally unmoved by the increase in the cost of doing criminal business. The notion of the importance of the margin was woven into the conference exchange.

Economists distinguish theoretical and empirical questions. Some predictive statements can be derived from theory; others cannot. Those that cannot are called "empirical questions." While theory instructs with respect to the direction of behavioral responses to price changes, it says nothing about the magnitudes of the responses to given changes in price. These are called supply and demand elasticities, and to know their magnitudes one must examine what occurs in the world. If the police enforce the law against the sale and consumption of illegal drugs more aggressively, this will cause the price of drugs to rise. In such a circumstance, will the consumption of drugs fall at all? Will consumption fall less than proportionately to the rise in price, or more than proportionately to the rise in price? Since this is an empirical question, only the examination of empirical evidence can suggest a proper response. Since drug-users are said to acquire their means for the purchase of drugs by engaging in theft, the efficiency of the police in protecting the nonaddict subset of the population from thievery requires the correct response to this empirical question.

Economists are attentive to risk preferences. People may prefer risk, or they may be averse to risk, or they may be neutral with respect to risk. It was suggested at the conference that, if the criminal justice system is at a socially optimal scale, those engaged in criminal activity will, at the margin, be risk preferrers, and the implication of this is that an increase in the severity of punishment would deter less crime than an increase in the *certainty* that the criminal *will* be punished.

The conference papers and the commentaries made upon them should be fruitfully useful in the design and application of public policy with respect to the containment of socially harmful criminal activity. The relevance of the discussions to policy were continuously implicit throughout the conference proceedings, and from time to time they were explicitly brought to the surface. In addition to being a significant contribution to the scholarly treatment of the economics of crime and punishment, this volume should also prove most imformative to the intelligent layman and those charged with the administration of criminal justice.

PART ONE:

MOTIVES OF CRIMINALS

PROBLEMS IN UNDERSTANDING CRIMINAL MOTIVES

Paul B. Horton

Ever since Eve opened the first fruit market and Cain discovered sibling jealousy, the question, "Why did he do it?" has been repeated and repeated without a satisfactory answer. In the classical world, possession by demons or manipulation by a clutch of supernatural deities provided explanations that were infinitely more satisfying than those we have today.

The current explanations of criminal motivation are neither satisfying nor useful. The sociopsychological literature on motivation is dominated by laboratory experiments which provide results little more transferable to real life than finesse in the parlor game of Monopoly is marketable in Wall Street.[1] When social scientists shift from laboratory exercises to a search for the motives underlying significant social behavior, the result is often limited only by the extent of their semantic imagination. Practically every number of motives has been announced by some scholar or other, ranging from Thomas's four wishes to Murray's 28! [2]

"Motive" is one of a cluster of words, like "purpose," "intent," and "impulse," which have no precise scientific meaning, and which are often defined in terms of the others in circular definitions that make nothing clear. More explicit definitions usually emerge as a succession of relatively incomprehensible verbiage. One journal article defines motivation as a process whereby a person, either through interaction with other persons and groups, or through reading or solitary reflection, comes symbolically to define a particular situation as calling for a particular action.[3] That's mighty helpful, isn't it? Another defines motives as "linguistic constructs organizing actions in particular situations." [4] So that's it!

Obviously, a motive is not a thing, not an entity; it is an inference or deduction drawn by an observer of another person's behavior. As such, motives are more likely to be found in the mind of the observer than to be established as components

[1] Bernard Berelson and Gary A. Steiner, *Human Behavior: An Inventory of Scientific Findings* (New York: Holt, Rinehart and Winston, 1964), Chapter 6, "Motivation."

[2] Henry A. Murray, ed., *Explorations in Personality: A Clinical Experimental Study of Fifty Men at College* (New York: Oxford University Press, 1938).

[3] Nelson N. Foote, "Identification as a Basis for a Theory of Motivation," *American Sociological Review,* vol. 16 (February 1951), pp. 14-21.

[4] Frank E. Hartung, "A Vocabulary of Motives for Law Violations," in *Crime, Law, and Society* (Detroit: Wayne State University Press, 1965), pp. 62-83; paraphrasing C. Wright Mills, "Situated Actions and Vocabularies of Motives," *American Sociological Review,* vol. 5 (December 1940), pp. 904-913.

of the behavior system of the actor. One man's motive is another's rationalization and still another's "con." Possibly this is why the term is practically absent from criminological literature. Most criminology textbooks have no index entry for "motives," and in those few with such an entry, the references are to casual, incidental uses of the term. This writer has found no recent work in criminology with a systematic treatment of "motives." The term seems to have expired along with "instinct," "will," and "character"—concepts which have proved equally unhelpful in behavioral science.

A second difficulty in searching for motives for criminal behavior is that criminological theory strongly implies that the motives for criminal behavior are inseparable from the motives for *all* behavior. Very often the difference between criminal behavior and conventional behavior lies not in the behavior but in the social context. Killing people may be rewarded with a chair in the death house or a chair in the White House, depending upon the circumstances of the killing. The desire to impress and entertain young ladies apparently provides the motive for much juvenile robbery and car theft, but precisely the same motive impels other young men to seek jobs and work like beavers. It is difficult to imagine *any* motive for criminal behavior, even among the less honored ones such as anger, greed, lust, or even revenge, which may not also be fulfilled, and is more often fulfilled, through acceptable law-abiding behavior than through criminal behavior. I believe we will never isolate identifiable motives for criminal behavior except possibly in the case of a few compulsion neuroses or organic anomalies, to which only a minor part of the crime problem can be attributed.

If the search for motives is futile, what approach does show promise? The search for "causes" is no great improvement. A cause is commonly defined as a condition which is both necessary and sufficient for the appearance of a particular consequence. Criminological research has found no factor in heredity, environment, or experience which is either *necessary* (in that the criminal behavior appears *only* when this factor is present) or *sufficient* (in that criminal behavior *always* follows whenever this factor is present). Thus, no true causes of crime have been established. What has emerged from hundreds of research studies is a series of statistical associations, correlations, and sequences. Thus we know that officially recorded juvenile delinquency is significantly associated with, among other things, unsatisfactory home life, poor school progress, and a pattern of conflict with authority. Among young people showing all three of these characteristics, the incidence of official delinquency mounts astronomically. This we call "multiple causation." Not having established what causes people to commit crimes, but having observed that a number of circumstances are associated with high crime rates, we lump them together as "multiple causes." Transmuting statistical associations into causes, however, is far from satisfying. By this test, burned-out street lights, flimsy door locks, and parked cars are "causes" of crime. As with motives, the search for "causes" is doomed to failure. As with motives, there is an interaction between circumstance and self which insures that no circumstance and no characteristic of self, and no combination thereof, will have predictable behavior outcomes for a particular individual.

Yet the search for statistical associations and for sequences and probabilities is not useless. People realized that eating spoiled food was often followed by distress long before they knew anything about bacteria or toxins. Heavy cigarette smoking is associated with an intriguing assortment of ways to die more quickly; this knowledge is functionally useful as a factor in individual decision, even when one has no real understanding of the chemical processes which may lead to death. The knowledge that family relationships, school progress, and responses to authority are strongly associated with juvenile delinquency provides a valuable focus for policy making. The more we know about the conditions favoring criminal behavior, the greater the possibilities for practical action. I suggest, therefore, that we abandon the attempt to isolate motives or causes and concentrate upon establishing the conditions associated with crime and the policy changes which might restrain or reduce crime and reform criminals. But sound policy flows from sound theory, and what is the state of criminological theory?

I shall not attempt a review of criminological theory here. One recent textbook devotes 82 pages to what the author terms a very condensed summary of current theories of crime causation. These are classified as physiopsychological theories, socioenvironmental and sociocultural theories, and sociopsychological theories; the author presents no fewer than 18 major theories or sets of related theories.[5] He then attempts to develop "an integrated theory of delinquency-crime causation" which requires 20 pages and includes 39 major propositions with 37 subheadings.[6] I see this not as an integrated theory, but as a series of descriptive propositions and highly probable sequences. This is not to disparage his effort, which is quite impressive. I cite this instead as evidence that no concise, truly integrated theory has yet been constructed to prove the relationship among the great variety of statistical associations and sequences which criminological research has assembled.

Robert K. Merton has suggested that after a discipline has passed the stage of discrete ad hoc theoretical interpretations, but has not yet accumulated the empirical basis for broad, integrated generic theory, a stage of middle range theory is appropriate.[7] Such middle range theory would attempt to relate the observed associations and sequences in as coherent a formulation as the data permit. It is just such a middle range theory that Richard D. Knudten attempts.[8] But the concept of middle range theory assumes that, with continued accumulation of empirical

---

[5] Richard D. Knudten, *Crime in a Complex Society* (Homewood, Ill.: The Dorsey Press, 1970), pp. 223-304.

[6] Ibid., pp. 305-325.

[7] Robert K. Merton, *Social Theory and Social Structure* (Glencoe, Ill.: The Free Press, 1957), pp. 103-117.

[8] Knudten, *Crime,* pp. 305-325.

data, a time will come when broad generic theorizing is possible. This model, in which an accumulation of data eventually permits a perceptive scholar to construct a theory that brings into orderly relationship a wide range of confusing and apparently contradictory phenomena, has been applicable many times in the history of science—Newton and gravity, Pasteur and bacteria, Einstein and relativity.

To propose such a theoretical breakthrough must be the cherished dream of every true scientist. But not all scientific evolution follows this model of the ordering of masses of data through integrating generic theory. Sometimes the opposite happens. For example, it may have appeared for a time that Pasteur's germ theory of disease provided *the* explanation of the cause of illness and the research paths to disease control. To a spectacular degree, it did just that. But after some decades it became clear that there were many diseases which it did not fit, and the virus theory of disease opened fresh avenues of research. More recently, the stress theory of illness led to still more insights and research leads. Thus in medicine during the past century, the direction has been away from relying on broad range generic theory as an explanation of *the* cause of illness, and toward multiple theories, each explaining a certain range of data with respect to a certain class of illnesses. Meanwhile the new discipline of social medicine arose to deal with the interrelationships between multiple causes and multiple treatments.

I suggest that medicine is a relatively simple field for research and theory construction, as compared with criminal behavior. I gravely doubt that anything more than middle range theory will ever be possible in criminology. The range of behavior and the permutations and combinations of interaction between actor, environment, and social experience are so numerous that any attempt at an integrated generic theory will necessarily be either a simplistic and incomplete explanation of criminal behavior, or will be a loosely connected series of descriptive observations and theoretical propositions which spill over dozens of pages and thousands of words. A venerable example of this first possibility is the Marxian theory of crime as a product of the capitalist system, a theory which is currently gaining favor with neo-Marxian scholars. But how, then, does one explain crime in pre-capitalist societies, or the persistence of crime in all contemporary Marxian societies? The most impressive example of a concise and consistent generic theory of crime causation probably is Edwin H. Sutherland's differential association theory,[9] but even in its more recent revisions by Cressey [10] and by Burgess and Akers,[11] it fails to account satisfactorily for all kinds of crime or criminals. Knudten's "integrated theory of delinquency-crime causation" is a good example of

[9] Edwin H. Sutherland, *Principles of Criminology,* 3rd ed. (Philadelphia: J. B. Lippincott Co., 1939).

[10] Edwin H. Sutherland and Donald R. Cressey, *Criminology,* 8th ed. (Philadelphia: J. B. Lippincott Co., 1970), Chapter 4.

[11] Robert L. Burgess and Ronald L. Akers, "A Differential Association-Reinforcement Theory of Criminal Behavior," *Social Problems,* vol. 14 (Fall 1966), pp. 128-147.

the second get-it-all-together type of eclectic theory; [12] while it is probably as useful as the present stage of knowledge will permit, it is unsatisfying to the searcher for concise generic theory. Most of the major theories in physical science can be stated in no more than a few dozen words, including all qualifications and limitations, but such neat simplicity is not a realistic expectation in the behavioral sciences.

Are we, then, doomed to wander forever in the theoretical wilderness and never reach the promised land of policy-validating theory and knowledge? Not necessarily. But first we must recognize that "crime" consists of many kinds of behavior with a wide range of predisposing circumstances and treatment possibilities. While continuing to search for reliable knowledge and relevant theory for each kind of criminal or crime, we may concurrently proceed to test a variety of restraints and treatments. Sometimes a single action, such as improved street lighting, may reduce the incidence of several kinds of crime. While we cannot go into a full discussion of crime prevention and treatment here, it may be relevant to suggest a few promising possibilities which have not been fully developed.

Would a determined attempt to eliminate the injustices and inequities of our society reduce the motivation for crime? Probably to some degree, but I am doubtful that any more than a modest crime reduction would follow from even a highly successful attack upon racism, poverty, and other social problems which are often cited as causal factors in crime. Official crime statistics show significant associations between high crime rates and race, income, et cetera, but studies of unreported crime suggest that the true incidence of criminal acts shows no more than a very modest association with race and income.[13] There are, in my opinion, pressing reasons for reordering the priorities of American society with a determined attack upon poverty, racism, ill health, substandard housing, and a number of other social problems. But as a means of reducing the motivation for crime, no more than modest gains can be expected from this course of action.

From the radical leftists comes the suggestion that crime can only be substantially reduced through a radical restructuring of the dominant value system of American society in which the drive for possessions and conspicuous consumption is replaced with a relative indifference to material possessions and status symbols. In all honesty, we must concede that they may be right. A relatively high incidence of property crime may be the price we must pay for a competitive materialistic society. But such major value transformations do not come through a conscious choice, but as the largely unplanned consequence of other social and cultural

---

[12] Knudten, *Crime,* pp. 305-325.

[13] James S. Wallerstein and Clement J. Wyle, "Our Law-Abiding Law-Breakers," reprint from *Probation* (New York: National Probation Association, April 1947); Lewis Yablonsky, *The Violent Gang* (New York: The Macmillan Co., 1962); James F. Short and Fred L. Strodtbeck, *Group Process and Gang Delinquency* (Chicago: University of Chicago Press, 1965); D. M. Downes, *The Delinquent Solution* (New York: The Free Press, 1966); Martin Gold, *Delinquent Behavior in an American City* (Belmont, Calif.: Brooks-Cole Publishing Co., 1970).

changes. Such alternative values have spread rather widely among young people within the past decade, but at the present quite rapid rate of change, several decades would be required for a new societal consensus. Furthermore, such value changes are not necessarily permanent. Waves of antimaterialistic sentiment have appeared a number of times in Western civilization and, to date, all have been temporary aberrations rather than lasting value transformations. Finally, there is no firm guarantee that a decline in materialistic values would reduce crime. While I know of no reliable data on the question, casual observation does not suggest that those young people who have rejected materialistic values are more law-abiding than other people. We note that rock music festivals have now virtually disappeared; among the reasons are local fears of the rowdyism and disorder which often accompanied them and the festival promoters' difficulties in controlling gate-crashing. Rock musicians, who so often extol the alternative values in their musical arrangements, seem to prefer solid materialistic values in their contractual arrangements. In his *Steal This Book*,[14] Abbie Hoffman advocates and gives extensive instructions in the techniques of the rip-off, but when someone ripped off *his* stereo system, his howls of outrage were indistinguishable from those of the most bourgeois suburbanite. A reduction in crime motivation through modification of our materialistic values is a possibility, but one which is neither imminent nor certain.

One faster and more certain approach would be the decriminalization of all "crimes without victims." These would include drug use, intoxication, all forms of private, consensual sex behavior among adults, including prostitution. These absorb a tremendous share of the resources of law enforcement and correctional personnel. Most authorities agree that a major portion of property crime is committed by addicts who need funds for a fix.[15] It is possible that no single measure would produce so immediate and sharp a drop in such crimes as robbery, burglary, and assault, as would the decriminalization of drug use. Furthermore, decriminalization of drug use would interrupt the secondary deviation process.[16] When the drug user is identified and labeled as a criminal deviant through arrest and prosecution, he tends to be isolated from conventional associations and institutional ties and cast into closer association with other deviant persons, thus confirming and extending his own deviation. It is likely, for example, that the demotivation which sometimes follows marijuana use is explained mainly in terms of secondary deviation. There is today a strong trend toward removing from the criminal law all such victimless crimes which are essentially matters of esthetics or morals without any clear public injury. This trend should be applauded and encouraged.

---

[14] Abbie Hoffman, *Steal This Book* (New York: Pirate Editions, 1971); distributed by Grove Press.

[15] See Max Singer, "The Vitality of Mythical Numbers," *The Public Interest,* Spring 1971, pp. 3-9, for a critical examination which reduces somewhat the usual estimates of such a crime.

[16] Edwin M. Lemert, *Social Pathology* (New York: McGraw-Hill Book Co., 1951), pp. 75-77; Howard S. Becker, *Outsiders* (New York: The Free Press, 1963), Chapter 1.

A somewhat neglected area of research and experiment is the process of resocialization of criminals. We have extensively studied the processes of stigmatization and criminalization, and conducted a number of experiments in rehabilitation along with detailed analyses of rehabilitation failures, but there has been little study of rehabilitation successes. We thus know far more about how and why the recidivist recidivates than about how and why the reformed criminal reforms. We do know that, insofar as we can tell from arrests and convictions, relatively few delinquents persist in criminal behavior throughout an entire lifetime. What happens to the reformed? Is it increased maturity, a lapse into an apathetic, timorous incapacity, a genuine resocialization, or what? We aren't certain. Experimentation and research on halfway houses, behavior modification procedures, group therapy techniques and other resocialization activities might tell us more about the process.

Still another approach consists of attempting to reduce the opportunities and temptations to crime while largely bypassing the actor's system of motives and needs. Amitai Etzioni refers to these as "shortcuts." [17] His idea is that fundamental solutions, such as changing the institutional structure of society or the motivation and need system of people, are so expensive and time-consuming that they are unlikely to be accomplished. Shortcuts include all relatively simple, quick, and fairly inexpensive ways of altering the behavior situation so that the undesired behavior is discouraged. The decriminalization of drug use might be one example. Others might include gun control, alarm systems and other security devices, marking of personal possessions for identification, thumb printing of check cashers, packaging and display card-mounting of small objects so as to make shoplifting more difficult, low-cost photocopy machines to discourage library book mutilation, and many other ways of reducing temptations or increasing risks. In both the short run and the long run, it may be more rewarding to concentrate upon changing the behavior situation than upon changing the motivation system of the actors.

It is disheartening that any paper should be so heavily negative—so greatly a recital of what we do not know and cannot do. But nothing is gained by presuming a knowledge and expertise which we do not possess. Better to accept our present limitations, and get on with the task of pushing beyond them as rapidly as we can.

---

[17] Amitai Etzioni, "Shortcuts to Social Change," *The Public Interest,* Summer 1968, pp. 40-51; Amitai Etzioni and Richard Remp, *Technological Shortcuts to Social Change* (New York: Russell Sage Foundation, 1972).

THEFT AND THE TWO HYPOTHESES

William E. Cobb

An important issue has arisen concerning the basic motivational characteristics of the criminal element in our society. The two approaches which seem to be receiving most attention have been characterized as the "economic hypothesis" and the "sickness hypothesis." [1] We will summarize here the arguments of those endorsing the two points of view and then make an attempt to merge the two into one hypothesis, acceptable to both sides and consistent with the basic behavior postulate of economic theory—utility maximization. This analysis will not resolve all areas of disagreement between the two factions, but will correctly define those areas of conflict. In the final section of the paper we will summarize some empirical work.[2]

I. The Two Hypotheses

The Economic Hypothesis. The economic hypothesis is founded on the principle that crime is just like any other enterprise: *the potential criminal evaluates all possibilities within the limits of all information which he possesses and chooses that activity which maximizes his utility.* This hypothesis has become entrapped in that maze of misconception which accompanies most attempts to explain "utility-inspired" motivation to the lay economist. There is apparent difficulty in differentiating between utility gain and monetary return. Economists have become infamous through their attempts to convert nonpecuniary costs and benefits into dollar equivalents. These attempts, however, do seem to have logical foundations. If an individual voluntarily trades some nonpecuniary property right—be it physical or psychological—for a pecuniary income, then it would seem logical to conclude (and impossible to disprove) that he expects his net utility change to be a positive one *at the time of the trade.* Few, if any, economists argue that receipt of dollars is the only motivating factor in any decision process. The basic argument in an economic (or utility maximization) approach is that an individual decision maker

---

[1] A good survey article is Gordon Tullock's "Two Hypotheses" which will appear in Gordon Tullock, ed., *The Economics of Crime* (Blacksburg, Va.: Center for Study of Public Choice, forthcoming).

[2] The empirical work was made possible by a National Science Foundation grant. Institutional interest in such projects is an important facet of research into, and reform of, the law enforcement system.

explicitly or implicitly considers *all* benefits and costs which he expects to result from a decision.

Of course the decision maker is allowed to miscalculate. Decisions are made with limited knowledge and may prove to be incorrect, an ex post revelation. Sociologists have coined a useful phrase with their creation of the term "bounded rationality." [3] "The essence of this notion is that individuals have perceptual as well as information-processing limits, and even though they may intend to act rationally, they can do so only in a limited fashion." [4]

Gary Becker has written, "Some persons become 'criminals,' therefore, not because their basic motivation differs from that of other persons, but because their benefits and costs differ." [5] Advocates of the economic hypothesis accept this proposition and argue that criminal activities can be altered by a change in the expected net utilities of individual decision makers. That is, in order to reduce crime we must lower the expected benefits, raise the expected costs, or effect some combination thereof which insures that crime has an expected negative influence on the utility of most potential criminals.

The Sickness Hypothesis. The sickness hypothesis attacks the problem of crime from a different perspective. Many sociologists adhere to this approach and vehemently attack the economic formulation:

> This misplaced faith in punishment may rest upon the unrealistic assumption that people *consciously decide* whether to be criminal—that they consider a criminal career, rationally balance its dangers against its rewards, and arrive at a decision based upon such pleasure-pain calculation. It supposedly follows that if the pain element is increased by severe punishments, people will turn from crime to righteousness. A little reflection reveals the absurdity of this notion. [6]

The same sociologists present empirical data which allegedly show that punishment has no deterrent effect whatever on crime. [7] Proponents argue that the expected payoff of crime may be negative (negative net utility) and that the criminal is sick because he disregards this negative effect. Since the potential criminal does not act within the realm of even bounded rationality, adjustments of the expected benefits and costs of crime will in no way alter his decision to

---

[3] H. A. Simon, "Bounded Rationality," *Administrative Behavior* (New York: The Free Press, 1957), pp. 33-41.

[4] K. E. Weick, *The Social Psychology of Organizing* (Reading, Mass.: Addison-Wesley Publishing Company, 1968), p. 9.

[5] Gary Becker, "Crime and Punishment: An Economic Approach," *Journal of Political Economy,* vol. 76 (March-April 1968), p. 176.

[6] Paul B. Horton and Gerald R. Leslie, *The Sociology of Social Problems,* 4th ed. (New York: Appleton-Century-Crofts, 1970), p. 167.

[7] See R. G. Caldwell, "The Deterrent Influence of Corporal Punishment upon Prisoners Who Have Been Whipped," *American Sociological Review,* vol. 9 (April 1944), pp. 171-177.

commit a crime.[8] Advocates of the sickness hypothesis conclude that rehabilitation is the only solution to the control of criminal behavior.

II. A Resolution of the Controversy

Extensive discussions with proponents of each of the two hypotheses reveals a basic communication gap between them. Few sociologists believe that punishment, in general, does not deter. To hold to such a position would be to reject scientific evidence which indicates that most, if not all, living organisms react to pleasure-pain stimuli. Common sense, as well as Pavlov, tells us that we do react to punishment. Would you ever illegally park your automobile if the penalty were raised from the present small fine to twenty years of imprisonment? On the other hand, would you illegally park more than you do now if the only punishment were a note on your windshield saying, "Shame on you"? Clearly punishment does have a deterrent effect on this type of crime.

The actual argument that sociologists are making is not that punishment does not deter, but rather that our current system of punishment is not effective. Almost invariably, one can eventually persuade advocates of the sickness approach to concede this point. As Gibbs has said:

> Sociologists have participated in the controversy between the classical and positivist schools, and many of them have clearly questioned the deterrent efficacy of punitive reactions to crime, capital punishment in particular. The pronouncements of some sociologists on capital punishment are questionable and unfortunate. In particular, the general question of the deterrent efficacy of punishment cannot be answered by research on the death penalty alone. Execution is, after all, only one type of punitive reaction to crime; but sociologists tend to extend their opinions on the death penalty to punitive reactions generally. *The point is that some sociologists do not treat the general question of deterrence as an open one.*[9] [Italics mine.]

Punishment does function as a deterrent. The problem with our system of criminal justice is that no one has attempted to determine the utility that a criminal loses as a result of various penalties. A year of imprisonment does not affect everyone in the same manner. A preacher convicted of petit larceny and given a suspended sentence might suffer greater utility loss than a vagrant incarcerated for 90 days for the same crime. As Charles R. Tittle has pointed out, "The crucial question is not simply whether negative sanctions deter, but rather under what conditions are negative sanctions likely to be effective."[10] Negative sanctions are

---

[8] This position is not limited to sociologists. A former criminal lawyer with whom this topic was discussed adamantly argued for this viewpoint.

[9] Jack P. Gibbs, "Crime Punishment, and Deterrence," *Social Science Quarterly,* March 1968, p. 515.

[10] Charles R. Tittle, "Crime Rates and Legal Sanctions," *Social Problems,* vol. 16 (Spring 1969), p. 411.

effective only if the negative utility which the potential criminal expects to result from their imposition is greater than the positive utility he expects to gain from the crime.

In his oft-cited article on crime, Gary Becker says of the economic hypothesis:

> This approach implies that there is a function relating the number of offenses by any person to his probability of conviction, to his punishment if convicted, and to other variables, such as the income available to him in legal and other illegal activities, the frequency of nuisance arrests, and his willingness to commit an illegal act. This can be represented as
>
> $$O_j = O_j\,(p_j, f_j, u_j),\tag{1}$$
>
> where O_j is the number of offenses he would commit during a particular period, p_j his probability of conviction per offense, f_j his punishment per offense, and u_j a portmanteau variable representing all these other influences.[11]

If sociologists were arguing that punishments do not deter crime, they would be arguing that

$$\partial O_j/\partial f_j = 0.\tag{2}$$

Clearly, this is not the case! They are, in fact, arguing that the change in committed offenses resulting from a change in punishments is very small and hence,

$$\partial O_j/\partial f_j < \partial O_j/\partial u_j,\tag{3}$$

or as is argued in some cases,

$$\partial O_j/\partial f_j < \partial O_j/\partial p_j.\tag{4}$$

Equation (3) represents the view that, although increases in punishment may deter, changes in the variables in u_j—income available to the potential criminal in legal activities, his willingness to commit an illegal act (moral code), et cetera— more effectively reduce the level of crime.

Equation (4) represents a similar argument that changes in the probability of apprehension reduce criminal offenses more than changes in the punishment per offense.

The formulation of the sickness hypothesis as seen in equations (3) and (4) does not run counter to the utility maximization approach used by economists. However, as elementary students of economics recognize, within a budget constraint, B, the relevant decision model requires:

$$\frac{\partial O_j/\partial p_j}{P_{p_j}} = \frac{\partial O_j/\partial f_j}{P_{f_j}} = \frac{\partial O_j/\partial u_j}{P_{u_j}},\tag{5}$$

and

$$(p_j \cdot P_{p_j}) + (f_j \cdot P_{f_j}) + (u_j \cdot P_{u_j}) = B,\tag{6}$$

where P_{p_j}, P_{f_j}, and P_{u_j} represent the prices of apprehension, punishment, and "rehabilitation," respectively. (Henceforth, ∂u_j will be called "rehabilitation.")

---

[11] Becker, "Crime and Punishment," p. 117.

That is, in order to minimize crime within a given budget, expenditures on crime prevention should be divided so that the above equalities hold.

The disagreement between proponents of each of the two hypotheses is one that can be empirically decided: Will a dollar of expenditures on crime reduction be more effectively spent on altering the probability of apprehension, on altering punishments per offense, or on altering factors included in the portmanteau variable, which we are calling rehabilitation?

III. Economics of Theft

Within the framework of the model just discussed, reduction in the level of criminal activity might be accomplished in three ways: (1) redistributing expenditures among the three variables p_j, f_j, and u_j, (2) increasing total expenditures (budget, B) while holding constant the distribution of expenditures, and (3) a combination of increasing or redistributing the budget.

These methods depend pivotally on the assumption that criminals are rational decision makers in the sense that they do not make decisions on a random basis. If criminal acts were random (irrational), they would not be a function of *any* decision variables, including p_j, f_j, u_j, and B.

It does seem plausible, however, that a person *always* seeks to maximize his *expected* net benefits and that acts in which ex ante costs exceed benefits will never be perpetrated. The problem which exists in all decision-making processes is that ex ante costs and benefits seldom are equivalent to ex post costs and benefits. Stated more simply, people have imperfect knowledge.

In most discussions "irrationality" usually is limited to the realm of bounded rationality. An irrational action is implicitly defined as one for which, due to imperfect knowledge, ex ante net benefits are positive but ex post net benefits are negative. As psychologists have noted, "rationality seems better understood as a post-decision rather than a pre-decision occurrence." [12]

Within this framework, the proposition that criminals act irrationally is identical to one that states that crime does not pay. If crime does not pay, one method of reducing the level of crime is to convince (educate) potential criminals that they are making incorrect calculations. If crime does pay, this method would convert to convincing (indoctrinating) potential thieves that they are incorrect in their calculations, when, in fact, they are making the correct choices. Equations (1), (5), and (6) will then convert to

$$O_j = O_j \, (p_j, f_j, u_j, k_j), \tag{7}$$

$$\frac{\partial O_j/\partial p_j}{P_{p_j}} = \frac{\partial O_j/\partial f_j}{P_{f_j}} = \frac{\partial O_j/\partial u_j}{P_{u_j}} = \frac{\partial O_j/\partial k_j}{P_{k_j}}, \tag{8}$$

and

$$(p_j \cdot P_{p_j}) + (f_j \cdot P_{f_j}) + (u_j \cdot P_{u_j}) + k_j(P_{k_j}) = B, \tag{9}$$

[12] Weick, *Social Psychology of Organizing*, p. 38.

23

where k_j represents the "knowledge" possessed by individual j, P_{k_j} represents the price of providing that knowledge, and $\partial O_j / \partial k_j$ represents the change in the number of offenses committed by him which result from a change in the "knowledge" which he possesses.[13]

The following empirical analysis examines only one small facet of the problem which this model encompasses. It is an attempt to determine whether education or indoctrination, as defined above, is the more viable method of reducing one type of crime—theft. That is, it is an attempt to measure some of the ex post costs and benefits of thieves in order to determine whether or not thieves are, as a group, making the "correct" choices.

Method and Scope. The method employed is a "simple" benefit-cost technique. The costs associated with the actual acts of committing theft, along with the costs of capture, conviction, and imprisonment, are compared to the benefits from these thefts. I have confined my analysis to those crimes classified as either grand larceny or burglary by the Federal Bureau of Investigation, in only one locality, Norfolk, Virginia, for the two years 1964 and 1966.

The first problem concerned what to include as the benefits of theft. After I obtained estimates of the market value of stolen merchandise, I made adjustments to find the value of this merchandise *to the thief*, this being somewhat less than the market value because of problems in disposing of stolen materials. It is this value of stolen property to the thief which best approximates the benefit he receives.

Costs to thieves are more difficult to evaluate. There are positive physical costs such as the actual work involved in committing thefts, the disposable income lost while incarcerated, and the fines which are levied in addition to incarcerations. There are negative physical costs (benefits) which accrue to thieves while they are incarcerated: free room and board, free medical and dental care, welfare payments to dependents, and wages earned within the prison.

To be added to the physical costs just mentioned are psychic costs, such as loss of freedom, and attainment of a "bad reputation," which may prove to be a negative cost.

Temporarily ignoring both psychic and negative costs, we find that the cost decision is narrowed to three variables: (1) the work involved in theft, (2) lost disposable income, and (3) fines. The first of these—the work or time involved in committing thefts—seems to be relatively negligible. It simply takes very little time to commit the average theft. For convenience, this cost will be assumed to be zero.

The cost side of the analysis now centers on two factors—lost disposable income as a result of incarceration and fines levied on convicted thieves.

---

[13] "Knowledge" here refers to what an individual believes to be true, not to an actual state of the world. In effect k_j is included in u_j of equation (1).

The Benefits: 1964. In 1964 there were 2,388 reported cases of burglary and 1,867 reported cases of grand larceny in the city of Norfolk.[14] These 1964 thefts may be divided into five categories as shown in Table 1.

The figures exhibited in the table show values for reported stolen property only. If we desire an examination of benefits to the criminal, an attempt must be made to place a value on property stolen but *not reported stolen.* The President's Commission on Law Enforcement and Administration of Justice has issued a report indicating that total unreported thefts might well exceed the total number of reported thefts.[15] The commission cites a figure for the cash value of unreported crimes which indicates that 50 percent of total dollars stolen is unreported.[16] Using this 50 percent figure, values in Table 1 are doubled to those shown in Table 2.

As shown in each of these two tables the Norfolk Police Department made significant recovery of stolen property in the period being investigated. Benefits to the criminal do not include recovered property, as it is assumed that the property was recovered from the thief and not from the individual to whom it was given or sold. The important figure is the difference between total property stolen and property recovered. Table 3 shows the net value of each of the categories.

The figures in Table 3 need one final adjustment before they suit our purposes. The values shown are those placed on the property by its owner. The value of stolen property to the thief is considerably less than this. Through interviews within the Norfolk Police Department and in an interview with a professional "fence" in the Norfolk area, it was determined that, on the average, thieves can sell stolen merchandise for only approximately 20 percent of its market value. For certain types of merchandise this figure is still lower—wearing apparel, for instance. The professional thief may receive greater percentages than these because he will normally have his own selling outlets. However, professionalism appears to be a rather rare exception in the area under study.

The consensus among those interviewed indicates that, for stolen property, 20 percent of the market value would approximate the value to the thief—cash and clothing being the two exceptions. Cash obviously retains its entire value, while clothing is almost valueless to the thief. In the case of clothing, most of the value to the thief involves that clothing which he retains for his own use. The fence who was interviewed suggested that, to the thief, stolen clothing would realistically be worth approximately 12 percent of its market value. Upon agreement by police officials, this figure was adopted.

---

[14] Norfolk Police Department, *Annual Police Report,* Norfolk, Virginia, 1964.

[15] President's Commission on Law Enforcement and Administration of Justice, *The Challenge of Crime in a Free Society* (Washington, D. C.: Government Printing Office, 1967), pp. 20-21.

[16] U.S. Task Force on Assessment of Crime, *Task Force Report: Crime and Its Impact, An Assessment* (Washington, D. C.: Government Printing Office, 1967), pp. 46-47.

Table 1
TOTAL REPORTED THEFTS EXCLUDING ROBBERY AND PETIT LARCENY, CITY OF NORFOLK, 1964

Category	Stolen	Recovered
Currency	$ 83,773	$ 9,988
Jewelry	187,744	35,462
Furs	8,149	32
Clothing	75,726	11,132
Miscellaneous	300,109	59,053
TOTAL	$655,501	$115,667

Source: Norfolk Police Department, *Annual Police Report,* Norfolk, Virginia, 1964.

Table 2
TOTAL REPORTED AND UNREPORTED THEFTS EXCLUDING ROBBERY AND PETIT LARCENY, CITY OF NORFOLK, 1964

Category	Stolen			Recovered
Currency	$ 83,773	× 2 =	$ 167,546	$ 9,988
Jewelry	187,774	× 2 =	375,548	35,462
Furs	8,149	× 2 =	16,298	32
Clothing	75,726	× 2 =	151,452	11,132
Miscellaneous	300,109	× 2 =	600,218	59,053
TOTAL			$1,311,062	$115,667

Table 3
NET TAKE FROM TOTAL REPORTED AND UNREPORTED THEFTS, CITY OF NORFOLK, 1964

Category	Net Take
Currency	$ 157,558
Jewelry	340,086
Furs	16,266
Clothing	140,320
Miscellaneous	541,165
TOTAL	$1,195,395

Applying these percentages to Table 3, the figures for net benefits shown in Table 4 are obtained, totaling $353,899. Of the 1,867 reported cases of grand larceny, 193 (10.3 percent) resulted in arrests. Of the 2,388 reported cases of burglary, 335 (14 percent) resulted in arrests.

Table 4

ADJUSTED NET TAKE FROM TOTAL REPORTED AND UNREPORTED
THEFTS, CITY OF NORFOLK, 1964

Category	Net Take		
Currency	$157,558 × 1.00 =	$157,558
Jewelry	340,086 × 0.20 =	68,017
Furs	16,266 × 0.20 =	3,253
Clothing	140,320 × 0.12 =	16,838
Miscellaneous	541,165 × 0.20 =	108,233
TOTAL		$353,899

Of those convicted, 195 were adults and these adults stole 82.04 percent of the total amount stolen by those arrested. Since the present study is concerned only with adults, this figure was used to adjust net benefits, attempting to exclude that portion of the total stolen by juveniles. Assuming that adults steal 82.04 percent of all merchandise stolen, total benefits to adults become $290,339.

The Costs: 1964. Of the 195 adults arrested, 31 served time in prison on felony convictions (both burglary and grand larceny are considered to be felonies), while 29 served time on a less serious misdemeanor charge. Investigation revealed that these 29 were probably guilty of the more serious charge, but that the court found it expedient, as it so often does, to reduce the charge. We have assumed that these individuals were guilty of committing one of the crimes being investigated.

Of the 31 convicted felons, 25 served 52.09 years in prison. The remaining six were convicted of multiple offenses. The average of the first 25 was used to approximate the length of time in prison for these six which resulted from crimes of burglary or grand larceny. Adding this approximation yields a total of 64.57 years served in prison.

A misdemeanor conviction involves a sentence of one year or less. An approximation of the time served by the 29 so convicted was 13.77 years. This is an approximation because records for some individuals could not be found. They were tried, convicted, and sentenced, but if they served the sentences, no one seems to know where they served them. Averages for those whose records were available were used for the seven individuals who "disappeared."

Total time served in jail for the 1964 thefts was 78.34 years. Along with these years of imprisonment went fines totaling $2,460 levied on misdemeanants.

Since our cost measure is essentially alternative income available to the convicted thief in legal occupations, an estimate of this income was obtained by approximating the average yearly income—prior to arrest—of the sixty men and women convicted for the 1964 thefts.

Employment records revealed the type of job most frequently held by these individuals. We then used studies by the Bureau of Statistics of the Department of Labor to obtain average hourly wages for each type of job—specifically in the Norfolk area. Results show that the sixty individuals imprisoned in 1964 could have earned, on the average, $1.62 per hour in legitimate jobs had they not gone to prison.

Records further indicated frequent periods of unemployment for these persons, and led us to a seemingly reasonable assumption that, on the average, each person worked only approximately thirty weeks per year. Assuming a forty hour work-week, we found that the average yearly gross income per person was $1,932. For the 78.34 years served, $151,353 was lost in addition to the $2,460 in fines. Total lost income as a result of incarceration was $153,813.

We also made our calculations on the bases of forty and fifty weeks worked per year, respectively, and these results are shown in Table 5.

The Benefits: 1966. Identical procedures were used to obtain an estimate of benefits from 1966 thefts.[17] These benefits were significantly higher than those of 1964: $460,121 compared to $290,339. Examination of the data revealed several possible explanations for this gap. Of some importance was the fact that a greater amount was stolen in 1966: $1,915,603 compared to $1,203,806. Possibly more significant was the fact that only 61 individuals served time for these thefts and their total sentences were only 67.45 years as compared to 78.34 years served for the 1964 thefts. The 1965 change in the Virginia State Code which raised from $50 to $100 the minimum theft classified as grand larceny must be considered significant here. (For the purpose of comparison, we continued to use $50 as the lower limit to crimes classified as grand larceny.)

The Costs: 1966. We determined the average hourly wage for the 61 individuals incarcerated in 1966 to be $1.55. Fines totaling $2,615 were levied. The calculation for each of the three assumptions concerning weeks worked per year are shown in Table 6.

The Benefits and Costs: 1964, 1966 Combined. We have added together the figures used in each of the individual calculations to give a broader base to our results. Table 7 compares and combines the results for 1964 and 1966.

Conclusions to Empirical Analysis. We must now ask if, indeed, those factors affecting cost which we "temporarily" disregarded can be ignored. Psychic costs present the major roadblock in our analysis. The bad reputation aspect can reasonably be omitted. Superficial investigation points to the fact that a criminal record may be of some benefit to the convict. In numerous cases, especially in the ghetto,

---

[17] Norfolk Police Department, *Annual Police Report,* Norfolk, Virginia, 1966.

Table 5
INCOME LOST AS RESULT OF INCARCERATION, 1964

Weeks Worked Per Year, Assumed	Gross Income Per Year, Average	Total Income Lost [a]	Total Income Lost, Plus Fines [a]
30	$1,932	$151,353	$153,813
40	$2,576	$201,804	$204,264
50	$3,220	$252,255	$254,715

a For the 78.34 years served.

Table 6
INCOME LOST AS RESULT OF INCARCERATION, 1966

Weeks Worked Per Year, Assumed	Gross Income Per Year, Average	Total Income Lost [a]	Total Income Lost, Plus Fines [a]
30	$1,860	$125,457	$128,072
40	$2,480	$167,276	$169,891
50	$3,000	$202,350	$204,965

a For the 67.45 years served.

Table 7
BENEFITS AND COSTS OF THEFT, CITY OF NORFOLK, 1964 AND 1966

Year	Total Income			Total Benefits From Theft
	Weeks worked per year			
	30	40	50	
1964	$153,813	$204,264	$254,715	$290,339
1966	128,072	169,891	204,965	460,121
1964 and 1966	$281,885	$374,155	$459,680	$750,989 [a]

a Total of *unrounded* data for both years.

the criminal is held in esteem when he returns to his community upon release from prison.

The real problem arises in consideration of the psychic costs of the loss of freedom. Until a realistic estimate can be made for this cost, our conclusions must be considerably weaker than we would like. Examining Table 7 for the two years combined and making the most likely assumption that the convicted criminals would have worked thirty weeks per year, the benefits from theft are more than double the costs, with a net difference of $469,104.[18] We find that, for the total 145.79 years served in prison, benefits exceed costs by this amount. For the individuals who served these sentences, the average evaluation of the cost of "loss of freedom" would have to be greater than $3,225 per year in prison before one could say that theft is not profitable.

Several studies have been proposed to determine the true cost of this loss of freedom aspect. In one preliminary report, James P. Gunning revealed that prisoners he worked with would pay only an average of $1,500 per year in return for freedom.[19] This would seem to be a close approximation to the cost associated with loss of freedom, but the sample size and procedure used to arrive at this figure make the result of little significance.

Finally, we have ignored the negative costs associated with incarceration. These costs would seem definitely to be determinable, but as yet little work has been performed here.[20]

What *do* these results show? Ignoring the psychic costs of the loss of freedom, thieves in Norfolk did make a net profit. Using Gunning's approximation, theft continues to be profitable with inclusion of this loss of freedom cost. Further study is needed but these conclusions indicate that thieves, as a group, are making the "correct" choices.

---

[18] This figure would be increased if the benefits and costs were discounted over the lifetime of the thieves involved—benefits from theft, on the average, accrue several months before costs are "levied." A further increase in the gap between benefits and costs would result if one considered the fact that "legitimate" income is taxable while income from crime is "tax exempt."

[19] James P. Gunning, "A Report on the Study of the Costs of Incarceration," Virginia Polytechnic Institute and State University, 1970 (mimeographed).

[20] Paul Nobblett, "Economics of Crime," Virginia Polytechnic Institute and State University, 1969 (unpublished).

THE PECUNIARY INCENTIVES
OF PROPERTY CRIME[1]

Gregory Krohm

In their investigations of the causes of crime, most researchers have invested a great deal of effort probing for the abnormal roots of criminal behavior. The viewpoint taken in this paper is that most chronic criminals are fully rational decision makers, that is, they are capable of scanning the set of occupational choices they feel are open to them and selecting that alternative which stands highest in their own scale of preferences. In comparing the relative desirability of various occupations, the individual weighs not only the tangible, pecuniary rewards, but also a variety of intangible factors. Our purpose here, however, is to quantify only the *monetary* costs and benefits derived from the commission of theft.

The types of pecuniary cost-benefit analysis used in this paper had its greatest predictive (that is, explanatory) power when applied to crimes where monetary payoffs dominate emotional or psychic benefits. For this reason, we restricted our study to the crime of burglary. Except where noted, it is based on data from Chicago during the year 1969. While we recognize the fact that persons who engage in burglary are not a homogeneous group, data limitations made it necessary to center the analysis on the "average" or "typical" burglar.

The first step in the study was to compare the gross (unadjusted for periods of unemployment) income of burglary and legitimate labor. When analyzing the monetary returns of crime, one must remember that, for a variety of reasons, a large portion of burglaries committed do not become part of official police tabulations. Because of this, the official figures were adjusted for the estimated proportion of unreported crimes. We made a similar adjustment on the police figures for property stolen in burglaries. This resulted in the following figures:

Adjusted number of burglaries	109,000
Adjusted value of property ultimately gained by burglars (net of recovered merchandise)	$22,450,000

In order to get some idea of the gross share of this loot per burglar, an estimate had to be made of the average number of participants in a burglary. Using two different sources, we estimated that slightly more than two participants were involved in the average burglary. Thus:

---

[1] This work was done as part of a research project funded by the National Science Foundation and directed by Gordon Tullock; it is a summary of a longer paper.

31

Adjusted number of burglaries	109,000
Average number of participants	× 2
Total crimes of burglary committed	218,000

Total property ultimately gained per crime of burglary:

$$\frac{\$22,450,000}{218,000} = \$102$$

It is generally true that the thief does not realize as income the entire fair market value of his loot. He will be satisfied with only a small fraction of its value in order to be freed from the trouble and risk of liquidating the goods himself. From the existing evidence it seems safe to assume that the thief will receive from his fence roughly 20 percent of the fair market value of the nonnegotiable loot. Since cash is not fenced and is worth its face value, it is especially important to know the proportion of cash stolen in order to calculate the burglar's net money income. We have estimated that approximately 20 percent of the total loot stolen is negotiable (cash).

In light of the above estimates, it is possible to approximate the burglar's income per offense by taking 20 percent (the fence value) of his nonnegotiable loot and adding to it the full value of all the negotiables taken:

Nonnegotiable portion of loot	$81.60 (80 percent of $102)
Fence value of the above loot	16.30 (20 percent of $81.60)
Negotiable property stolen	+20.40
Net values of loot to burglar	$36.70

To make the income from burglary more comparable to other forms of employment, it would be desirable to measure the gains by the amount of time spent in obtaining them. However, the time spent working on a burglary is difficult to pin down. Even though the typical residence burglar probably spends no more than an average of twenty minutes actually committing the burglary, a thief may spend a good deal of time preparing for a "score." Since the purpose of this paper is to measure pecuniary returns and not job amenities, a single act of burglary will hereafter be defined as a "day's work." The amount of leisure time or the intensity of labor in this contrived unit are not considered.

It is now appropriate to compare the above estimate of net income earned per "day's work" at burglary with the income the burglar could have earned in the best legitimate occupation open to him. Research has indicated that the best legitimate job open to *most* burglars was that of an unskilled blue-collar worker. In 1969, unskilled laborers in Chicago's manufacturing firms were earning $26.80 for an *eight-hour day*. This figure is based on the simplifying assumption that tax payments are roughly matched by non-wage benefits, for example, vacation pay, hospitalization, et cetera. A second figure was obtained using the actual earnings of ex-convicts. Averaging the two estimates produced an alternative income of $23.30 for a "day's work." For those burglars under 18 years of age, a group whose legitimate employment prospects are historically very poor, the alternative income was approximated by the legal minimum wage of $1.60 per hour or $11.62 a day (after taxes).

Next, crude estimates were made of some of the unemployment risks which confront both the burglar and his legitimate counterpart. As stated at the beginning of this paper, quantifiable income flows, not psychic ones, are the focus of this study. For that reason, prison terms were treated simply as periods of mandatory unemployment. The unemployment rate among persons having the same earning potential as the average burglar was considered a risk which the thief would have to face were he to choose honest employment.

From police and court data we have concluded that the chance of an "adult" (seventeen or older) burglar being sent to prison for *any single offense* is .0024. This is considered his chance of becoming unemployed per burglary he becomes involved in. For juveniles (under seventeen years of age), the risk was much lower, 0.0015. An adult who was actually sent to the penitentiary spent an average of 26.8 months (1964 data). Convicted juveniles, on the other hand, could expect to be institutionalized for about nine months.

Although a person may find it less distasteful in many ways to lose his legitimate job than to go to prison, the negative effect on one's average career earnings is the same. Moreover, statistics show that unemployment is no small threat to persons having the socioeconomic-demographic characteristics of the typical burglar.

One method of evaluating the income effects of both prison and conventional unemployment is to reduce money income in proportion to the statistical risk of being unemployed. The burglar's expected income, over the run of his career, is significantly reduced by this percentage of work time lost in prison. His expected legitimate income is reduced to a lesser extent by the average rate of unemployment.

The long-term average daily earnings of the fictitious "typical" burglar in crime and in his best form of honest employment are shown in the following table:

	Illegitimate	Legitimate
Adult average daily earnings—before and after adjusting for unemployment		
Income ignoring the risk of unemployment	$36.70 [2]	$23.30
Proportional work time lost	65%	7%
Average income adjusted for lost work time	12.85	21.67

[2] Data limitations made it impossible to adjust for the fact that adults steal more per offense than do juveniles. If such an adjustment were made, the adult earnings would rise and juvenile earnings fall.

	Illegitimate	*Legitimate*
Juvenile average daily earnings—before and after adjusting for unemployment		
Income ignoring risk of unemployment	$36.70 [2]	$11.62
Proportional work time lost	32%	22%
Average income adjusted for lost work time	24.96	9.06

The above figures understate the burglar's real income since it ignores the income in kind which the incarcerated burglar receives from the state. If we merely include per diem state expenditures on housing and feeding prisoners, the returns to crime would increase drastically:

	Adults	*Juveniles*
Average criminal income adjusted for unemployment	$12.85	$24.96
Income in kind	17.50	17.50
Total income	$30.35	$42.46

After a final note of warning regarding the provisional nature of the data, we can make the following general statements: (1) burglary is a highly superior source of income vis-à-vis legitimate employment if an individual has little aversion to risk or, alternatively, a low rate of time discount (drug addicts are very common examples); (2) after we adjust the average earnings to reflect the time spent unemployed, the comparative income advantage of burglary vanishes for adults, unless one includes income in kind; (3) the income incentives to commit burglary are especially large for juveniles. These findings are consistent with the fact that most burglaries are committed by youths who have little to lose from seeking their fortunes in crime. With age comes increased legitimate opportunities and less reason to choose burglary as an occupation.

HOW PROFITABLE IS BURGLARY?

J. Patrick Gunning, Jr.

The hypothesis to be tested in this paper is that the profits of professional burglary are high enough to induce persons, who would otherwise have been productive citizens, into a life of crime. There appeared to be two ways of testing the hypothesis, given the nature of the data. Since some burglars are undoubtedly social deviants, a direct test would require that the deviants be separated from the professionals. In light of the preliminary nature of this study, such a separation would have been largely extracted from the data, and to that extent, the test would have lost much of its scientific objectivity. Consequently, it was necessary to make indirect tests of the hypothesis.

The first method that was used to test the hypothesis was merely to assume that all burglars were professionals. If we accept as reasonable the assumption that burglary is at least no *more* profitable to the social deviant than to the professional (because the financial costs and benefits of burglary are presumably not the basic motivation for a deviant's crime), and if we could show that the overall profits from burglary were higher than the economic return to alternative occupations, we could then make a reasonable case for increasing the penalties to convicted professional burglars.

The second method involved the use of an objective proxy for the extent of professionalism in a burglary. The proxy was the amount stolen in the burglary. On the whole, it seems reasonable to expect that a much larger percentage of burglaries of over $1,000 are committed by professionals than burglaries of under $1,000. Furthermore, a comparison of the profitability of the over-$1,000 burglaries with other burglaries might provide a basis for discrimination by judges with respect to their sentencing decisions, even if the size of the crime were totally unrelated to what this study has called "professionalism."

I. Method

In general, burglary during any given time can be said to have been profitable if the benefits accruing to burglars exceeded the opportunity costs of burglarizing. Formalizing this concept, the profits derived from burglary (π) equal the benefits (B) minus the opportunity costs (OC) of burglary. Or:

$$\pi = B - OC. \tag{1}$$

35

The benefits of burglary for any given time consist mainly of the sale price of the loot that is sold and of the "use value" of the loot that is kept. By far the most important element in the calculation of the opportunity costs is the expected value of the penalty for getting caught. For instance, in Delaware, in 1967, the number of hours spent in jail by convicted burglars was greater than the estimated dollar value of stolen loot to burglars. Although it was a simple matter to estimate the probability of capture and the expected sentence, it is beyond the scope of this paper to attempt to determine burglars' evaluations of the harshness of imprisonment. Estimating the demand schedule for the right to remain free from jail is not unlike estimating the demand schedule for moonlight on a romantic summer evening—both of these "goods" simply cannot be bought and sold in markets.

We request, therefore, that the reader make his own judgment. In order to make the reader's judgment easier, some algebraic manipulations have been performed on the opportunity cost of burglary. Essentially, we have defined opportunity cost in terms of wages that could have been earned by imprisoned burglars. Equation (2) shows that the opportunity costs of burglary are equal to some multiple (λ) of the sums of prisoner's alternative wage rates, times their respective sentences in hours ($\Sigma w_i s_i$), times an adjustment factor (40/168) which expresses the assumption that each prisoner would work a forty-hour week.*

$$OC = \frac{40}{168} \lambda \Sigma w_i s_i. \tag{2}$$

A way of expressing this relationship verbally is to say that the total opportunity cost of burglary during a given time is equal to some multiple of the amount of money which could have been earned by the average burglar during the time that he spent in jail for his crimes times the number of burglars. Substituting equation (2) into equation (1), we get:

$$\pi = B - \frac{40}{168} \lambda \Sigma w_i s_i. \tag{3}$$

We now ask the following question: How small must λ be to assure that burglary will be economically profitable (i.e., to assure that $\pi > O$)? Now, if $\pi > O$, B must be greater than opportunity costs. That is,

$$B > \frac{40}{168} \lambda \Sigma w_i s_i. \tag{4}$$

Transforming equation (4) gives:

$$\lambda < \frac{168}{40} B / \Sigma w_i s_i. \tag{5}$$

---

* An adjustment for seasonal and part-time employees was also made. For a full description, see my more complete paper, "The Economic Basis for the Punishment of Burglars," available through the Center for Study of Public Choice, Virginia Polytechnic Institute and State University, Blacksburg, Virginia.

Using equation (5), burglary will be profitable if λ is smaller than the right side of the expression. Thus, the reader needs only to compare the ratio of benefits to earnings with the percentage of his alternative wage that he believes the average burglar would be willing to give up in exchange for his freedom. For example, if the observed λ is 2.0, then, for burglary to be economically profitable, the average burglar must not be willing to pay more than 2.0 times what he could have earned during his jail term. Consequently, if the reader feels that the average burglar would, in fact, be willing to pay more than 2.0 times the amount that he could have earned, then the reader must conclude that burglary is unprofitable.

II. Testing the Hypothesis

First Test of the Hypothesis. The first test of the hypothesis that burglary is at least as profitable as other income-yielding alternatives was computed using figures for all burglars. If we substitute the actual numerical values into equation (5), we get an estimated benefit-earnings ratio of 1:28.

If the reader believes that the average burglar would not have been willing to pay as much as 1.28 times his average alternative wage to stay out of jail for a time equal to the length of his sentence, then he could conclude that burglary in Delaware in 1967 was a profitable activity.

Second Test of the Hypothesis. The second test compared the profit on all burglary to the profit on large (over $1,000) burglaries. The benefit-earnings ratio for over-$1,000 burglaries was found to be 2.04. Regarding large burglaries alone, if the reader believes that burglars who stole large amounts were unwilling to pay more than 2.04 times their alternative earnings to stay out of jail, then he should conclude that burglary is a profitable occupation.

It is apparent from the two tests that large burglaries are more profitable, or less unprofitable, than small burglaries. However, before one could put much faith in this comparison, one would have to know the relative evaluation of freedom by individuals with different incomes. Burglars in the over-$1000 category had larger incomes, and it seems reasonable to expect that the percentage of income that an individual is willing to pay to avoid incarceration rises with income. Furthermore, the number of persons convicted and sentenced for large burglaries in this study was only eight, so that the possibility of error in the second test is quite large.

III. Conclusion

On the basis of this pilot, the need for a more comprehensive study is obvious. It is sad but true that none of our current criminal laws are based on a truly scientific economic analysis. This is the case in spite of the fact that some crimes seem to be almost entirely motivated by financial considerations. Consider such crimes as fraud, embezzlement, employee pilfering, shoplifting, and false advertising. It is clear to me that an increase in penalties for these crimes would substantially reduce the crime rate and lead to lower enforcement costs. If it is true that burglars who steal large amounts are primarily motivated by financial considerations, a substantial increase in penalties for large thefts seems warranted. Although it would be impossible to avoid treating some social deviants inappropriately, it is conjectured that such a risk is well worth the potential savings in criminal cost to society.

COMMENTS ON THE
PAPERS IN SEMINAR

William C. Bailey

I intend first to examine some of Professor Horton's arguments regarding the motives of criminals as they relate to (1) the nature of, and the adequacy of, the concept of motivation in criminological research; (2) the nature of causation and our present understanding of causal factors in criminology; (3) the state of theory in criminology today and the direction it is taking; and (4) the "promising possibilities" Professor Horton suggests criminologists might consider.

Motivation and Criminology

Let me say at the outset that I do not envy Professor Horton's assignment to examine the "motivations of criminals." As he points out, an examination of the sociological literature reveals very few attempts to deal specifically with the motives of offenders. With the exception of a brief discussion by Albert K. Cohen and James F. Short in 1971 on the sociological perspectives of crime and delinquency, I too have found no systematic motivational analysis in the recent literature. Cohen and Short present a series of three general propositions of criminal motivation couched in a symbolic interactionist framework. Their general formula for motivation is as follows: "In any given situation, the actor tends to select, from the possibilities open to him, that mode of action that is most likely to reduce the disparity between his self-image and his self-demands, and thereby to maintain or enhance a satisfactory self-judgment." [1]

Despite the fact that few theorists have explicitly set forth a general theory of the motivations of offenders, close examination of many contemporary theories of crime and delinquency clearly reveals the importance assigned to motivation. Sutherland and Cressey, for example, state that the product of differential association not only includes the learning of "techniques of committing a crime, which are sometimes very complicated and sometimes very simple," but also "the specific direction of *motives,* drives, rationalizations, and attitudes." [2] Similarly, the central role of motivation is quite evident in Daniel Glaser's theory of differential identifica-

---

[1] Albert K. Cohen and James F. Short, Jr., "Crime and Juvenile Delinquency," *Contemporary Social Problems,* 3rd edition, ed. Robert K. Merton and Robert Nisbet (New York: Harcourt Brace Jovanovich, Inc., 1971), p. 123.

[2] Edwin H. Sutherland and Donald R. Cressey, *Principles of Criminology,* 8th edition (Philadelphia: J. B. Lippincott Co., 1970), p. 75.

tion (published in 1956), Robert K. Merton's classic anomie theory (1957), Richard A. Cloward and Lloyd E. Ohlin's opportunity theory (1960), Albert K. Cohen's theory in *Delinquent Boys* (1955), Gresham M. Sykes's and David Matza's theory of neutralization (1957), Walter C. Reckless's theory of containment (1967),[3] et cetera. In short, there would appear to be no shortage of theories in the sociological literature addressing motivation in crime and delinquency. Nor does a brief survey of the psychiatric literature on crime reveal any such vacuum.[4]

In summary, contrary to Horton's assessment, it would appear that the concern for the motives of offenders has not "expired" from the criminological literature. Nor would it appear that the sociopsychological literature on motivation holds no promise in the search for motives underlying "significant social behavior"— including crime and delinquency—as he also argues.

As Horton correctly points out, much sociopsychological research on motivation has been of a laboratory type, but this does not automatically rule out its relevance to the "outside world," as some would argue. As Morris Zelditch, Jr., points out, the vehicle of inference to the outside world from the laboratory is theory, not the direct similarity of the laboratory to the outside world, as is often mistakenly assumed.[5] Dr. Horton may well be correct that finesse in the game of Monopoly ill prepares one to successfully wheel and deal on Wall Street, but few would deny the important developments in the areas of perception, attitudes, power and influence, attraction, status and communication, leadership, norm formation, role formation and role strain, intergroup relations and socialization that have come from social psychology.

One final point of Professor Horton's discussion of motivation should be noted before we move on. In his analysis, he concludes that because "motives are more likely to be found in the mind of the observer than established as components

---

[3] See Daniel Glaser, "Criminality Theories and Behavioral Images," *American Journal of Sociology,* vol. 61 (March 1956), pp. 433-44; Robert K. Merton, *Social Theory and Social Structure* (New York: Free Press of Glencoe, 1957); Richard A. Cloward and Lloyd E. Ohlin, *Delinquency and Opportunity* (New York: Free Press of Glencoe, 1960); Albert K. Cohen, *Delinquent Boys* (New York: Free Press of Glencoe, 1955); Gresham M. Sykes and David Matza, "Techniques of Neutralization: A Theory of Delinquency," *American Sociological Review,* vol. 22 (December 1957), pp. 664-74; and Walter C. Reckless, *The Crime Problem* (New York: Appleton-Century-Crofts, 1967).

[4] See, for example, Karl Menninger, *The Crime of Punishment* (New York: The Viking Press, 1968) and Seymour Halleck, *Psychiatry and the Dilemmas of Crime* (New York: Harper and Bros., 1967). Sociologists have typically ignored the psychiatric literature because of their unfamiliarity with psychiatric jargon and their rejection of the importance which psychiatrists assign to the subconscious roots of human motivation. This literature must not be overlooked, however, for not all of this profession seem wholly preoccupied with this level of explanation. Halleck, for example, in the impressive work cited above states that "while some aggressive and some sexual activity is often correlated with weakening control mechanisms . . . the act of law violation is often a deliberate, planned and complicated operation. . . ." (p. 61)

[5] Morris Zelditch, Jr., "Can You Really Study an Army in the Laboratory?" Stanford, California, 1968, mimeographed.

40

in the behavior system of the actor," the motivation concept is of no value as a scientific tool.

To this conclusion I must take strong exception. Certainly the assessment of motives rests upon the inference or deduction of the observer, but this is equally true in assessing all inner mental states. But so what? What Horton appears to be saying is that since a motive is not a thing or an entity that can be observed directly, its existence is simply a product of the observer, and again, only limited by his semantic imagination. If we were to accept Horton's suggestion and throw out motives on these grounds, we would also be forced to rule out of existence the equally important, but nonobservable, concepts of values, beliefs, interests, needs, attitudes, sentiments, aptitudes, intelligence, aspirations, individuality, frustration, anxiety, happiness, anger, pride and so on, which all rest upon inference. Furthermore, what proportion of the basic terms, tools and concepts in the social as well as the physical sciences do not rest upon inference and deduction of one form or another?

Criminology and the Search for Causes

Once disposing of the utility of motivational inquiry, Horton next argues that the search for causes in criminology has provided no great insight into understanding crime and delinquency. A cause, he states, is commonly defined as a condition which is both necessary ("in that the criminal behavior appears *only* when this factor is present") and sufficient ("in that criminal behavior *always* follows whenever this factor is present") for the appearance of a particular consequence.[6] In criminology, he claims, no true causes of crime and delinquency have yet been established.

Here I must take strong exception with him. The definition of cause that he presents is only one of many, and fortunately not the one that guides most scientific inquiry.[7] To require that a condition be both necessary and sufficient in order to consider it a *true cause* (and I am not sure of the difference between a true cause and *cause*) of a consequence is to rule out the possibility of ever establishing causation. Who among us in our own work or in examining that of others has ever discovered a condition in which a certain consequence occurs only when a single factor is present, and the presence of that single factor, and that factor alone, is

---

[6] I would define "necessary" and "sufficient" conditions slightly differently. A factor is a "necessary" condition if it must be present for an effect to occur regardless of the presence of additional causal factors. A factor is a "sufficient" condition if its presence (and only its presence is required) is invariably followed by the occurrence. For a brief discussion of necessary and sufficient conditions see Travis Hirschi and Hannah Selvin, *Delinquency Research: An Appraisal of Analytic Methods* (New York: The Free Press, 1967).

[7] For an excellent discussion of social causation, see Robert M. MacIver, *Social Causation* (Boston: Ginn and Co., 1942). For a brief summary of the concept cause and social causation, see *A Dictionary of the Social Sciences,* ed. Julius Gould and William L. Kolb (New York: The Free Press, 1964), pp. 646-47.

sufficient to produce the observed consequence? To put it in other words, how many of us have ever observed a perfect correlation in a bivariate case? [8] Notice that we must use the term bivariate here, for a requirement that a causal relationship be both necessary and sufficient implies but a single cause and a single effect. I submit that if those of us in search of causal relationships accept Dr. Horton's standard of causation, we might as well call it quits right now, pack up and go home. Not only must we do so, but so must our big brothers in the hard sciences, for necessary and sufficient conditions are equally unheard of in those fields. [9]

With Horton's view of causation it is easy to see how no conclusion could be possible other than that no true causes of crime have yet been established from the many hundreds of research studies in criminology and, further, that the future search for causes is doomed to failure. Horton goes on to say that all that has emerged from these hundreds of studies is a "series of statistical associations, correlations and sequences." (I would argue that in seeking cause, all we can ever hope to "observe" is association, correlation and sequences.) Horton says that since none of these sequences and covariances is perfect, since we cannot know what really causes people to commit crimes, we have "lumped them together as multiple causes."

Here too, I must take strong exception to Horton's description of how multiple causes are simply the lumping together of bits and fragments of empirical evidence. His use of the concept of multiple causation greatly departs from its common use in contemporary criminology literature. The "throw it all together" practice he equates with the assumption of multiple causation has not enjoyed popularity among respectable scholars since Robert MacIver's classic statement on this question over thirty years ago, and Albert Cohen's later statement on multiple factor approaches over twenty years ago. [10] As Hirschi and Selvin suggest, the principle of multiple causation should be viewed as the only rational assumption one can make with evidence currently available, and not as a "cop out" after having fallen short of our ideal of single causation. They state:

> All studies have shown that more than one independent variable is needed to account for delinquency. In this field, as in others, perfect relations are virtually unknown. The researcher who finds a less than perfect relation between variable X and delinquency should not conclude that X is not a cause of delinquency, but merely that it is not the only cause. [11]

One additional argument Horton makes about multiple causation deserves consideration before we move on. He states that the multiple causation approach

---

[8] Further, even when a perfect correlation is observed, error is usually still present.

[9] See Hirschi and Selvin, *Delinquency Research*, pp. 117-19.

[10] MacIver, *Social Causation*, and Albert K. Cohen, "Juvenile Delinquency and the Social Structure" (Ph.D. diss.: Harvard University, 1951), pp. 5-13.

[11] Hirschi and Selvin, *Delinquency Research*, p. 118. They are, of course, assuming that the causal order and lack of spuriousness criteria are satisfied.

of "transmitting statistical associations into causes is far from satisfying. By this test, burned-out street lights, flimsy door locks, and parked cars are 'causes' of crime." I would certainly have to agree with him that the simple transmitting of correlation into assumptions of causation is far from satisfying, but few reputable scholars would argue otherwise. One of the first lessons any introductory philosophy student learns is that "in no way" can one automatically assume causation from an observed correlation; nor can one ever prove causation in an absolute sense, as David Hume and others convinced us long ago. All anyone (the scientist included) can do is to try to meet the minimum requirements of demonstrating concomitant variation and proper temporal sequence, and deal with the question of spuriousness as best he can.

In sum, Horton informs us of a truism (that correlation does not mean causation) that has been recognized for generations, and one that no enlightened scholar would dare to question. In short, the issue he raises here is dead, and has been for many years.

After declaring the search for both motives and causes of crime doomed to failure, Professor Horton next informs us that the "interaction between circumstance and self insures that no circumstance and no characteristic of self and no combination thereof will have predictable behavior outcomes for a particular individual." (This conclusion invariably follows whenever we require both a necessary and sufficient condition to be isolated in seeking cause.) So does this slam the door on both causation and prediction as Horton suggests? Fortunately not, for in criminology, as in all fields, the probability of a correct prediction has been substituted for absolute prediction. Even in the hardest of the physical sciences, prediction in every case is never possible. As the beginning chemistry student soon learns, 1,000 replications of the most simple experiment, under the most controlled conditions possible, invariably yields 1,000 different results, if, of course, the measuring devices are adequately refined. This, too, is the situation, obviously, in the soft sciences. But in both the physical and social sciences, this fact is well recognized and in each discipline reasonable standards of prediction (given the state of theory and measurement) have been adopted.

Absolute prediction, at least at the moment, is clearly not a viable goal in any discipline. The important question to be addressed, and one to which Horton might better have addressed himself, is, "What constitutes a reasonable degree of prediction in criminology?" Clearly this must be tackled before any of the policy research Horton suggests we undertake can be realistically considered. Certainly he is not suggesting that if we cannot identify perfectly the "conditions favoring criminal behavior" (not causes, but *conditions favoring* criminal behavior) in order to "restrain, reduce and reform criminals," we should do nothing. If such favoring conditions had to be both necessary and sufficient in order to produce 100 percent predictions in "restraining," "reducing," and "reforming" criminals, Horton's own argument would rule out the policy research he recommends. Certainly, law enforcement and corrections persons would quickly welcome suggestions that would reduce crime by less than 100 percent and reform fewer than all offenders.

The State of Criminological Theory

Before questions of influencing policy can be seriously considered, Horton correctly suggests that we first must ask, "What is the state of theory in criminology?" His answer to this question is that "no concise, truly integrated theory has yet been constructed which relates the great variety of statistical associations and sequences which criminological research has assembled." He cites an ambitious attempt by Richard D. Knudten in a recent criminology text [12] to construct "an integrated theory of delinquency-crime causation," which, he says, unfortunately falls short of the mark.

I take no issue with either of these points. First, Knudten does not successfully provide an adequate, integrated theory of crime and delinquency. And secondly, criminology has not reached the level of grand theory. I do, however, disagree with Dr. Horton's assessment of the direction of theory development and research in contemporary criminology. A casual survey of criminology texts and periodicals over the past few years clearly reveals, in my assessment, an increasing indifference to the search for grand theory, or even for the Merton-type middle-range theory, toward which Horton sees us still actively working.

For some time, most scholars of crime have come to the realization that it is ridiculous to ask questions like, "What is *the* cause of crime?" As MacIver pointed out over three decades ago, "The only thing that is alike in all crimes is that they are all violations of law." [13] The only thing all violators have in common is that they are all violators. A survey of the scope of criminal law allows no other conclusion. One would be hard put, for example, to find any element of human behavior that is not, or has not been at some time, somewhere, forbidden by statute, nor any element of human behavior that is, or has been, universally condemned by criminal law. Accordingly, questions like "What is *the* cause of criminal behavior?" may be more appropriately stated, "What is *the* cause of human behavior?" Unfortunately, no satisfactory answer to either question has yet been posed, nor may it ever be.

Recognizing these facts, Don C. Gibbons argues:

> Criminological attention must turn away from the study of crime and criminality to the examination of various types of role-careers in criminality. We aver that the situation of criminology is similar to that of medicine—there is not one form of sickness, there are many. There is not one cause of illness, there are a number of causes each related to a par-

---

[12] Richard D. Knudten, *Crime in a Complex Society* (Homewood, Ill.: The Dorsey Press, 1970).
[13] MacIver, *Social Causation,* p. 119.

44

ticular form of sickness. So it is with criminality, for the rubric is a broad one indeed, containing under it a very large number of behavioral forms having little in common with each other. If this is so it is doubtful that a general theory of criminal etiology can be discussed which will explain all of the disparate forms taken by criminality. Instead, specific theories or subtheories are required in order to account for different criminal role careers.[14]

Gibbons is not alone in his plea for abandoning grand-level theorizing and concentrating on etiologically homogeneous groups of offenders. A similar approach is suggested and provides the framework of organization in popular criminology texts by Marshall B. Clinard and Richard Quinney (1967), Herbert A. Bloch and Gilbert Geis (1970), Paul W. Tappan (1960), Walter C. Reckless (1967), and Richard R. Korn and Lloyd W. McCorkle (1959).[15]

The focus away from grand theory and toward research and theory on criminal types is also clearly evident in the periodic literature. To cite but a few very noteworthy efforts in this direction, we might mention the work of (1) Julian B. Roebuck and Mervyn L. Cadwallader (1961) and John E. Conklin (1972) on armed robbers; (2) Edwin M. Lemert (1953, 1958) on check forgers; (3) William Wattenberg and James Balistrieri (1952) and Erwin Schepses (1960) on young auto thieves; (4) Mary Owen Cameron (1964) and Gerald D. Robin (1963) on shoplifters; (5) David W. Maurer (1964) on pickpockets; (6) Julian B. Roebuck and Ronald Johnson (1964), Edwin M. Schur (1957), Walter P. Gibson (1946) and David W. Maurer (1940) on "short" and "big" con men; (7) Edwin H. Sutherland's (1937, 1940, 1941, 1945, 1949, 1956) classic work on the professional thief and white-collar crime; Donald R. Cressey (1953) on embezzlers; and so on.[16]

---

[14] Don C. Gibbons, *Society, Crime and Criminal Careers* (Englewood Cliffs, N.J.: Prentice-Hall, 1968), pp. 12-13.

[15] See Marshall B. Clinard and Richard Quinney, *Criminal Behavior Systems* (New York: Holt, Rinehart and Winston, 1967); Herbert A. Bloch and Gilbert Geis, *Man, Crime and Society* (New York: Random House, 1970); Paul W. Tappan, *Crime, Justice, and Correction* (New York: McGraw-Hill Book Co., Inc., 1960); Reckless, *The Crime Problem;* and Richard R. Korn and Lloyd W. McCorkle, *Criminology and Penology* (New York: Holt, Rinehart and Winston, 1959).

[16] See Julian B. Roebuck and Mervyn L. Cadwallader, "The Negro Armed Robber as a Criminal Type: The Construction and Application of a Typology," *Pacific Sociological Review,* vol. 4 (Spring 1961), pp. 12-26; John E. Conklin, *Robbery and the Criminal Justice System* (Philadelphia: J. B. Lippincott, 1972); Edwin M. Lemert, "The Behavior of the Systematic Check Forger," *Social Problems,* vol. 6 (Fall 1958), pp. 141-49, and idem, "An Isolation and Closure Theory of Naive Check Forgery," *Journal of Criminal Law, Criminology, and Police Science,* vol. 44 (September-October 1953), pp. 296-307; William Wattenberg and James Balistrieri, "Automobile Theft: A Favored Group Delinquency," *American Journal of Sociology,* vol. 57 (May 1952), pp. 575-79; Erwin Schepses, "The Young Car Thief," *Journal of Criminal Law, Criminology, and Police Science,* vol. 50 (March-April 1960), p. 569; Mary Owen Cameron, *The Booster and the Snitch* (New York: Free Press, 1964); Gerald D. Robin, "Patterns of Department Store Shoplifting," *Crime and Delinquency,* vol. 9 (April 1963), pp. 163-72; David W. Maurer, *The Whiz Mob* (New Haven: College and University Press, 1964); Julian B. Roebuck and Ronald Johnson, "The Short Con Man," *Crime and Delinquency,*

I point out these examples to illustrate that the more microscopic type of analysis that Horton suggests we follow is widely accepted today in criminology, and has been for some years. The hope is that the accumulation of evidence on the lower levels will in time permit ever larger theoretical systems to be constructed. It may well be, as Horton and others suggest, that theory beyond the middle range will never prove possible. But obviously this remains to be seen. In this writer's assessment, to discourage those who would now pursue middle range theory and even grand level theory is not wise. Quite probably, adequate middle range and grand theory will only come as a result of extensive work at the lower levels. But certainly the shortcomings of Knudten, Sutherland [17] and others do not preclude continued effort in this direction. I think there is plenty of room in the field of criminology for work at all levels of analysis.

Some Promising Possibilities?

Having "demonstrated" the shortcomings of theory in criminology, Professor Horton asks, "Are we then doomed to wander forever in the theoretical wilderness and never reach the promised land of policy-validating theory and knowledge?" Fortunately not, he tells us, for by recognizing the wide range of what he calls "predisposing circumstances" of crime and treatment possibilities, we might examine some "promising possibilities" which have yet not been fully developed. (It is of interest to note here that Horton previously ruled out the possibility of finding causes of crime, but apparently he feels predisposing conditions can be determined and used in policy formulation. Further, are not predisposing conditions along with motives and causes really only products of the observer, limited only by his imagination?)

What are the promising possibilities that Horton suggests, and what is their meaning for those in criminology? The latter question is something of a mystery for we are not sure from his discussion what our role as scientists and citizens should be within these possibilities. But what are the promising possibilities?

Horton first suggests, but later rejects, consideration of the question as to whether eliminating the injustices and inequities of our society would reduce the

---

vol. 10 (July 1964), pp. 235-48; Edwin M. Schur, "Sociological Analysis of Confidence Swindle," *Journal of Criminal Law, Criminology, and Police Science,* vol. 48 (September-October 1957), pp. 296-304; Walter B. Gibson, *The Bunco Book* (Holyoke, Mass.: Sidney H. Radner, 1946); David W. Maurer, *The Big Con* (New York: Bobbs-Merrill Co., 1940); Edwin H. Sutherland, "White Collar Criminality," *American Sociological Review,* vol. 5 (February 1940), pp. 1-12; idem, "Crime and Business," *Annals of the American Academy of Political and Social Science,* vol. 217 (September 1941), pp. 112-18; idem, "Is 'White Collar Crime' Crime?" *American Sociological Review,* vol. 10 (April 1945), pp. 132-39; idem, *White Collar Crime* (New York: Dryden Press, 1949); idem, "Crime of Corporations," *The Sutherland Papers,* ed. Albert Cohen, Alfred Lindesmith, and Karl Schuessler (Bloomington, Ind.: Indiana University Press, 1956); and Donald R. Cressey, *Other People's Money* (New York: Free Press, 1953).

[17] Knudten, *Crime in a Complex Society,* and Edwin H. Sutherland, *The Professional Thief* (Chicago: University of Chicago Press, 1937).

motivation for crime. (Notice that he is now asking an empirical question about *motivations* where he earlier rejected such an inquiry.) He concludes that only "a modest crime reduction would follow from even a highly successful attack on racism, poverty and other social problems which are often cited as causal factors in crime." [18] He reasons that the "incidence of criminal acts shows no more than a very modest association with race and income," as revealed by surveys of self-reported deviance. Accordingly, racism, poverty, et cetera, must not be of much causal significance.

Dr. Horton would have to draw this conclusion given his preoccupation with a single cause for a single effect, crime. Might it not be, however, as nearly all criminologists believe, that the causes of crime and delinquency in this society are *not* necessarily uniform throughout the socioeconomic structure? More specifically, might it not be that the motives behind the theft of food and clothing by lower-class, urban, ghetto youth differ from those of bored, middle-class, surburban adolescents who might spend a Saturday afternoon seeing who can steal the biggest brassiere from the local department stores?

Clearly, studies of self-reported crime and delinquency reveal that violations are not confined to racial minorities and the lower class, but this fact alone does not automatically lead us to the conclusion that "a highly successful attack on racism, poverty and other social problems" would not have appreciable effect in reducing crime in this society.

Professor Horton next moves on to ask whether a radical restructuring of our value system in this country would reduce crime, as the radical left (as well as others, I might add) suggests. He concedes that it might have such an effect, but for various reasons, he argues that such a change is not immediately possible and in any case the results of such a change would be uncertain. He suggests two alternative approaches, however, that would be both faster and more certain.

First, by "decriminalizing" all "crimes without victims," including drug use, intoxication, and all forms of private consensual sex behavior among adults, and perhaps abortion, he claims we could greatly reduce our crime problem. Obviously, Horton is perfectly correct, for certainly the easiest and quickest way to deal with a crime problem is to define the problem out of existence. To illustrate, the FBI figures indicate that by simply eliminating the statutes for prostitution and commercialized vice, sex offenses (except for forcible rape), narcotics, gambling, liquor violations, public drunkenness and vagrancy, the number of arrests in 1970 would have been cut from 4,644,006 to 2,904,126—a decrease of 37.5 percent. [19] Decriminalization of drug offenses alone (which were responsible for 265,734 arrests in

[18] It is important to note the significance which the President's Commission on Law Enforcement and the Administration of Justice (*The Challenge of Crime in a Free Society* [Washington, D. C.: U.S. Government Printing Office, 1967]) assigned to poverty, racism, and other social problems in contributing to law breaking. All are factors that Horton summarily dismisses.

[19] Federal Bureau of Investigation, U.S. Department of Justice, *1970 Uniform Crime Report for the United States* (Washington, D. C.: U.S. Government Printing Office, 1971), p. 122.

1970) would also probably have the effect, as Horton points out, of (1) reducing the number of drug-related crimes such as burglary, theft and robbery, (2) discouraging the secondary deviance process, and (3) freeing police to deal with "more important" matters.

I, too, applaud the trend in this country of removing "victimless crimes" from the books, but as I pointed out above, it is not clear what role the research criminologist should play in this "promising possibility." Nor is our role clear with regard to a second "promising possibility" Horton suggests, this being to "reduce the opportunities and temptations to crime while largely bypassing the actor's system of motives and needs." The so-called shortcut measures he suggests which include gun control, alarm systems, and security devices, are "relatively simple, quick and fairly inexpensive ways of altering the behavior situation so that undesirable behavior is discouraged." In both the short run and the long run he believes that the payoff will be higher if we alter the behavior situation of the actor rather than his motivational system.

In my assessment, if those in medical science had accepted such a suggestion in dealing with physical rather than social ills, I am quite sure that the profession of medicine would not have advanced beyond crude first aid. Shortcuts such as Horton suggests are certainly tempting for a fledgling discipline like criminology, but fortunately most specialists in this field have set their ambitions somewhat higher than simple first aid.

A final "promising possibility" that Dr. Horton suggests, and one that seems especially promising compared to his other recommendations, is a greater research concentration in the area of corrections. As he correctly points out, success in this area has been quite limited. Clearly, innovation and experimentation with halfway houses, group therapy, et cetera, are needed, but in my opinion, this should not be done at the expense of continued research into the etiology of crime and delinquency. Here, too, our first aid analogy would seem appropriate, for all too many prevention and corrections programs have not been guided by sound theoretical principles, but rather by faith and intuition. I cite as examples here Mobilization for Youth, an over 14 million dollar project and the Mid-City Project—all very well known efforts, but unfortunately, also well known as failures.

Conclusion

Like Professor Horton, I too find it disheartening to have to end my remarks on his paper on such a negative note. First, I find his wholesale rejection of further consideration of the motives of offenders as highly premature. Second, his argument for abandoning causal research in crime and delinquency is quite unconvincing. Adhering to his conception of cause would clearly put us all out of business immediately. Third, his assessment that theory in criminology falls short of grand scale is quite accurate. But the future course of action he suggests in research and theory is one that has been recognized for years and, in fact, has been put into action with very fruitful results. Finally, I find Professor Horton's suggestion of some "promising possibilities" quite unpromising. I agree to the urgent need for innovative work in the fields of prevention and corrections, but I do not see the "shortcut" maneuvers he suggests to increase risks to potential offenders and reduce temptations as the most rewarding path to follow in either the short or the long run.

With Mr. Cobb's paper on the "economic and sickness hypotheses" regarding theft, I would like first to examine briefly his characterization of the differing hypotheses of crime held by economists and sociologists, and second, to assess his attempt to resolve the conflict between these two theoretical perspectives and merge both into one hypothesis "acceptable to both sides." Lastly, I want to examine the methodology of his benefit-analysis investigation of theft.

The Two Hypotheses

In Mr. Cobb's view, there is a wide gap between the economists' and sociologists' assessments of "the basic motivational characteristics of the criminal element in this country." The economic hypothesis of crime "is founded on the principle that crime is just like any other enterprise: *The potential criminal evaluates all possibilities within the limits of all information which he possesses and chooses that activity which maximizes his utility."* Here, man is viewed as a rational being who chooses those behavioral alternatives—criminal or conventional—which he expects to result in maximum reward and minimum cost, or in other words, maximum profit. This model of behavior, of course, permits miscalculation of anticipated costs and benefits (imperfect knowledge) and variation among individuals in the cost and benefit contingencies associated with any given action and consequence.

Proponents of the economic hypothesis, according to Cobb, believe that criminal activities can be altered by changes in the net utility of individual decision makers, or, in other words, by putting into the "red" the net gain potential criminals might expect.

In contrast, Cobb sees sociologists typically adhering to what he calls the sickness hypothesis. Unfortunately, he does not bother to inform us of the major principles of this hypothesis, nor am I quite sure what theoretical model of crime he believes most sociologists commonly accept. What he does say is that proponents of the sickness hypothesis argue that the threat of punishment has no deterrent effect whatever on crime because, even though the expected payoff of crime may be negative (negative net utility), "the criminal is sick because he disregards this negative effect." Mr. Cobb goes on to say that proponents of this model conclude that "rehabilitation is the only solution to the control of criminal behavior."

I must say that I am somewhat bewildered by Cobb's discussion of sociologists and the sickness hypothesis. First, in his discussion of this hypothesis he fails to mention one sociological theory of crime or to name a single theorist in sociology who fits this model. And, I might add, from his description of the sickness hypothesis I can think of no example myself. I know of no major theory of crime in sociology that views the criminal as *sick* because he disregards negative sanctions. Nor am I completely sure whether to interpret Cobb as saying that sociologists view criminals as sick because they disregard the expectation of negative net utility, or because they are sick they disregard negative net utility.

Furthermore, I know of no major theory of crime in sociology that views rehabilitation as "the only solution to the control of criminal behavior." What about preventive measures? Are they not another approach to crime control? In fact, do not most sociological discussions of crime control clearly suggest a preference for prevention over rehabilitation? I submit that an examination of any text in criminology or juvenile delinquency will reveal this to be the case.

What Cobb seems to be saying by introducing the economic and sickness hypotheses is that economists and sociologists differ in the relative importance they would assign the threat of legal sanctions as a deterrent to crime. I must emphasize relative importance here for it would be a serious mistake to view all sociologists as of one opinion on this question, and the same probably applies for economists as well. Clearly a casual survey of the recent sociological literature on crime will reveal a wide variety of opinions on the question of crime and deterrence. Furthermore, such a survey will reveal no careful scholar citing any empirical evidence presently available as conclusive proof "that punishment has no deterrent effect whatever on crime."

In sum, I must take strong exception to Cobb's assessment of current thinking of sociologists on the question of crime and deterrence. The position of Paul B. Horton and Gerald R. Leslie, whose discussion of this issue in 1960 is cited by Cobb, should not be construed to reflect the views of all sociologists nor even most sociologists, as Cobb would lead us to believe. In short, I can only conclude that Cobb's lack of familiarity with the current criminological literature is responsible for many of the conclusions he draws.

A Resolution of the Controversy?

Having presented the economic and sickness hypotheses, Cobb moves on to the task of resolving the controversy he sees between these two models. A communication gap is suggested as the major factor separating proponents of the two hypotheses. Sociologists, he concludes, "do not really believe that punishment in general does not deter." The actual argument that sociologists are making, he says, "is not that punishment does not deter, but rather that our current system of punishment is not effective."

Again, I must take issue with Mr. Cobb for I do not see a gap in communication lying at the heart of the difficulty here. I agree with his view that few sociologists would deny a role to "punishment in general" in influencing social behavior, crime included. To do so would be to disregard completely the accomplishments in behavioral psychology. But more importantly, such denial would reject a sizeable body of theory and research in nearly every subfield of sociology. Here I refer to the influence of the theoretical works of George C. Homans in 1961, John W. Thibaut and Harold H. Kelley in 1959, Paul F. Secord and Carl W. Backman in 1964 and others who attempt to explain social behavior in terms of rewards exchanged and costs incurred in interaction.[20]

For most sociologists, the question of "punishment in general" is not the question of importance here. Rather, the real issue is the role that one class of negative sanctions—legal sanctions—do play, and can play, in the prevention and control of crime. As Cobb points out, many sociologists in the past have seriously questioned the role of legal sanctions as deterrents. Some have even gone so far as to conclude that there is no hope whatsoever of legally punishing persons into conformity. Fortunately, most criminologists have come to view the issue of deterrence as an open question, and one not yet resolved.

It is of interest to note here that Cobb is critical of sociologists for their unwillingness to view the issue of deterrence as an open question. I might level the same criticism against Cobb. After recognizing, as Charles R. Tittle suggests, that we should now be asking "under what conditions are negative sanctions likely to be effective," he repeatedly concludes that "punishment does function as a deterrent."

After concluding that sociologists really do believe that punishment in general does deter crime, Cobb next attempts to merge the economic and sickness hypotheses through using Becker's interpretation of the economic hypothesis. Becker argues essentially that the number of crimes committed by a person is a function of five factors: (1) the probability of conviction (punishment), (2) the nature and severity of the punishment, (3) the income available to the actor from alternative legal and illegal activities, (4) the frequency of nuisance arrests, and (5) the actor's willingness to commit an illegal act.[21]

I seriously question if Becker's hypothesis and Cobb's discussion of it add significantly to our understanding of crime. All Becker and Cobb suggest is that the number of offenses a person would commit is influenced by the threat of legal sanctions, income available from other sources, and one's willingness to commit an offense in the first place, whatever that means. I do not take issue with the

---

[20] George C. Homans, *Social Behavior: Its Elementary Forms* (New York: Harcourt, Brace and World, 1961); John W. Thibaut and Harold H. Kelley, *The Social Psychology of Groups* (New York: John Wiley and Sons, 1959); and Paul F. Secord and Carl W. Backman, *Social Psychology* (New York: McGraw-Hill Book Co., 1964).

[21] Gary Becker, "Crime and Punishment: An Economic Approach," *Journal of Political Economy,* vol. 76 (March-April 1968), pp. 169-217.

probable importance of the first four factors Becker enumerates. All of these considerations, in one form or another, have long been recognized by deterrence theorists since the writings of Cesare Beccaria in 1809, Jeremy Bentham in 1843, and others on the etiology of crime and its control. I might also add to this list, Adam Smith's 1896 *Lecture on Justice, Police, Revenue and Arms* which would appear to be of some relevance here.[22]

What particularly bothers me about Becker's scheme, and I see Cobb adding nothing to it, is his inclusion of the catchall variable, a person's willingness to commit an illegal act in the first place, without specifying the importance of this factor alone and in comparison to the factors that he does enumerate, and without discussing the important factors that influence one's willingness to commit illegal acts. It is precisely these questions that have provided the major source of debate between classical and positivist criminologists over the last century and a half.

It is of interest to note that in Becker's lengthy essay, "Crime and Punishment: An Economic Approach," he mentions Beccaria and Bentham only in passing in the last paragraph of his paper. Cobb does not mention these writers nor the classical school of criminology in his theoretical discussion.

Some Methodological Comments

In the empirical section of his paper, Cobb presents a very interesting analysis of the ex post costs and benefits to thieves, as a group, for two years in Norfolk, Virginia. The method employed is a "simple" benefit-cost technique. In discussing this section of the paper I would like to confine myself to some methodological comments and to the conclusions he draws from his investigation.

The Benefits of Theft. Cobb first attacks the problem of determining the benefits of two types of theft: burglary and grand larceny. In assessing benefits he recognized three important considerations. First, not all thefts are reported to the authorities. Accordingly, Cobb makes the appropriate adjustments in the police figures by using the estimate of the President's Commission that reported costs of theft underestimate the true value by half.

Second, Cobb recognized that the market value of stolen goods to the thief is considerably less than the value placed on stolen goods by theft victims. Excluding stolen cash and clothing, he puts the estimated value of stolen goods to the thief at 20 percent. Finally, Cobb adjusts the total benefit to thieves by the value of stolen goods recovered by the police.

I suggest that a few additional benefit considerations and questions might have been examined, even though adjustments for some of these would not have

---

[22] Cesare Beccaria, *Essay on Crimes and Punishment* (New York: Gould Press, 1809; Bobbs-Merrill edition, 1963, New York); Jeremy Bentham, *Principles of Penal Law,* 1st ed. (Edinburgh: W. Tait, 1943); and Adam Smith, *Lecture on Justice, Police, Revenue, and Arms* (Oxford: Clarendon Press, 1896).

been possible in his analysis. First, it should be recognized that not all victims of theft recognize their loss. This would appear particularly true for theft from businesses. Norman Jaspan and Hillel Black, for example, tell us that the biggest part of retail shrinkage does not result from shoplifters, but rather from employee theft.[23] Of course, reliable estimates of such losses are not available, but more importantly for our purposes here, seldom do such losses ever show up in the police statistics.

Second, even of the thefts that are recognized, not all are reported to the authorities. The National Opinion Research Center victim survey of 1967, for example, reveals that only about 32 percent of burglaries and 44 percent of larcenies are reported to the police. Cobb attempts to deal with this problem by doubling the loss figures reported by the Norfolk police, a procedure suggested by the President's Commission. Whether this adjustment allows for an adequate assessment of total dollar loss is not clear. The nonreporting of theft, it should be noted, is not a random matter. Quite probably, the greater the value of stolen goods, the more likely the theft will be reported. Whether the adjustment procedure suggested by the President's Commission adequately compensates for this fact is not clear. Further, it is not clear if this estimate procedure allows for the tendency of victims to overestimate the value of their stolen goods when reporting to the authorities.

Third, there would appear to be some disagreement over the value of fenced goods. Cobb puts the value at 20 percent for most items, but some suggest a figure of one third and still others a value as high as 40 percent. Unfortunately, there is no "hard" evidence that allows us to answer this question. Certainly though, some types of stolen items have a higher fenced value than others. As a professional fence recently pointed out to me in an interview, a "hot" pistol (say, worth $100 retail) is worth quite a bit more to him than a $100 vacuum cleaner, "which you can't give away." The same could apply to the value of jewelry compared to other "hard to move" items. In short, the fenced value of 20 percent that Cobb uses for jewelry, furs and miscellaneous items (which is the largest single category of theft) would seem somewhat suspect.

The question of fences brings up another issue that must be examined. In Cobb's analysis, benefits to thieves are assessed as if all stolen goods are fenced at the going rate. This would appear to be a highly questionable assumption. Again we are faced with a lack of evidence, but I would submit that probably proportionately few stolen goods are fenced by thieves. Further, I would argue that proportionately few thieves steal with the intention of fencing the loot. Many probably steal with the intention of keeping the goods for themselves, and of course, much stolen property is discarded, particularly by young thieves. All of these factors make it extremely difficult to assess the cash value of stolen goods to thieves.

---

[23] Norman Jaspan and Hillel Black, *The Thief in the White Collar* (Philadelphia: J. B. Lippincott Co., 1960).

There is one additional aspect of "fencing" goods that Cobb glosses over without due consideration. In his analysis he implies that fences are readily available to retrieve stolen goods, and that thieves know of their whereabouts. I put these questions to an introductory sociology class very recently with these results. First, only approximately two-thirds of the class knew what a fence was. Second, only a few out of a class of over 100 thought that they knew where they could sell stolen goods (to a fence, that is). And third, even though each of these students had been personally involved in some theft, and some in major thefts, none had ever tried to fence stolen goods.

In sum, Cobb's attempt to construct an index of the economic benefits of theft is highly commendable, but it would appear to suffer from some major shortcomings that must be recognized.

The Costs of Theft. As Cobb points out, the costs to thieves are extremely difficult to evaluate. He recognizes a number of areas of consideration: the physical costs of the actual work involved in committing thefts; the disposable income lost while incarcerated if apprehended and convicted; fines levied in addition to, or in place of, incarceration; and the psychic costs of the loss of freedom and the negative stigma of a "bad reputation." To these I might add the costs of nuisance arrests (he and Becker cite this as a factor earlier in the paper), the cost of lawyer's fees, the cost of bail, the psychic costs of guilt and shame, and the costs of physical injury that might result from unwilling victims and the police.

Mr. Cobb chooses only to examine two cost factors in his analysis: the loss of disposable income as a result of incarceration, and fines levied on convicted thieves. Using these two factors he constructs his overall index of costs to thieves by combining the figures for fines for convicted thieves with the figures for the total lost disposable income of incarcerated offenders calculated according to the work histories of the convicted thieves.

Some Conclusions

Having constructed indices of total income benefits and total income losses for two years, Cobb compares these estimates to see if theft "pays" in Norfolk, Virginia. For both years combined, total losses are put at $281,885, while benefits equal $750,460, a net difference of $468,575. From these figures, he argues that for those who served prison sentences, the average yearly costs would have to exceed $3,225 per year before one could say that theft is not profitable. Clearly, he concludes, thieves are making a wise economic choice.

But what of psychic costs? Cobb sees the loss of freedom as a major road block in his analysis, but he dismisses "bad reputation" as a possible cost. Why? Because in many cases, he says, and especially in the ghetto, "ex-cons" are held in esteem.

I must take strong issue with Cobb for summarily dismissing legal stigma as a cost. On the contrary, I see it as an important cost consideration. First, while probably some persons with a police record are viewed with esteem in the ghetto, probably many others are seen as losers. Second, theft is definitely not solely confined to ghetto residents. Investigations of confessed thieves reveal that no socioeconomic class in this society has a corner on this market.[24] Hence, the costs of legal stigma cannot be so easily disregarded. Nor does Gunning's 1970 research on the costs of the loss of freedom seem of much importance, as Cobb recognizes. Clearly additional research is required in this important area. Ignoring psychic costs, though, Cobb concludes that thieves in Norfolk are making a wise economic choice. I must conclude that because of some major problems in Cobb's benefit index of theft, I am unconvinced of this conclusion.

Charles H. Logan

I never have understood why some economists, like Cobb, insist on transforming ordinary prose into symbolic formulas, which are harder to type, take longer to read, and often, as in the present instance, add nothing in the way of precision. Gary Becker's statement that the number of offenses is a function of probability of conviction, punishment if convicted, and "other variables" is still just a vague generalization whether he states it that way or as:

$$O_j = O_j\,(p_j, f_j, u_j).$$

A more serious consequence of reducing our thinking to manipulation of the terms of economic equations is that it produces dangerous simplifications. In Cobb's decision model, for example, he is forced to consider the prices of apprehension, punishment, and rehabilitation purely in terms of one common dimension: expenditures. But when nonmonetary costs are also considered, it is clear that the financially cheapest arrangement may entail the greatest overall human cost. Unfortunately, such multidimensional cost accounting does not fit into neat economic models.

The most fascinating part of Cobb's paper—the determination of whether or not theft does, in fact, "pay"—is an illustration of this, perhaps inherent, problem of simplification. Cobb's ingenious calculations and adjustments produce what can

---

[24] See James S. Wallerstein and Clement Wyle, "Our Law-Abiding Law-Breakers," *Probation*, vol. 25 (April 1947), pp. 107-12; Ivan F. Nye, *Family Relations and Delinquent Behavior* (New York: John Wiley, 1958); Robert A. Dentler and Lawrence Monroe, "The Family and Early Adolescent Conformity and Deviance," *Marriage and Family Living*, vol. 23 (August 1961), pp. 241-47; Harwin L. Voss, "Ethnic Differentials in Delinquency in Honolulu," *Journal of Criminal Law, Criminology, and Police Science*, vol. 65 (September 1963), pp. 322-327; and Albert J. Reiss and Albert L. Rhodes, "The Distribution of Juvenile Delinquency in the Social Structure," *American Sociological Review*, vol. 36 (October 1961), pp. 720-32.

be accepted as perhaps the best available estimate of the net monetary benefits of theft to thieves in the aggregate (though I'm surprised that he did not include tax "exemption" in his calculations). But, as Cobb realizes, this does not really tell us—or potential thieves—whether or not theft "pays" in the largest sense of the term.

It is necessary to ask about the usefulness of attempting to calculate the net economic costs and benefits of theft. Suppose we could say for sure that theft is twice as profitable in Baltimore as it is in Cumberland. This might tell us something about the effectiveness of law enforcement in these two cities, but not necessarily, since the profitability of theft is determined by other factors as well. Likewise, the information might be of some interest to thieves who take a scientific approach to their work, but if they are intelligent they will realize that the figures are not relevant to individual thieves, only to thieves as a group. If criminologists are equally intelligent, they too will refrain from drawing inferences about the rationality of the average theft from figures that prove the overall profitability of stealing. Such an inference (that stealing is an individually profitable, hence rational, act) might be correct; but it is also at least equally possible that a small number of individuals gain the bulk of the profits while the majority of thieves are losers, who, therefore, are behaving "irrationally" in the economic sense. At any rate, it is evident that Cobb's paper has little to do with individual thieves, and nothing directly to do with motivation.

Professor Horton also seems to touch only casually on the question of motivation, but first I want to respond briefly to his treatment of the question of causation. I do not share Horton's pessimism about the search for causes, primarily because I don't subscribe to the strict determinist's view that only necessary and sufficient conditions or unique and invariant relations can be identified as causes. Hirschi and Selvin have referred to this as one of several false criteria of causation that have plagued delinquency research. Moreover, Horton's caricature of "multiple causation" is not what I understand by the term. Apparently he uses it to refer to the kind of thinking described by Albert K. Cohen in his critique of the "multiple factor approach" to crime—namely, the lumping together of isolated variables, each found to be associated separately with crime, into an unintegrated whole without regard to their interaction. This is clearly an inadequate form of explanation, but it is not an inevitable result of adopting the principle of multiple causation.

It is perhaps largely an academic debate whether imperfect statistical associations can ever be called "causal effects." In advocating their use to guide practical action and policy, Horton is in effect saying that even though associated conditions must not be thought of as causes, they can, in practice be treated as if they were, especially where the form, direction, magnitude, and probability limits of the associations are well established, along with knowledge of how the relationships change under specified conditions. Horton cites medicine as a scientific model, but he does not follow through on the implications of this model. Medicine rarely establishes absolutely necessary and sufficient conditions, but it does not for that reason abandon the search for causes.

Returning to the topic of motivation, Horton is quite correct in emphasizing that the search for a particular set of general motives that are common and unique to criminal behavior is a futile one. This has long been the fatal stumbling block of most psychiatric and psychoanalytic approaches to explaining criminal behavior. An attempted study of "criminal motives" is even further complicated by the fact that there is no simple one-to-one relation between motives and actions. Even the most trivial act usually has a conglomeration of disparate motives behind it. It does not follow from the fact, however, that the same general motives (love, hate, fear, et cetera) are involved in both criminal and noncriminal behavior; nor can we say that because no two conglomerations of motives are ever alike, there cannot be found some specific *motivational element* common and unique to criminal acts.

I would go even further. Not only is it possible to isolate a motivational element (as distinct from a motive) common and unique to criminal acts, it is necessary to do so in the very definition of what we mean by "criminal."

"Criminality" must be defined differently for different purposes. In the past, criminologists have followed the easiest course by simply adopting legal definitions of behavior as criminal or noncriminal. But these are basically moral and political judgments formed for the purpose of sanctioning and controlling behavior, rather than scientific definitions formed for the purpose of explaining criminal acts. In recognition of this, it has lately become fashionable for criminologists to argue that criminality is therefore simply an officially ascribed status and not an intrinsic characteristic of any persons or actions. These criminologists despair of the possibility of ever explaining criminal behavior as such—instead we can only explain why and how behavior comes to be labeled as criminal.

I do not think we should give up so easily. I believe that we can define criminality in a sociologically meaningful way that both distinguishes criminal from noncriminal conduct in terms of an intrinsic characteristic, and that makes the etiology of an act at least slightly different when that act is criminal from when it is not. The key to this lies in focusing on the motivational and perceptual aspects of criminal conduct.

We may distinguish "conduct" from "behavior" by saying that while "behavior" is anything a person does, "conduct" refers to the act plus the subjective meaning of the act to the actor. Criminal conduct, then, may be defined simply as conduct that the actor perceives to be criminal, or which he believes exposes him to the risk of punitive legal sanctions. Both law and criminology already give some recognition to this principle; I propose that it be carried to its logical extreme (by criminologists, not by jurists).

This definition should also be applied to potential or contemplated conduct. An individual who is on the verge of committing an act may or may not, at that moment, be perceiving the act as criminal. This perception and definition of the act need not be so conscious and explicit as the discussion so far may seem to imply. Defining an act as criminal need not involve lawyer-type thinking. It might simply be a glimmering consideration in the back of the mind that this is an act about which the legal authorities might have something to say if they were present and observing.

But in any case, it is this perception of the act by the actor that becomes the unique and common defining element of criminal conduct. Therefore, insofar as this process of definition is part of what we mean by motivation, this implies that a consideration of motives is central to both the definition and explanation of crime. The etiological question facing criminologists interested in crime at the individual level, then, is: Given that a person (implicitly or explicitly) perceives or defines an act as criminal, what then determines whether he or she will commit it?

When criminal conduct is defined in the way I have proposed, it can be seen to be a special type of normal risk-taking behavior, to be explained by some variation of a general theory of risk-taking behavior—or, more broadly, a general theory of rational conduct. I think one outcome of this conference will be to show the desirability of pursuing just such a model, in preference to other models, in explaining crime.

Serapio R. Zalba

In contrast to the more specific reactions of Professors Bailey and Logan to the papers by Professor Horton and Mr. Cobb, I intend to take a different approach, and touch on a number of more general issues which the papers generated.

Models of Behavior

In criminology today there are approaches to understanding and analyzing criminal behavior other than the economic and sickness models. Criminality can be considered learned behavior which has continued to persist because of the rewards it has conferred—social and psychological, as well as monetary. Economists might argue that I am really speaking about utility, and that I am therefore using an economics model. Another way of looking at it, however, is to say that the means— the behaviors—by which an offender has maximized his utility in the past, have become habitual, or patterned. Because of this, some behaviors become valued as a familiar way of doing things. Thus, perhaps to a considerable extent, choices of "economic" behaviors may not be made on a rational basis. These patterns of choice and behavior become known to others, who, in turn, come to recognize the idiosyncracies of the individual personality.

We all behave in our daily lives as though this is true. We come to know persons significant to us whose behavior patterns we have observed to the point where we can reasonably predict their reactions to events, to gifts, to disappointments, indeed, to a wide variety of stimuli. If we *are* able to do this, then there is some orderliness to human behavior not predicated on strictly rational economic grounds.

Motivation

It should not be surprising that the primarily sociologically oriented criminological literature does not stress motivation—a psychological concept. Yet, economists continually make use of the concept of motivation, in that one of the premises of economic analysis is that one seeks to maximize his utility, and minimize his cost—basically the pleasure/pain principle. There is a meeting ground for the disciplines of psychology and economics where utility is defined to include expressive components, group support and approval, interpersonal affection, and self-respect deriving from behaving in accordance with one's own ethical values. The Maslow schema of the hierarchy of needs is one relatively contemporary approach toward motivation that can be applied usefully in criminology.

If criminality can be considered employment, or an occupation, then perhaps we should consider the findings from numerous studies on job satisfaction. Despite common preconceptions, the main reasons given by people in a wide variety of occupations as to why they left employment were not economic ones. Instead, they had to do with what Frederick Herzberg calls "motivating" factors,* rather than what he terms the "hygienic" factors of pay, vacation, fringe benefits, et cetera. Aside from the desire of employees for a "reasonable" level of financial remuneration required for a minimal standard of living for their occupational group, it is clear that their more salient motivations lie in the amount of discretion they can use in their work, by the opportunities afforded for creativity—"doing their own thing"— and by the quality of their peer relationships on the job.

This may be equally true if we examine criminality as an occupation. While a criminal needs a minimum level of income to maintain himself physically so that he may pursue his criminal career, increases or decreases in expected net financial income from crime may have much less to do with the crime rate than does the social meaning of a specific criminal behavior, the offender's lack of skills for satisfying his wants in a more socially acceptable way, or the offender's underlying views of himself or others that lead to his destructive behavior.

Cobb attempted to give the economic motivation for criminal acts the greatest salience by considering only crimes against property, but it seems clear that there are other important nonmonetary benefits of crime besides the development of a tough reputation. Among the other nonmonetary benefits are: (1)

---

* Frederick Herzberg, *Work and the Nature of Man* (New York: World Publishing Co., 1966).

acting out angry and aggressive feelings and impulses, making the crime an expressive, rather than instrumental act; (2) removing oneself from interpersonal situations where one feels inadequate (such as a marriage, or family situation) by getting caught and being incarcerated; (3) dealing with a sense of guilt by managing to get caught and punished in the commission of crimes; and (4) going along with others who represent a social or subcultural membership group. There are other motivations that could be identified. Those who actually work with offenders are aware of the impulsively nonrational nature of much crime, including crimes against property.

Attempts to determine the meaning a crime has to the offender make it very apparent that the same act—for example, shoplifting—can have very different meanings to different people. It can even mean different things to the same person at different times. (See the figure below for a schematic representation.) While this may be an inconvenience to those of us attempting to identify regularities in criminal behavior and its deterrence, ignoring it is a fool's gambit. It may be that certain motivations are more typical or probable for certain kinds of crimes— indecent exposure, for example—and that the interventions that are effective in deterring such crimes can thus be identified.

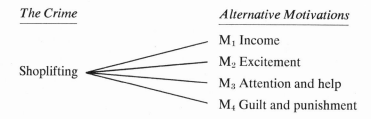

| *The Crime* | *Alternative Motivations* |

- M_1 Income
- M_2 Excitement
- M_3 Attention and help
- M_4 Guilt and punishment

This is an empirical matter that is worth pursuing. What are the central tendencies as to the motivations for the various kinds of crimes? It does not seem profitable to pretend that the economic motive is the primary explanation of criminal activity, even when we qualify this by referring to the nonmonetary motives, such as the disutility of incarceration, et cetera. It is a simple sociological trick to label anything that is done as being functional, otherwise it would not continue to occur. It would be a neater trick still to demonstrate the extent to which variances in crime rates for *different crimes,* and for *different kinds of people,* are explained by variances in economic profitability. Even such an ostensibly economic crime as passing bad checks, in my correctional experience in probation, parole, jails, and prisons, as often as not is motivated by nonmonetary considerations. Often the major motivation is to make a fool of the person being tricked into cashing the worthless check. In many cases the money is dissipated almost compulsively, even though it may be a relatively scarce commodity for the offender.

Interventions by society and its agents should be related to the kind of utility the crime represents to the largest numbers of persons commiting the crime. This can be done by making use of a variety of interventions, making noncriminal means viable and attractive to the potential offender, by trying to change the most salient motivations of certain kinds of offenders, and by making the costs of criminal means to personal ends too costly in view of the rewards.

Family as a Factor

In their presentation here, both Horton and Cobb failed to recognize the family as an important consideration in understanding crime and its prevention. The family may, for example, serve as a social constraint on the individual with anti-social propensities. A potential offender's roles as husband, father, head of the household, primary provider, et cetera, may serve to structure his time, leaving less opportunity for impulsive criminal activity. The family may also meet some of his needs for affection and belonging, leaving him less vulnerable to recruitment into criminal activities by persons whose companionship he needs or desires. For some persons, on the other hand, the family may make such overwhelming demands on them that crime, prosecution, and incarceration are a social solution for them, rather than an indication of unsuccessful occupational performance as a criminal.

The Range of Interventions

As indicated earlier in this paper, when interventions into criminal careers or deterrents to crime are considered, it may be useful to think about a range of interventive alternatives, related to the differential motivation or condition of the actual or potential offender. Where the crime is one of great impulse, strong passion, or even mental disorder, deterrence may consist of making weapons difficult to obtain, minimizing access to victims, or other interventions into the environment or the circumstances in which specific crimes tend to be committed. Long-term incarceration may be indicated for the dangerous, uncontrollable person.

For the more professional criminal who commits crimes primarily for the monetary benefits it affords him, some of the steps suggested by Cobb might be effective, unless criminality has become an ingrained way of life supported by peers who are the only realistic source of social satisfactions. In cases where the latter condition prevails, deterrence is unlikely, though incarceration will keep the criminal out of public circulation. It may be possible to maintain the more neurotic offender in the community, at a lesser cost to society (approximately one-tenth the cost of incarceration) through the use of counseling-supervision techniques, including probation, halfway houses, work furlough, and other programs.

Raising the economic costs of crime through increasing the probability of detection, conviction, and punishment, and through increasing the severity of punishment, is most likely to be effective with persons whose crimes are most rational—that is, the professionals. But even here, some of the professionals are

61

so socialized into lives of crime that threatening them with severe penalties, or incarcerating them for long periods of time, is just part of the game to which they are already committed.

Etzioni's Shortcuts

Professor Horton has referred to Etzioni's "shortcuts," and they are persuasive. In one specific program in Cleveland, for example, the rate of auto thefts was drastically reduced through a public program with two thrusts: first, community service radio announcements were made, describing recently stolen autos and requesting that persons seeing the described autos report their whereabouts to the police; and second, a publicity campaign was launched to warn the general public to remove their keys from parked autos and lock their doors.

We have not been particularly successful with either rehabilitative programs or punitive-deterrent approaches; neither has inspired much faith on the part of the public or governmental officials. It is easy to suspect that strong supporters of one or the other approach have predetermined biases in the direction of either humanitarianism or retribution. While it is important to test further whether there are specified populations for which rehabilitation programs or punishment-deterrence programs are effective in lowering crime rates and recidivism, we might better allocate community resources toward programs such as Horton described: those that reduce the number of "attractive nuisances" in the community which encourage the commission of crimes.

The Greater Rationality of Criminals

Cobb suggests that crime *does* pay and that many criminals are making rational occupational choices. He also implies that at a certain socioeconomic level criminals are making *better* economic choices than are noncriminals. This presupposes that despite his earlier disclaimers regarding total utility as being the goal of economic choice, he still discounts the values of social conformity, reputation, perceptions of self-worth, and internalized ethical precepts to the individual.

If he really wishes to develop a model of criminality based on economic theory, he will need to develop *families* of supply curves of criminality, where different values are given to different kinds of costs and benefits (for example, family contact, violation of societal norms, expression of hostility). This would necessarily be true if supply curves for nonmaterially profitable crimes were elastic.

The presupposition in Cobb's paper is that economic motives are the most salient ones. This hypothesis should be tested across a number of different kinds of crimes, to determine if variances in the material costs and benefits of crime are predictive of its occurrence.

62

PART TWO:

DOES PUNISHMENT DETER?

CRIME CONTROL:
THE CASE FOR DETERRENCE

Llad Phillips

Deterrence is the theoretical foundation for many programs of crime control. Yet the principle of deterrence has remained controversial, perhaps in large measure because the evidence on deterrence has been regarded as inconclusive. While some investigators have found criminal activity to be related inversely to the certainty and severity of punishment, others have not.[1] When one considers that etiological factors as well as control instruments probably determine offense rates, the relationship observed between crime rates and deterrence is not likely to be simple. Moreover, the intensity of criminal activity may have as much to do with determining the degree of control as control has to do with determining criminal activity. With these complications in mind, analysts who have found a simple negative relationship between certainty, severity and criminal activity appear, indeed, fortunate. Those who have found no correlation, or a "surprisingly" positive one, have simply demonstrated that there is more to the explanation of criminal activity than control.

In my analysis of deterrence here, I intend to focus on two difficulties which must be considered in "identifying" the deterrent effect.[2] The first of these is the

---

[1] Studies which have interpreted the evidence as favoring deterrence include Jack P. Gibbs, "Crime, Punishment, and Deterrence," *The Southwestern Social Science Quarterly,* vol. 48, no. 4 (March 1968); Charles R. Tittle, "Crime Rates and Legal Sanctions," *Social Problems,* vol. 16, no. 4 (Spring 1969); Llad Phillips and Harold L. Votey, Jr., "An Economic Analysis of the Deterrent Effect of Law Enforcement on Criminal Activity," *The Journal of Criminal Law, Criminology, and Police Science,* vol. 63, no. 3 (September 1972); and idem, "The Control of Criminal Activity: An Economic Analysis," Chapter XXX in *Handbook of Criminology,* ed. Daniel Glaser (Chicago: Rand McNally & Co., forthcoming). Studies which have found the evidence for deterrence wanting include Theodore G. Chiricos and Gordon P. Waldo, "Punishment and Crime: An Examination of Some Empirical Evidence," *Social Problems,* vol. 18, no. 2 (Fall 1970) and in the particular case of capital punishment, Thorsten Sellin, *Capital Punishment* (New York: Harper and Row, 1967) and Karl F. Schuessler, "The Deterrent Influence of the Death Penalty," *The Annals of the American Academy of Political and Social Science,* vol. 284 (November 1952). One scholar has interpreted the evidence as for in some cases and against in others; see, respectively, William J. Chambliss, "The Deterrent Influence of Punishment," *Crime and Delinquency,* vol. 12, no. 1 (January 1966) and idem, "Types of Deviance and the Effectiveness of Legal Sanctions," *Wisconsin Law Review,* vol. 1967, no. 3 (Summer 1967).

[2] For a nontechnical discussion of the general identification problem, see Lawrence R. Klein, *An Introduction to Econometrics* (Englewood Cliffs, N. J.: Prentice-Hall, 1962). For a review of some of the methodological difficulties encountered in identifying deterrence, see Franklin E. Zimring, *Perspectives on Deterrence,* Public Health Service Publication No. 2056 (Washington, D. C.: U.S. Government Printing Office, January 1971).

specification of the simultaneous, or action-reaction, relationship which potentially exists between criminal activity and crime control. The second is the standardization (control) of the causal factors which determine crime rates. Resolving these two difficulties will permit the isolation of the deterrent effect. Furthermore, we can use the analysis developed to deal with these two complications to help explain the apparently conflicting findings of researchers who sought simple correlations between certainty, severity and crime.

These two "identification" difficulties may be adequately resolved by a research strategy which separates by function the etiological factors determining offense rates from the deterrent controls. This approach is applied to homicides committed with firearms. It will be demonstrated that variations in two major contributing variables, namely the assault rate and the fraction of assaults involving firearms, determine the fluctuations in this crime rate. While many factors could lead to the eruption of aggressive behavior, the intensity of response and the choice of a deadly weapon in particular may be especially susceptible to deterrent control. We shall concentrate our empirical analysis in this paper on the deterrence of the use of firearms in assault.

The particular approach we used to handle the problem of identifying the deterrent effect was to develop a probability model which relates the likelihood of murders involving firearms to the assault rate and the likelihood of gun use in assault. This enabled us to separate causal and deterrent factors in homicide. Then we developed the form in which the likelihood of gun use in assault depended upon the certainty and severity of punishment.

We used econometric techniques to assess the relative contribution of gun use in assault to the homicide rate, and to demonstrate that certainty and severity of punishment apparently explain, to a significant degree, the choice of weapon.

I. Identification of the Deterrent Effect

We constructed a simple conceptual model of crime generation and crime control to illustrate that both the offense rate and the certainty of punishment depend on the factors causing crime, the resources devoted to apprehension and conviction, and the severity of punishment. The severity of penalty and quantity of crime control resources which will minimize the total social cost of crime are derived.

We have used this conceptual framework to demonstrate why, under various circumstances, it is likely that an investigator could find a negative, a positive, or no simple correlation between the offense rate and the certainty or severity of punishment. We do advocate the development of an analytical model as a foundation to guide the empirical analysis of deterrence.

We may handle the problems of simultaneity and standardization which arise in the identification of deterrence if it is feasible to separate the impact of deterrent and causal factors on the crime rate. This is possible in the case of homicides committed with a firearm. The logic of the approach is developed as a basis for the probability model derived in section II.

A Model of Crime Generation and Crime Control. For simplicity we suggest that society is restricted to the selection of two means to control a given crime: the criminal justice resources devoted to apprehension and conviction indexed by L, and the severity of punishment, SV. In addition to the resources, L, the offense rate, OF, which may be viewed as a burden or load on the criminal justice system, determines the effectiveness of the system as measured by the conviction ratio, CR,[3] expressed by

$$CR = CR (OF, L),$$ (1)

where an increase in resources will increase the effectiveness, i.e.,

$$\frac{\partial CR}{\partial L} > O.$$

Given the resources, L, if the offense rate (burden) increases, the conviction ratio (effectiveness) will fall but at a decreasing rate, i.e.,

$$\frac{\partial CR}{\partial OF} < O, \frac{\partial^2 CR}{\partial OF^2} > O.$$

The certainty of punishment (CR), the severity of punishment (SV), and the etiological factors indexed by SE are postulated to determine the offense rate, OF,[4] expressed by

$$OF = OF (CR, SV, SE),$$ (2)

where the offense rate increases with the causal factors,

$$\frac{\partial OF}{\partial SE} > O,$$

[3] This effectiveness, or production-function, approach is in some ways similar to Becker's cost-function approach. Becker's cost function increases with "activity" where the latter is the product of the ratio of offenses cleared by conviction and the offense rate. See Gary S. Becker, "Crime and Punishment: An Economic Approach," *Journal of Political Economy,* vol. 76, no. 2 (March-April 1968), p. 174. One can obtain a similar cost function by inverting equation (1) and multiplying by the cost per resource. As an example of the estimation of a specific functional form for equation (1) for various crimes, see Harold L. Votey, Jr. and Llad Phillips, "The Law Enforcement Production Function," *Journal of Legal Studies,* vol. 1, no. 2 (June 1972), and idem, *Economic Crimes: Their Generation, Deterrence, and Control* (Springfield, Va.: U.S. Clearinghouse for Federal Scientific and Technical Information, 1969).

[4] This development of the crime generation function closely parallels Becker's "Crime and Punishment," p. 177. For an example of the estimation of a specific formulation of equation (2) where apprehension ratios were used to standardize arrest rates, see Llad Phillips and Harold L. Votey, Jr., "Crime, Youth, and the Labor Market," *Journal of Political Economy,* vol. 80, no. 3 (May-June 1972). In specifying equation (2) we include as deterrence any decrease in OF with an increase in CR or SV, whether it arises from fear, education or whatever source. For a discussion of possible effects, see Gordon Hawkins, "Punishment and Deterrence: The Educative, Moralizing, and Habituative Effects," *Wisconsin Law Review,* vol. 1969, no. 2 (1969).

Figure 1

CRIME GENERATION AND CRIME CONTROL

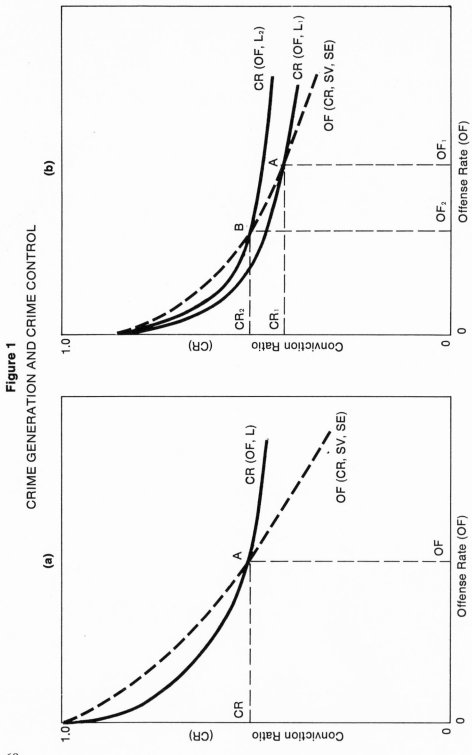

and decreases with the deterrent instruments,

$$\frac{\partial OF}{\partial CR} < O \text{ and } \frac{\partial OF}{\partial SV} < O,$$

but at a decreasing rate,

$$\frac{\partial^2 OF}{\partial CR^2} > O \text{ and } \frac{\partial^2 OF}{\partial SV^2} > O.$$

Given the conditions generating crime, SE, and society's choices of resources, L, and penalties, SV, to control crime, equations (1) and (2) determine the conviction ratio and the offense rate as indicated by point A in Figure 1(a). If society increases the resources allocated to fight crime, the effectiveness of law enforcement will increase and the offense rate will fall. This is indicated in Figure 1(b) by the translation upward in the crime control function from $CR(OF, L_1)$ to $CR(OF, L_2)$, which shifts the equilibrium from point A to point B. This decrease in crime which accompanies an increase in the resources allocated to control crime is illustrated directly by the solid line in Figure 2. Of course, increasing the resources to fight crime costs money, but the decline in offenses cuts the losses from crime. For a given cost per unit resource, w, and a dollar loss per offense, r, the combinations of offense rates and crime fighting resources with a total social cost, TC, is,

$$TC = wL + rOF, \tag{3}$$

and is illustrated by the dashed line in Figure 2. The minimum attainable social cost of crime is indicated by point C. A lower offense rate could be obtained by allocating more resources to criminal justice as indicated by point D, but only at a higher cost (upper dashed line). A similar analysis can be undertaken to trace the effects of varying severity of penalties on offense rates and conviction ratios. Of course, increasing the penalty may increase the costs associated with incarceration, as expressed by

$$C = C(SV), \tag{4}$$

which must be included in total social cost (equation 3). The attainable combinations of severity of penalty and offense rates can be illustrated in a figure similar to Figure 2. The severity of penalty which minimizes the total social cost of crime, *ceteris paribus,* will be indicated by the tangency between this locus of attainable combinations and the locus of constant cost combinations of severity of penalty and offense rates, analogous to point C in Figure 2. The argument is developed fully in the appendix.

Simple Correlations Between Conviction Ratios and Offense Rates. For the sake of illustration, consider two communities with a similar crime generation function, i.e., comparable conditions causing crime, SE, and comparable severity of punish-

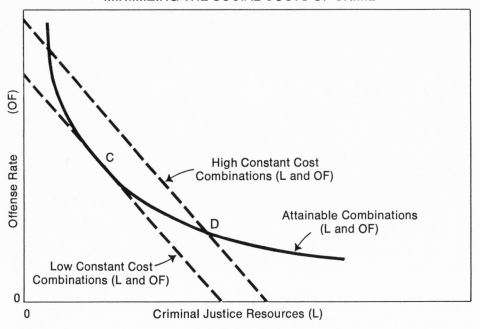

Figure 2

MINIMIZING THE SOCIAL COSTS OF CRIME

Offense Rate (OF)

High Constant Cost
Combinations (L and OF)

C

D

Attainable Combinations
(L and OF)

Low Constant Cost
Combinations (L and OF)

Criminal Justice Resources (L)

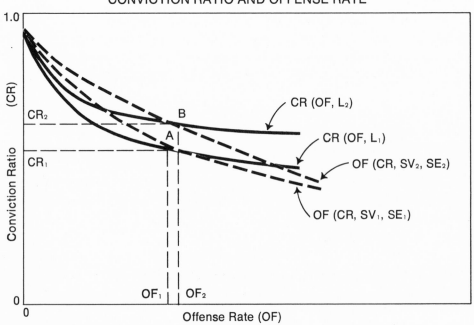

Figure 3

POSITIVE CORRELATION BETWEEN
CONVICTION RATIO AND OFFENSE RATE

Conviction Ratio (CR)

1.0

CR_2

CR_1

B

A

CR (OF, L_2)

CR (OF, L_1)

OF (CR, SV_2, SE_2)

OF (CR, SV_1, SE_1)

OF_1 OF_2

Offense Rate (OF)

ment, SV. If the second community devotes more resources to combating crime than the first, then the conviction ratio, CR_2, will be higher and the crime rate, OF_2, lower in the second community. A simple inverse correlation between conviction ratio and offense rate will obtain. This is illustrated in Figure 1(b). Suppose, however, that the conditions generating crime in the second community are worse than those in the first and/or that the severity of penalty is lower. Then, even though the second community allocates more resources to combat crime than the first, and attains a higher conviction ratio, the crime rate in the second community may still be higher than that in the first community. We find a "surprising" positive correlation between the conviction ratio and the offense rate. This is illustrated in Figure 3.

The contrasting stories told by Figures 1(b) and 3 may explain why Gibbs found a significant negative correlation between the certainty of punishment and homicide rates across states in 1960, when Chiricos and Waldo did not find this result in 1950 or 1963, despite the fact they corroborated Gibbs's 1960 result. As time passes, the conditions causing homicide can vary from state to state; so can the resources devoted to combating this crime.[5] If there is a relative upsurge of robbery in a given state, resources may be shifted away from controlling homicide and other crimes to combat this new menace. To isolate and identify the deterrent effect it is necessary to standardize for other factors that affect offense rates, such as etiological variables and the level of activity of the authorities.

Charles R. Tittle, in his study of seven major felonies, made an effort to standardize for causal factors by controlling for age, sex, education, urbanization, and industrialization. Of course, these controls are effective only if they account significantly for variation in offense rates from state to state. The explanatory power of these controls was not reported. Only the simple association between offense rates and certainty of punishment is listed for all crimes. Furthermore, Tittle made no attempt to control for the number of criminal justice personnel per capita, although he did mention the possible effect this variable could have on the results.[6]

The importance of standardizing for variations in causal factors and criminal justice personnel also extends to studies of deterrence over a period of time. Chiricos and Waldo report the effect which percentage changes in certainty for a 10-year period have on percentage changes in crime rates for six major felonies.[7] There is no attempt to control for changes in causal factors or personnel per capita, although changes in these factors might certainly dominate the effect that changes in certainty would have on offense rates.

---

[5] For an example of how conditions and resources can vary over a period of time, see Llad Phillips, Harold L. Votey, Jr., and John Howell, "A Simultaneous Equation System to Evaluate the Impact of Law Enforcement on the Generation of Crime," a paper presented at the Western Economic Association meetings, Vancouver, B. C., 1971.

[6] Tittle, "Crime Rates," p. 420.

[7] Chiricos and Waldo, "Punishment and Crime."

We can extend the argument that it is necessary to control for causal factors and for the level of activity of the authorities to studies of the deterrent effect of severity. In summary, in the absence of an experimental design that controls for other factors, it is hazardous to draw conclusions from simple correlations between the certainty of punishment or the severity of punishment, on the one hand, and offense rates, on the other.

Separating Deterrent and Causal Factors. We can use various means to handle the identification problems posed by fluctuations in causal factors and simultaneity between the offense rate and the conviction ratio. One approach is to estimate equation (1) and equation (2) using simultaneous equation methods.[8] A different approach is feasible if we can separate the components of the crime generation function so as to isolate the deterrent and causal variables as indicated by

$$OF = OF(CR, SV, SE) = OF_1 (CR, SV) \cdot OF_2(SE). \tag{5}$$

It will be shown that this condition is approximated for homicides committed with firearms, denoted by OF in (5). We have adopted the research strategy to demonstrate that most of the variation in homicides committed with a firearm can be explained by the assault rate, $OF_2(SE)$, and the fraction of assaults involving guns, $OF_1(CR, SV)$. Certain parts of the country have more instances of violence than others.[9] The assault rate, $OF_2(SE)$, varies from state to state and over a period of time as the etiological factors, SE, vary. While the causes of fights are manifold, and their eruption is somewhat spontaneous, the severity or seriousness of the fight may be more subject to control. If the consequences of lethal assault (which is more likely if a firearm is used) are certain and severe, the frequency of attacks with a firearm may be reduced.[10] Consequently, *ex hypothesi,* an approximate separation of etiological and deterrent factors may be attainable. By studying the fraction of assaults which result in homicides at the hand of a gun, $OF/OF_2(SE)$, it is possible to standardize for causal factors if we divide equation (5) by the assault rate resulting in

$$OF/OF_2 = OF_1, \tag{6}$$

and thereby concentrate on deterrence, which should be a major source of variation in OF_1, i.e.,

$$OF_1 = OF_1(CR, SV). \tag{7}$$

---

[8] For a discussion of this technique, see John Johnston, *Econometric Methods,* 2nd edition (New York: McGraw-Hill Book Co., 1972); for an application of this technique, see Phillips, Votey and Howell, "Simultaneous Equation System."

[9] For examples, see Sheldon Hackney, "Southern Violence," *The American Historical Review,* vol. 74, no. 3 (February 1969), and Lyle W. Shannon, "The Spatial Distribution of Criminal Offenses by State," *The Journal of Criminal Law, Criminology, and Police Science,* vol. 45, no. 3 (September-October 1954).

[10] For a discussion of the dependence of the fatality rate of assault upon the weapon used, see Franklin E. Zimring, "The Medium is the Message: Firearm Caliber as a Determinant of Death from Assault," *The Journal of Legal Studies,* vol. 1, no. 1 (January 1972).

Of course, the conviction ratio depends on the total homicide rate, OF_H, i.e.,

$$CR = CR(OF_H, L), \tag{8}$$

but since the dependent variable in equation (7) is the fraction of assaults committed with a gun, which accounts for only a fraction of the variance in the homicide rate, simultaneity is reduced and single equation methods are defensible. In summary, the approach embodied in equations (6) and (7) standardizes for causal factors, amplifies (or concentrates) the effects of deterrence, and reduces simultaneity. The details of the model are developed in the next section.

II. A Probability Model Relating Murder, Assault, Gun Use and Deterrence

Murder can be subdivided into two dimensions: type of weapon used and circumstance. (In this paper we are considering only murder and nonnegligent manslaughter; negligent homicides are excluded.) [11] A majority of the murders committed in this country in the last 10 years have involved firearms, and the fraction has been increasing. Knives are the second most frequently used weapon. Studies of the circumstances which led to homicide indicate that most of the cases involved family or acquaintances who became involved in a fight.[12] In 1970, known and suspected felonious murders (defined as killings resulting from robberies, sex motives, gangland slayings, and other felonious activities) comprised 28.8 percent of the total murder offenses.[13] The probability of murder [$P(M)$], which can be measured as the average rate (per 100,000 people, for example) for a given time period, can be expressed as the sum of the probability of murder at the hand of a gun, $P(M \wedge G)$, and the probability of murder committed with a knife or some other weapon, $P(M \wedge K)$:

$$P(M) = P(M \wedge G) + P(M \wedge K). \tag{9}$$

The probability of murder, $P(M)$, can also be expressed as the sum of the probability of murder arising from assaults involving family or acquaintances, $P(M \wedge A)$, and the probability for felonious murder, $P(M \wedge F)$:

$$P(M) = P(M \wedge A) + P(M \wedge F). \tag{10}$$

In a similar fashion, the probability of murder involving guns, $P(M \wedge G)$, can be written as the sum of the probability of murder involving a gun and arising from assault, $P(M \wedge G \wedge A)$, and the probability of murder involving a gun and arising from felonious circumstances, $P(M \wedge G \wedge F)$:

$$P(M \wedge G) = P(M \wedge G \wedge A) + P(M \wedge G \wedge F). \tag{11}$$

---

[11] For definitions, see U.S. Department of Justice, Federal Bureau of Investigation, *Uniform Crime Reports* (Washington, D. C.: U.S. Government Printing Office, 1970), p. 61.

[12] See George D. Newton and Franklin E. Zimring, *Firearms and Violence in American Life*, A Staff Report to the National Commission on the Causes and Prevention of Violence (Washington, D. C.: U.S. Government Printing Office, 1969), Chapter 10; and FBI, *Uniform Crime Reports*, 1966 and 1970.

[13] FBI, *Uniform Crime Reports*, 1970.

Following this approach one can define the probability of murder committed with a knife or other weapon as

$$P(M \wedge K) = P(M \wedge K \wedge A) + P(M \wedge K \wedge F). \tag{12}$$

The probability of a murder resulting from an assault involving a gun, $P(M \wedge G \wedge A)$, depends upon the probability of assault, $P(A)$, the probability of a gun being used in the assault, $P(G/A)$, and the probability of a fatality or murder resulting from the attack with the gun, $P(M/G \wedge A)$. Thus, it follows that [14]

$$P(M \wedge G \wedge A) = P(M/G \wedge A) \, P(G/A) \, P(A). \tag{13}$$

Substituting equation (13) in equation (11) one obtains

$$P(M \wedge G) = P(M/G \wedge A) \, P(G/A) \, P(A) + P(M \wedge G \wedge F), \tag{14}$$

which may also be expressed as

$$P(M \wedge G) = P(M/G \wedge A) \, P(G \wedge A) + P(M \wedge G \wedge F), \tag{14}$$

since $P(G \wedge A) = P(G/A) \, P(A)$.

Equation (14) can be used to investigate to what extent the increasing rate of murders involving firearms can be attributed to the criminal element (felonious murders) or to assaults with guns by average citizens. In addition, equation (14) can be used to determine how much of the increase in murders with firearms is attributable to increased gun use in assault and how much is attributable to an increase in the rate of assault. Given observations on the rate of murders involving firearms, the fraction of assaults involving firearms, and the rate of assault, behavioral content can be introduced into equation (14) by making assumptions (such as constancy or linear trends) about the fatality rate for firearms attacks and the rate of felonious murders involving firearms. The specific assumptions and their appropriateness under the circumstances are discussed below when equation (14) is estimated. The effect of gun use in assault on the rate of murders involving guns can be separated from the impact of the assault rate on the murder rate by dividing by the assault rate in equation (14), yielding:

$$P(M \wedge G)/P(A) = P(M/G \wedge A) \, P(G/A) + P(M \wedge G \wedge F)/P(A). \tag{15}$$

Equation (15) is the specific form of equation (6) discussed above.

A parallel analysis can be developed for the probability of murders committed with a knife or other weapon, resulting in an equation similar to equation (14):

$$P(M \wedge K) = P(M/K \wedge A) \, P(K/A) \, P(A) + P(M \wedge K \wedge F), \tag{16}$$

or equivalently,

$$P(M \wedge K) = P(M/K \wedge A) \, P(K \wedge A) + P(M \wedge K \wedge F). \tag{16}$$

---

[14] This follows directly from the definition of conditional probabilities: $P(M \wedge G \wedge A) = P(M/G \wedge A) \, P(G \wedge A) = P(M/G \wedge A) \, P(G/A) P(A)$.

74

The rate of murders committed with a knife or other weapon will depend upon the fatality rate for knife and other weapon attacks, $P(M/K \wedge A)$, the fraction of assaults committed with knives and other weapons, $P(K/A)$, the assault rate, $P(A)$, and the rate of felonious murders committed with knives and other weapons, $P(M \wedge K \wedge F)$. Since the fraction of assaults committed with a gun and the fraction of assaults committed with a knife or other weapons sum to one, that is, $P(G/A) + P(K/A) = 1$, it is possible to express equation (16) as

$$P(M \wedge K) = P(M/K \wedge A) \, P(A) - P(M/K \wedge A) \, P(G/A) \, P(A) \quad (17)$$
$$+ P(M \wedge K \wedge F).$$

This indicates the direct dependence of murders committed with a knife or other weapon upon the fraction of assaults committed with a firearm.

A gun can be used in an assault only if the assailant possesses or owns a gun; in others words, possession or ownership is certain if a gun was used, $P(O/G \wedge A) = 1$; hence,

$$P(G \wedge A) = P(G \wedge O \wedge A). \quad (18)$$

Moreover, since by definition,

$$P(G \wedge O \wedge A) = P(G/A \wedge O) \, P(A/O) \, P(O), \quad (19)$$

and also by definition,

$$P(G \wedge A) = P(G/A)P(A), \quad (20)$$

from equations (18), (19) and (20) one obtains, after rearranging terms, the following expression for gun use in assault:

$$P(G/A) = \frac{P(G/A \wedge O)P(A/O)P(O)}{P(A)}. \quad (21)$$

In this study we are assuming that gun possession or ownership alone has a negligible influence in inducing assault, that is,

$$P(A/O) \simeq P(A). \quad (22)$$

Hence from equation (21) it follows that

$$\frac{P(G/A)}{P(O)} \simeq P(G/A \wedge O). \quad (23)$$

The fraction of assaults involving firearms, $P(G/A)$, is used as a proxy for the probability that an assailant who possesses or owns a gun will use it, $P(G/A \wedge O)$. As indicated by equation (23) one must standardize $P(G/A)$ for the probability of owning or possessing a gun. Unfortunately, cross-section data on firearms ownership is available only by region and not by state. Franklin E. Zimring has discussed the limitations of using hunting licenses as an index of firearms ownership.[15] We have hypothesized that it is reasonable to use the rate of fatal

---

[15] Franklin E. Zimring, "Games with Guns and Statistics," *Wisconsin Law Review,* vol. 1968, no. 4 (1968).

firearms accidents, GAX, as an index of gun ownership.[16]

$$P(O) = f(GAX). \tag{24}$$

The rate of fatal firearms accidents, GAX, is used to standardize the fraction of assaults involving firearms, $P(G/A)$, for variations in gun availability.

The conditional probability that an assailant who possesses or owns a gun will use it should be particularly sensitive to the deterrent effect of the certainty and/or severity of punishment, if such an effect exists, since $P(G/A \wedge O)$ is standardized for etiological factors (the assault rate and gun ownership). To separate the effect of the certainty and severity of punishment on gun use, an expression is derived which relates these deterrent factors to the odds that the assailant will not use a gun, $\dfrac{1 - P(G/A \wedge O)}{P(G/A \wedge O)}$. Hence, by combining equations (23) and (24) we can re-express standardization for gun ownership as

$$\frac{1 - P(G/A)}{P(G/A)} = \frac{1 - P(G/A \wedge O)}{P(G/A \wedge O)} \cdot f(GAX). \tag{25}$$

The probability that an assailant who possesses or owns a gun will use it, $P(G/A \wedge O)$, is postulated to vary inversely with the conviction ratio, CR, and the severity of sentence, SV, expressed by

$$P(G/A \wedge O) = \frac{1}{1 + CR^{\Theta} \, SV^{\Phi}}, \Theta > O, \Phi > O, \tag{26}$$

where Θ and Φ are parameters

and $P(G/A \wedge O) \rightarrow 1$ if $CR \rightarrow O$ or $SV \rightarrow O$,

and $P(G/A \wedge O) \rightarrow \dfrac{1}{1 + SV^{\Phi}}$ if $CR \rightarrow 1$,

and $P(G/A \wedge O) \rightarrow O$ if $SV \rightarrow \infty$, $CR > O$.

From (26) it follows that

$$\frac{1 - P(G/A \wedge O)}{P(G/A \wedge O)} = CR^{\Theta} SV^{\Phi}. \tag{27}$$

---

[16] The percentage of households owning firearms in 1968 as given in Newton and Zimring, *Firearms and Violence*, p. 10, and the death rate from firearm accidents from 1959-61 as given in Albert P. Iskrant and Paul V. Joliet, *Accidents and Homicide* (Cambridge, Mass.: Harvard University Press, 1968), p. 146, show a correlation in rank in the four regions:

Region	Percentage of Households Owning Firearms	Death Rate from Firearm Accidents
South	59	2.2
Midwest	51	1.8
West	49	1.0
East	33	0.55

The odds that an assailant will not use a gun increases with the certainty and severity of punishment if Θ and Φ, respectively, are positive, but at a decreasing rate if Θ and Φ are less than 1. Combining (25) and (27) one obtains

$$\frac{1-P(G/A)}{P(G/A)} = CR^{\Theta}SV^{\Phi}k\, GAX^{\Psi}, \tag{28}$$

assuming a multiplicative form for f(GAX). Equation (28) is the specific form of (7) discussed above and may be linearized by taking logarithms.

III. Empirical Analysis and Hypothesis Testing

Data for the fraction of murders and assaults committed with firearms in the United States are available for the last ten years.[17] Combined with the rates of murder and assault, these data permit a limited investigation of the variation in murders with variations in assault and gun use. We have used the more extensive cross-section data available for the states to analyze the extent to which gun use in assault depends on gun ownership and on the certainty and severity of punishment.

Time-series Analysis: Murder, Assault and Gun Use. Equation (14) was estimated with the alternative assumptions that the rate of felonious murders committed with a firearm, $P(M \wedge G \wedge F)$, was (a) constant or (b) trended to compare the relative contribution of criminals and average citizens to murders. The fatality rate for firearms attacks, $P(M/G \wedge A)$, was assumed to be constant for the period. This is probably a reasonable assumption for the decade of the 1960s (for which data were available) but would be more hazardous for a time-series analysis of longer duration where the possibility of bringing better medical attention to victims more rapidly might be a factor of importance.[18]

The results are reported below, with t-statistics for the parameter estimates in parentheses. The coefficient of determination $(\overline{R}^2)$ is corrected for degrees of freedom. The Durbin-Watson (D-W) statistic is indicated, although the time-series is short. The F-distribution statistic for the regression is reported. The time index is denoted by t.[19]

---

[17] FBI, *Uniform Crime Reports*, 1961 through 1970.

[18] FBI Director Hoover suggested that the reduction of the murder rate since the 1930s may well be the result of both improved police service (bringing quick medical attention for the victim) and improved medical treatment. See FBI, *Uniform Crime Reports*, 1963, p. 6.

[19] The rate of murders involving guns is reported per person hence the intercept (1.35×10^{-5}) is the rate per person. Equivalently, the intercept could be expressed as 1.35 per 100,000 persons. Equation (15) was also estimated with results comparable to equation (29).

$$P(M \wedge G)/P(A) = .0896\, P(G/A) + 1.44 \times 10^{-5}\, 1/P(A)$$
$$\qquad\qquad (23.8) \qquad\qquad (16.4)$$
$$\overline{R}^2 = .637,\ \text{D-W} = .92$$

$$P(M{\wedge}G) = .0927\,P(G{\wedge}A) + 1.35 \times 10^{-5} \tag{29}$$
$$(27.8) \qquad\qquad (13.5)$$
$$\overline{R}^2 = .988,\ D\text{-}W = .88,\ F(1,8) = 772$$

$$P(M{\wedge}G) = .112\,P(G{\wedge}A) + 1.25 \times 10^{-5} - .094 \times 10^{-5}\,t \tag{30}$$
$$(7.2) \qquad\qquad (9.8) \qquad\qquad (-1.29)$$
$$\overline{R}^2 = .989,\ D\text{-}W = 1.21,\ F(2.7) = 418$$

These equations were estimated for the period from 1961 to 1970. During this period murders with firearms increased from 2.5 to 6.1 per 100,000 persons. The estimates above indicate that the criminal element (felonious murders) can not be blamed for this increase since $P(M{\wedge}G{\wedge}F)$ was approximately constant (1.35×10^{-5}).[20] Thus, most of the increase in murders with firearms is attributable to assaults with firearms among family and acquaintances. This conclusion was checked by estimating equation (14) after differencing (Δ is the difference operator):

$$\Delta P(M{\wedge}G) = .0954\,\Delta P(G{\wedge}A) - .022 \times 10^{-5} \tag{31}$$
$$(4.61) \qquad\qquad (-.02)$$
$$\overline{R}^2 = .716,\ D\text{-}W = 1.35,\ F(1,7) = 21.2.$$

The intercept is insignificant and thus confirms an insignificant trend in felonious murders committed with a firearm. Estimating equation (14) in first differences is an important test, since $P(G{\wedge}A)$ and t are highly collinear.[21]

The estimate of the fatality rate for firearms attacks, $P(M/G{\wedge}A) = .0927$, compares favorably with estimates from independent studies. Newton and Zimring report an average fatality rate of .122 for attacks with guns in Chicago for the years 1965 through 1967.[22]

Recalling that $P(G{\wedge}A) = P(G/A)\,P(A)$, we can use equation (29) to calculate how much the estimated gun murder rate would have increased between 1961 and 1970 if the fraction of assaults involving guns had increased to the 1970 level while the assault rate had remained at the 1961 level. We can compare this to the estimated gun murder rate which would have obtained in 1970 if the fraction of assaults involving guns had remained at the 1961 level while the assault rate increased to the 1970 figure. Finally, the interaction effect is indicated by comparing these two calculations to the estimated gun murder rate when both gun use and the assault rate are allowed to increase to 1970 levels.[23] The calculations are reported in Table 1.

---

[20] In 1962 murders known or suspected to have arisen from felonious activities comprised 27 percent of total murders. In 1970 this fraction was 28.8 percent. Thus $P(M{\wedge}G{\wedge}F)$ was probably increasing more than equation (29) indicates.

[21] The simple correlation coefficient between $P(G{\wedge}A)$ and t is .98. The correlation coefficient between $P(G{\wedge}M)$ and $P(G{\wedge}A)$ is .99 while the correlation coefficient between $P(G{\wedge}M)$ and t is .96.

[22] Newton and Zimring, *Firearms and Violence*, p. 41. In 1967 the fatality rate for attacks with guns was .197 in Houston and .089 in New York; see ibid., p. 44.

[23] From equation (29) we have,

$$\Delta P(M{\wedge}G) = .0927\,[P(G/A)\,\Delta P(A) + P(A)\,\Delta P(G/A) + \Delta P(G/A)\,\Delta P(A)].$$

Table 1
ESTIMATES OF THE RATE OF MURDERS INVOLVING FIREARMS
(per 100,000)

		Rate	Net Increase
Base year	1961	2.46	—
Fraction of gun assaults increasing with assault rate constant	1970	3.46	1.00
Fraction of gun assaults constant with assault rate increasing	1970	3.76	1.30
Both the fraction of gun assaults and the assault rate increasing	1970	5.98	1.22

The blame for the increase in murders by firearm is divided approximately equally among an increase in gun use, an increase in the assault rate, and the reinforcement or interaction effect that results when both are increasing simultaneously.

Equation (16) was estimated in a fashion similar to equation (14) with the assumption that the fatality rate for assault with a knife or other weapon, $P(M/K \wedge A)$, was constant, and with the alternative assumptions that the rate of felonious murders committed with a knife or other weapon, $P(M \wedge K \wedge F)$, was (a) constant or (b) trended. Equation (16) was also estimated in first differences. The results are reported below:

$$P(M \wedge K) = .0130\, P(K \wedge A) + 1.06 \times 10^{-5} \qquad (32)$$
$$(7.7) \qquad\qquad (5.4)$$
$$\overline{R}^2 = .865,\ D\text{-}W = .93,\ F(1,8) = 58.7$$

$$P(M \wedge K) = .0293\, P(K \wedge A) - .137 \times 10^{-5} - .142 \times 10^{-5}\, t \qquad (33)$$
$$(2.77) \qquad\qquad (-.17) \qquad\quad (-1.56)$$
$$\overline{R}^2 = .886,\ D\text{-}W = 1.13,\ F(2,7) = 35.8$$

$$\Delta P(M \wedge K) = .0245\, \Delta P(K \wedge A) - .0926 \times 10^{-5} \qquad (34)$$
$$(2.21) \qquad\qquad (-.92)$$
$$\overline{R}^2 = .326,\ D\text{-}W = 1.87,\ F(1,7) = 4.86$$

The increase in murders with knives and other weapons is attributable to the increase in attacks involving ordinary citizens with these weapons and not to an increase in attacks by the criminal element. The estimate of the fatality rate for attacks with a knife and other weapons was much lower—$P(M/K \wedge A)$ ranges from .0130 to .0293—than that for guns. This estimate compares favorably to the average fatality rate of .024 for attacks with a knife in Chicago for the years 1965-67.[24] The estimated fatality rate for attack with a knife or other weapon (.0130) is approximately one-seventh that for attack with a gun (.0927), the ratio reported by the FBI.[25] We have plotted the actual and estimated values for murder with a firearm and for murder with a knife or other weapon in Figure 4.

[24] Newton and Zimring, *Firearms and Violence*, p. 41.
[25] FBI, *Uniform Crime Reports*, 1963, p. 7.

Figure 4

ACTUAL AND ESTIMATED MURDER RATES,
UNITED STATES, 1961-1970

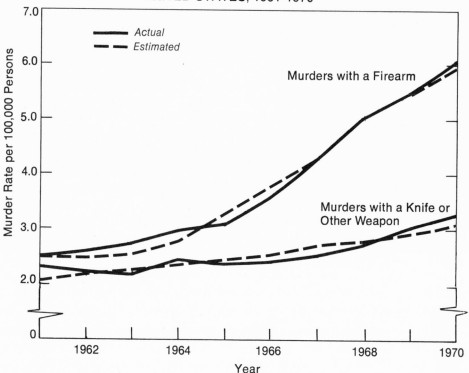

Cross-section Analysis: Murder, Assault and Gun Use. Data by state for the fraction of assaults committed with firearms is available only for the year 1965.[26] Combined with the assault and homicide rate, and the fraction of homicides committed with firearms, these data permit the estimation of equation (15) which can be compared to the time-series results. The rate of felonious murders committed with a firearm, $P(M \wedge G \wedge F)$, was presumed constant. The regression result is

$$P(M \wedge G)/P(A) = \underset{(11.05)}{.121} \, P(G/A) + \underset{(5.89)}{.59 \times 10^{-5}} \, \frac{1}{P(A)}. \qquad (35)$$

$$\overline{R}^2 = .559$$

---

[26] See Statement of the Honorable Bob Casey, *Hearings Before Subcommittee No. 5 of the Committee on the Judiciary,* House of Representatives, 90th Congress, pp. 478-489. Using data from this statement, $P(G/A)$ was calculated as the fraction of assaults and homicides committed with firearms, that is, the fraction of total assaults committed with firearms whether they resulted in a fatality or not. $P(M \wedge G)/P(A)$ was calculated as the ratio of homicides committed with firearms to the sum of all homicides and assaults. $\frac{1}{P(A)}$ was calculated from the assault rate published in FBI, *Uniform Crime Reports,* 1965.

The estimate of the fatality rate for firearms attacks, $P(M/G \wedge A) = .121$, compares favorably to the time-series estimate of .093, and to the Newton and Zimring value of .122, referred to above in the discussion of the time-series results.[27] We could improve the specification of equation (35) if we attempted to account for variations from state to state in murders arising from felonious activities, $P(M \wedge G \wedge F)$.

Cross-section Analysis: The Deterrence of Gun Use in Assault. Equation (28) was estimated using the calculated probability of gun use in assault; as noted earlier, these figures were available by state for 1965 only. We used the estimates pertaining to criminal homicide of certainty of imprisonment, CR, and severity of punishment, SV, circa 1960, as compiled by Jack P. Gibbs. We used the three-year average of death-rate firearms accidents between 1959 and 1961 compiled by Iskrant and Joliet for GAX. Denoting natural logarithms by 1n, the regression result is

$$\ln \frac{1-P(G/A)}{P(G/A)} = -2.76 + .620 \ln CR + .831 \ln SV - .172 \ln GAX \quad (36)$$
$$(-2.57) \quad (3.20) \quad (4.54) \quad (-1.88)$$
$$\overline{R}^2 = .402, F(3,44) = 11.55.$$

The elasticities Θ, Φ, and Ψ for certainty, severity and gun accidents, respectively, all have the expected sign. The estimated coefficients for certainty and severity are significantly different from zero at the one percent level. The fact that they are greater than zero but less than one implies that the odds that an assailant will not use a gun increase with the certainty or severity of punishment but at a decreasing rate. The coefficient on the proxy for gun density is not significant at the one percent level but is significant if the criterion is relaxed to the 5 percent level.[28]

It is particularly significant that the coefficients on certainty and severity are not significantly different from one another.[29] They have an approximately equal deterrent effect on gun use in assault. This is a direct refutation of the hypothesis devolving from the classical tradition that certainty would have a greater deterrent effect than severity.[30]

---

[27] See note 22 above.

[28] These levels of significance were calculated using a one-tailed test for the t-statistic.

[29] The variance (var) of $\Phi - \Theta = $ var $\Phi + $ var $\Theta - 2$ cov $\Phi\Theta = .335 + .0366 - 2(.0041)$ and hence the t-statistic to test the hypothesis that the difference between Φ and Θ is zero is $t = .211/.248$.

[30] See George B. Vold, *Theoretical Criminology* (New York: Oxford University Press, 1958). This notion is certainly more characteristic of the Italian criminologist, economist, and mathematician Cesare Beccaria than of Jeremy Bentham. In arguing that "one of the greatest curbs on crime is not the cruelty of punishments, but their infallibility," Beccaria seems to have been referring more to inexorable executions of the law by the judge than to the certainty of apprehension; Cesare Beccaria, *On Crimes and Punishment* (Indianapolis: Bobbs-Merrill Co., 1963). Bentham clearly expected a strong tradeoff between certainty and severity: "To enable the value of the punishment to outweigh that of the profit of the offense, it must be increased, in point of magnitude, in proportion as it falls short in point of certainty." Jeremy Bentham, *The Principles and Morals of Legislation* (New York: Hafner Publishing Co., 1948), p. 184.

These findings do not depend critically on standardizing for gun density. Dropping ln GAX from equation (36) one obtains

$$\ln\frac{1-P(G/A)}{P(G/A)} = -\underset{(-2.74)}{3.01} + \underset{(3.08)}{.605}\ln CR + \underset{(4.82)}{.893}\ln SV.$$ (37)

$$\bar{R}^2 = .369, F(2,45) = 14.7$$

All the conclusions about certainty and severity that we drew from equation (36) are also true for equation (37). In addition, we see that deterrence explains by far the largest fraction of the variance in gun use in assault.[31] Gun density, which may be imperfectly measured by gun accidents, plays a lesser role.

IV. Comments and Conclusions

Evidence for deterrence based on simple correlations between offense rates and the certainty and/or severity of punishment is unsatisfactory. Since we would expect an increase in the offense rate to decrease the conviction ratio, *ceteris paribus,* and, similarly, a decline in the conviction ratio to increase the offense rate, negative simple correlations are encouraging but inconclusive. Insignificant or positive simple correlations are clear warnings that it is necessary to standardize the analysis for variations in the factors causing crime and for variations in the resources devoted to its control.

By focusing on the probability of gun use in assault we can standardize for etiological factors and concentrate on deterrence. If the certainty and severity of punishment for criminal homicide have a deterrent effect, this should be reflected in the intensity of the assault and the likelihood that the assault will result in fatality. If the assailant chooses to use a firearm, the assault is serious and much more likely to result in murder.

The statistical analysis indicates that in the last ten years, murders committed with a firearm have been increasing much more rapidly than those committed with knives and other weapons. Most of the increase can be attributed to assaults with firearms among family and friends, rather than to circumstances involving felonious activities such as robbery. The increase in murders committed with a firearm can be attributed approximately in equal measure to the increase in the assault rate and the increase in the fraction of assaults involving firearms. The variation from state to state in the ratio of murders by firearm to total assaults is explained largely by the fraction of assaults involving firearms. Thus, on the basis of both time-series and cross-section analyses, it is reasonable to conclude that gun use in assault is a major factor contributing to violence in America.

On the basis of the analysis developed in this paper, gun use in assault can be deterred. Variations in the odds that an assailant will use a gun are significantly

---

[31] The simple correlation between ln $[1-P(G/A)/P(G/A)]$ and ln GAX is $-.29$.

affected by the certainty and the severity of the penalty for criminal homicide. The deterrent effect of severity is not significantly different from that of certainty. The odds that the assailant will use a gun are less if the gun density (measured by the rate of fatal gun accidents) is lower, but gun density plays a lesser role than deterrence. Increasing the certainty and severity of punishment will decrease gun use in assault, but at a diminishing rate. These results suggest that more empirical analysis in quest for evidence on deterrence is indicated.

Appendix

The total cost of a crime to society is the sum of the losses from the crime, r^oOF, and the costs of controlling the crime which consists of the costs of allocating resources to the tasks of apprehension and conviction, W^oL, plus the costs associated with applying the penalty, $C(SV)$. This total cost (the sum of equations (3) and (4)) may be represented as

$$TC = W^oL + r^oOF + C(SV).$$

It is presumed that society wishes to minimize the total cost of crime subject to the technological conditions which govern the effectiveness of applying resources to criminal justice, as represented by equation (1),

$$CR = CR(OF, L),$$

and subject to the conditions generating and controlling crime, as represented by equation (2),

$$OF = OF(CR, SV, SE).$$

The partial rates of change with respect to each argument presumed for equations (1) and (2) (as denoted by a roman numeral subscript corresponding to the order of the argument) are:

$$CR_I \left(\text{i.e. } \frac{\partial CR}{\partial OF} \right) < 0, \, CR_{I,I} \left(\text{i.e. } \frac{\partial^2 CR}{\partial OF^2} \right) > 0,$$

$$CR_{II} \left(\text{i.e. } \frac{\partial CR}{\partial L} \right) > 0, \, CR_{II,II} \left(\text{i.e. } \frac{\partial^2 CR}{\partial L^2} \right) < 0,$$

$$OF_{III} \left(\text{i.e. } \frac{\partial OF}{\partial SE} \right) > 0,$$

$$OF_I \left(\text{i.e. } \frac{\partial OF}{\partial CR} \right) < 0, \, OF_{I,I} \left(\text{i.e. } \frac{\partial^2 OF}{\partial CR^2} \right) > 0,$$

$$OF_{II} \left(\text{i.e. } \frac{\partial OF}{\partial SV} \right) < 0, \, OF_{II,II} \left(\text{i.e. } \frac{\partial^2 OF}{\partial SV^2} \right) > 0.$$

This minimization problem can be solved using a Lagrangian function which summarizes the approach:

$$LA[L, SV, OF, CR, \lambda_1, \lambda_2] = r^oOF + W^oL + C(SV) + \lambda_1[CR - CR(OF,L)] + \lambda_2[OF - OF(CR, SV, SE)]. \quad \text{(A-1)}$$

83

From the first order conditions for a minimum we have

$$\frac{CR_{II}}{1/OF_I - CR_I} = -\frac{W^o}{r^o} \qquad (A-2)$$

and

$$\frac{OF_{II}/OF_I}{1/OF_I - CR_I} = -\frac{dC/dSV}{r^o}. \qquad (A-3)$$

These tangency conditions can be interpreted quite simply from the total differential, dOF, derived from equations (1) and (2), that is,

$$OF = OF[CR(OF, L), SV, SE], \qquad (A-4)$$

and

$$dOF = \frac{CR_{II}\, dL + OF_{II}/OF_I\, dSV + OF_{III}/OF_I\, dSE}{1/OF_I - CR_I}. \qquad (A-5)$$

The partial change in the offense rate with an increase in criminal justice resources, $\partial OF/\partial L$, as derived from equation (A-5) which accounts for simultaneity, is

$$\frac{\partial OF}{\partial L} = \frac{CR_{II}}{1/OF_I - CR_I}, \qquad (A-6)$$

and is the slope of the solid line in Figure 2 which depicts the locus of attainable combinations of L and OF. Given the assumption CR_{II} is positive, this slope will be negative if

$$1/OF_I - CR_I < O.$$

The negativity condition for this term is the requirement for stability, that is, OF(CR, SV, SE) cuts CR(OF,L) from above in Figure 1(a). Since diminishing returns are presumed (that is, $CR_{II,II} < O$), the slope of attainable combinations depicted in Figure 2 will become less negative with increasing L, i.e., $\dfrac{\partial^2 OF}{\partial L^2} > O$, assuming the term $1/OF_1 - CR_I$ remains negative as L increases (that is, that the situation remains stable). Of course $-W^o/r^o$ is the slope of the line of constant cost combinations of L and OF depicted in Figure 2.

It is possible to give a similar interpretation to the condition represented by equation (A-3). From equation (A-5) we find that the rate of change of offenses with the severity of the penalty (accounting for simultaneity) is

$$\frac{\partial OF}{\partial SV} = \frac{OF_{II}/OF_I}{1/OF_I - CR_I}, \qquad (A-7)$$

which could be represented as the slope of the locus of attainable combinations of SV and OF. Given the assumptions that OF_{II} and OF_I are both negative, this slope will be negative, that is, $\dfrac{\partial OF}{\partial SV} < O$, if the situation is stable. The term $-dC/dSV/r^o$ is the slope of the locus of constant cost combinations of severity of penalty and offense rate.

PUNISHMENT AND DETERRENCE OF DEVIANCE*

Charles R. Tittle

Few issues in social science have evoked so much ideological debate as the question of whether punishment deters deviance. This controversy has been a two-edged sword. While it has kept alive an interest in the problem, it has at the same time inhibited thorough empirical investigation and has led to premature conclusions. Despite the fact that the question is essentially an empirical one, comparatively little research has been undertaken. As a result, social-scientific and lay opinion has always rested on a tenuous base, and the criminal law has been founded on a set of unproven assumptions.

For most of this century social scientists have been generally persuaded that punishment is relatively unimportant as a behavioral influence. For instance, a well-known criminological classic declares that punishment "does not deter . . . [nor] does it act as a deterrent upon others . . . ,"[1] and a popular contemporary text concludes that legal punishment is of limited effectiveness because "it does not prevent crime in others or prevent relapse into crime."[2] But recent changes in perspective have led to some reassessment of that position, and research since 1960 has provided empirical challenge to the orthodox view.

I. Previous Research

The argument that punishment has little or no deterrent effect typically stems from two kinds of evidence. The best known concerns the relationship between capital punishment and homicide.[3] Included in this literature are investigations comparing crime rates of political units which differ in legal provision for the death penalty,[4] comparisons over a period of time of political units which use capital punishment

---

* This paper is a revised version of a paper coauthored with Charles H. Logan.

1 Frank Tannenbaum, *Crime and the Community* (Boston: Ginn and Co., 1938), p. 478.

2 Walter C. Reckless, *The Crime Problem,* 4th ed. (New York: Appleton-Century-Crofts, 1967), p. 508.

3 Edwin H. Sutherland and Donald R. Cressey, *Principles of Criminology* (Philadelphia: J. B. Lippincott, 1966), pp. 335-53.

4 Karl F. Schuessler, "The Deterrent Influence of the Death Penalty," *The Annals,* vol. 284 (November 1952), pp. 54-62, and Thorsten Sellin, "Homicides in Retentionist and Abolitionist States," in *Capital Punishment* (New York: Harper and Row, 1967), pp. 135-38.

for some periods but not others,[5] sequence studies focusing on the frequency of homicide following publicity about executions,[6] and illustrative case or historical episodes.[7] These investigations all indicate that capital punishment, at least as it has been practiced in recent decades, adds nothing in deterrent power beyond what is already accomplished by the next most severe penalty. From this base, many generalize that punishment per se must be ineffective.

A second well-known body of data is relevant to whether punishment other than death or permanent separation from society deters those punished from future offenses. In one study, corporal punishment was found to be unrelated to further offense,[8] and a study of the relationship between cumulative time in prison (days in) and cumulative time between discharges and reconvictions (days out) reported no correlation between the two.[9] Recidivism rates for releasees were also generally reported to be very high.[10] In addition, experimental animal studies provided a basis for discounting the deterrent power of negative sanctions. Although the effectiveness of punishment as a conditioning tool has been controversial, the typical interpretation in the past was that negative reinforcement was at best inefficient.[11]

Some information prior to 1960 supported the view that the threat of detection and punishment had some influence on deviance. For example, historical case material showed that crime sometimes increased when police were immobilized, and that it tended to decrease when police surveillance was increased or when technical innovations were employed.[12] Nevertheless, most students of the subject interpreted the bulk of the data as contrary to a deterrent hypothesis.[13]

[5] Schuessler, "The Deterrent Influence"; Nigel Walker, *Crime and Punishment in Britain* (Edinburgh: University of Edinburgh Press, 1965), pp. 238-41; and Hans Mattick, *The Unexamined Death* (Chicago: John Howard Association, 1963).

[6] Leonard Savitz, "A Study in Capital Punishment," *Journal of Criminal Law, Criminology, and Police Science,* vol. 49 (November-December 1958), pp. 328-48; and Robert H. Dann, "The Deterrent Effect of Capital Punishment," *Friends Social Science Bulletin,* no. 29 (Philadelphia, 1935), as described in Mattick, *The Unexamined Death.*

[7] See Paul B. Horton and Gerald R. Leslie, *The Sociology of Social Problems* (New York: Appleton-Century-Crofts, 1965), pp. 165-69; and Harry E. Barnes and Negley K. Teeters, *New Horizons in Criminology* (Englewood Cliffs, N. J.: Prentice-Hall, 1959), pp. 315-17.

[8] See Robert G. Caldwell, "The Deterrent Influence of Corporal Punishment upon Prisoners Who Have Been Whipped," *American Sociological Review,* vol. 2 (April 1944), pp. 171-77.

[9] Norval Morris, *The Habitual Offender* (Cambridge, Mass.: Harvard University Press, 1951).

[10] Eleanor and Sheldon Glueck, *Criminal Careers in Retrospect* (New York: The Commonwealth Fund, 1943), p. 121; George B. Vold, "Does the Prison Reform?" *The Annals,* vol. 293 (May 1954), pp. 42-50; and Harry C. Westover, "Is Prison Rehabilitation Successful?" *Federal Probation,* vol. 22 (March 1958), pp. 3-6.

[11] B. F. Skinner, *Science and Human Behavior* (New York: Macmillan, 1953); Albert Bandura, "Punishment Revisited," *Journal of Consulting Psychology,* vol. 26 (1962), pp. 298-301.

[12] Jackson Toby, "Is Punishment Necessary?" *Journal of Criminal Law, Criminology, and Police Science,* vol. 55 (September 1964), pp. 332-37; Johs Andenaes, "General Prevention— Illusion or Reality?" *Journal of Criminal Law, Criminology, and Police Science,* vol. 43 (1952), pp. 176-98; and Jerome Hall, *Theft, Law, and Society,* 2nd ed. (Indianapolis: Bobbs-Merrill, 1952), pp. 284-87.

[13] John C. Ball, "The Deterrence Concept in Criminology and Law," *Journal of Criminal Law, Criminology, and Police Science,* vol. 46 (September-October 1955), pp. 347-54.

II. Contemporary Viewpoints

Within the past few years, students of deviance have turned their attention away from the deviant act and have focused on social reaction to deviance.[14] Interest in negative sanctions as independent variables has blossomed, and many have come to question earlier interpretations and assumptions. Consequently, critical reassessment of the death penalty and recidivism research has taken place, and we now have a body of research concerned with the role of sanctions in generating conformity.

Review of the capital punishment research has identified a number of deficiencies that make it less useful in resolving the deterrence issue than previously thought.[15] One of the most important defects of that body of work is its inattention to the probability, or perceived probability, of imposition of the penalty. It has been noted that the effect of a legal provision for a death penalty may not be the same as the effect of a death penalty that is imposed with a reasonably high degree of certainty. Only Karl F. Schuessler attempted to take this dimension into account. Using a crude index of the certainty of execution, he found a negative $(-.29)$, although nonsignificant, correlation between certainty of execution and the homicide rate—even though he was dealing with an attenuated distribution and a collection of low probability cases.[16] It is possible that if capital punishment were inflicted in a large proportion of the cases in which homicides occur, it would prove to be a deterrent. But since there are no systematic data from societies which have been both efficient in apprehension of offenders and willing to impose the death penalty, it is impossible to know whether it would be a deterrent under such conditions.

A second weakness of the capital punishment literature is its reliance upon anecdotal material.[17] The prevalence of crime in the face of possible capital punishment tells only how many offenses were not deterred; it does not indicate the number of contemplated deviant acts that may have been deterred. Similarly the number of convicted murderers who maintain that they did not consider the penalty before committing homicide reveals nothing about the number of potential murderers who may have taken it into account.

Finally, even if the death penalty research were impeccably valid, it would still reveal little about the deterrent power of punishment. The studies, without exception, really test whether capital punishment, as it is practiced in the modern

[14] Jack P. Gibbs, "Conceptions of Deviant Behavior: The Old and the New," *Pacific Sociological Review,* vol. 9 (Spring 1966), pp. 9-14.

[15] See Paul W. Tappan, *Crime, Justice, and Correction* (New York: McGraw-Hill, 1960), pp. 253-55; Walker, *Crime and Punishment,* p. 241; Frank E. Zimring, *Perspectives on Deterrence,* Public Health Service Publication No. 2056, NIMH Center for Studies of Crime and Delinquency (Washington, D. C.: U.S. Government Printing Office, 1971); and Charles H. Logan, "Legal Sanctions and Deterrence from Crime" (Ph. D. diss., Indiana University, 1971).

[16] See Schuessler, "The Deterrent Influence," and Quinn McNemar, *Psychological Statistics* (New York: John Wiley and Sons, 1955), pp. 149-50.

[17] See Walker, *Crime and Punishment,* p. 238, and Zimring, *Perspectives.*

world (that is, with a low probability of being used), adds anything additional to imprisonment as a deterrent. A valid test of the deterrent effect of capital punishment would be to pit it against the alternative of no punishment. We cannot interpret the fact that the threat of death apparently deters murder to no greater extent than the simple threat of imprisonment to mean that capital punishment does not deter at all; nor can we interpret it to mean that sanctions of all types are poor deterrents for all types of deviance. This latter point is especially applicable, since homicide is usually considered to be a unique kind of deviance.[18] Thus, although the death penalty literature provides sufficient justification for dispensing with capital punishment in modern society, it affords little basis for conclusions about the general question of whether sanctions influence behavior.

The use of recidivism literature as support for the pessimistic view of punishment has also undergone critical review. Among the most important problems in drawing general conclusions from this material is simply that recidivism data are applicable only to the question of specific deterrence (effect on the one punished) and not to general deterrence (effect on behavior in a population). Not only is it inappropriate to generalize from one level to the other, but it is actually reasonable to postulate that punishment might stimulate further deviance by the victim at the same time that it serves as a deterrent to those not punished.[19] The same mechanisms that labeling theorists point to as generators of secondary deviance, stigmatization, and rejection,[20] may also deter the nonstigmatized from engaging in the behavior that resulted in the label. In any case, specific deterrence is of far less importance than is general deterrence. Even complete specific deterrence would have little effect upon crime rates because only a small proportion of offenders are ever in a position to become recidivists.[21]

A second problem in drawing conclusions from recidivism studies, particularly studies of prison releasees, is that recidivism may be a by-product of prison life itself. These ancillary conditions may negate the effect of the punishment. For instance, the deterrent objective of incarceration—to increase fear of sanction—may be undermined by socialization into deviant subcultures and by exposure to deviant role models while incarcerated.[22] On the other hand, future conformity may

---

[18] William J. Chambliss, "Types of Deviance and the Effectiveness of Legal Sanctions," *Wisconsin Law Review,* Summer 1967, pp. 703-19.

[19] Charles R. Tittle, "Crime Rates and Legal Sanctions," *Social Problems,* vol. 16 (Spring 1969), pp. 409-23; and Bernard A. Thorsell and Lloyd W. Klemke, "The Labeling Process: Reinforcement and Deterrent?" *Law and Society Review,* vol. 6 (February 1972), pp. 393-403.

[20] Edwin M. Lemert, "The Concept of Secondary Deviation," in *Human Deviance, Social Problems, and Social Control* (Englewood Cliffs, N. J.: Prentice-Hall, 1967), pp. 40-60.

[21] Leroy Gould and Zvi Namenwirth, "Contrary Objectives: Crime Control and Rehabilitation of Criminals," in Jack Douglas, *Crime and Justice in American Society* (Indianapolis: Bobbs-Merrill, 1971), pp. 256-57.

[22] Donald Clemmer, *The Prison Community* (Boston: Christopher Publishing Company, 1940), and Stanton Wheeler, "Socialization in Correctional Communities," *American Sociological Review,* vol. 26 (October 1961), pp. 697-712.

be the product of rehabilitative efforts undertaken during incarceration rather than deterrence based on fear of punishment. Recidivism rates may, therefore, indicate more about the conditions under which the punishment is administered than about the punishment itself.

Further, a valid test of the specific deterrent effect of legal sanctions would involve comparisons of the recidivism of those punished with the recidivism of offenders who had experienced no contact with the law at all. Although there are really no data on this point (the government crime reports reveal, however, that rearrest is highest for those whose cases were previously dismissed or who were acquitted),[23] it hardly seems plausible that offenders who go undetected will be less likely to repeat an offense than those who are caught and punished.[24] True, comparison of recidivism of probationers with incarcerees suggests less effect for incarceration,[25] but there may well be a selective factor involved,[26] and probation is itself a form of legal punishment. Hence, one would conclude most appropriately from such comparisons that incarceration adds nothing in deterrent power to that which is achieved with the lesser penalty—rather than that incarceration or punishment in general fails to deter.

But even if these three considerations were not relevant, the recidivism literature would still not justify an antideterrent conclusion. Logical defects and interpretive difficulties have always plagued this type of work.[27] Moreover, the data are not so contrary to the deterrence argument as is usually assumed. While there are many variations and complexities, the available follow-up data suggest that instead of the widely believed 65 percent to 85 percent return-to-prison rate, only about 35 percent actually return.[28] And, a recent FBI study suggests that legal sanction may be more of a specific deterrent than even the FBI is willing to admit. By means of arrest reports, all offenders released from custody in 1963 were followed for six years. Although 65 percent were re-arrested on some charge during the follow-up period, only 23 percent, or 40 percent of those rearrested during the first four years, had been reconvicted by the end of the fourth year. Furthermore, extrapolation indicates an overall reconviction rate for the remainder of the offenders' lives somewhat below 35 percent.[29]

---

[23] See United States Department of Justice, *Uniform Crime Reports* (Washington, D. C.: U.S. Government Printing Office, 1967), p. 37.

[24] Herbert L. Packer, *The Limits of the Criminal Sanction* (Stanford: Stanford University Press, 1968), p. 46.

[25] Martin A. Levin, "Policy Evaluation and Recidivism," *Law and Society Review,* vol. 6 (August 1971), pp. 17-46.

[26] Leslie T. Wilkins, *Evaluation of Penal Measures* (New York: Random House, 1969).

[27] See Walker, *Crime and Punishment,* pp. 242-60, and Wilkins, *Evaluation.*

[28] Daniel Glaser, *The Effectiveness of a Prison and Parole System* (Indianapolis: Bobbs-Merrill, 1964), pp. 13-35; and Wilkins, *Evaluation.*

[29] FBI, *Uniform Crime Reports,* p. 41. Since the *Uniform Crime Reports* neglect to report reconvictions in subsequent years, one must extrapolate. In so doing, however, we must take note of the possibility that the number of reconvicted may have risen as people arrested during

Finally, recent comprehensive reviews of the experimental evidence concerning punishment conclude that, contrary to earlier beliefs, and even some current ones,[30] punishment can be highly effective in eliminating behavioral responses.[31] But more important, contemporary laboratory work points up the limitations of conditioning principles for human beings, and suggests that vicarious reinforcement (social learning) rather than operant conditioning, is more likely to be operative. Research on social learning has shown that vicarious negative reinforcement may play a very important role in the determination of human behavior.[32]

The research undertaken before 1960, therefore, provides little basis for judging the deterrent power of sanctions. At best, the evidence indicates that the issue is problematic. Certainly the data do not justify sweeping conclusions as to the inefficacy of sanctions.

III. Recent Research

Along with a critical review of past research, contemporary perspectives have spawned a series of studies, most of which contradict previously held views that negative sanctions have little effect on behavior.

Direct Investigative Evidence. The experimental researchers working on the problem of vicarious learning have compiled some of the most interesting data on this subject. Numerous experiments have shown that observing others being rewarded or punished can influence the future behavior of the observers just as if they had been directly reinforced. Apparently this is the result of the individuals' having psychically experienced the feelings of those whom they observed being rewarded or punished. Presumably this same process is operative in non-laboratory contexts, and it may even extend to vicarious conditioning from verbal reports. If so, it implies that general deterrence, to the extent that it occurs, is

---

the first four years came to trial at a later date and as additional arrests were made. Given that lag time in the judicial process is rarely more than two years, and that most of those rearrested during the six years covered by the follow-up were taken into custody during the first two years (66 percent), it is reasonable to assume that the vast majority of rearrestees had been tried by the end of the fourth year. If we assume, moreover, that the 40 percent rate of reconviction of arrestees applies only to those arrested during the first two years of the follow-up, and if we project this conviction rate to cover all those arrested from the third through the sixth years, we arrive at a total reconviction rate of 26 percent for the original sample of releasees. Furthermore, during the fifth and sixth years an increment of only about 2 percent per year in additional arrests was added. Hence the reconviction rate of offenders released in 1963 would appear to be well below 35 percent even if one projects the follow-up far beyond the original six years.

[30] For example, see James B. Appel and Neil J. Peterson, "What's Wrong with Punishment?" *Journal of Criminal Law, Criminology, and Police Science,* vol. 56 (1965), pp. 450-53.

[31] See N. H. Azrin and W. C. Holz, "Punishment," in *Operant Behavior: Areas of Research and Application,* ed. Werner K. Honig (New York: Appleton-Century-Crofts, 1966), pp. 380-447; Albert Bandura, *Principles of Behavior Modification* (New York: Holt, Rinehart and Winston, 1969), pp. 293-353.

[32] Bandura, *Behavior Modification,* pp. 118-216, and Albert Bandura and Richard H. Walters, *Social Learning and Personality Development* (New York: Holt, Rinehart and Winston, 1963).

possible because citizens vicariously identify with punished individuals. And of course the same process might account for the failure or weakness of general deterrence, since much deviance is actually rewarded and most goes unpunished.

Other relevant data have been reported in a series of sociological and sociopsychological studies. The first involved an investigation by William J. Chambliss of obedience to parking regulations on a midwestern university campus in 1966. He found that significant reductions in parking violations by faculty members followed an increase in the certainty of apprehension and severity of penalties. The effect was especially strong for those who were frequent violators, but a significant proportion of the professors were unaffected because they seldom or never violated the rules.[33]

The second study was an attempt to assess the effects of a "sanction threat" and a "conscience appeal" on compliance with income tax laws. Taxpayers were randomly assigned to treatment and control groups. Before tax returns were submitted, one group was interviewed and asked questions suggesting the possibility that they might be punished if they misreported their incomes. A second group was reminded of their moral responsibility, while a third group was interviewed but asked none of the questions suggesting a "sanction threat" or a "conscience appeal." A fourth group was not interviewed. The "sanction appeal" and "conscience appeal" groups both reported significantly higher incomes than the control groups, but the appeal to conscience was found to produce greater reported income than the sanction threat. The effectiveness of the inducements was also found to vary by social characteristics of the subjects, particularly socioeconomic status. It was also discovered that among some subjects (35 percent) the "sanction threat" led to greater deduction claims, apparently as a result of attempts to recover "losses" suffered from more honest reporting.[34]

Although this particular study can be criticized because the "threat" and "conscience appeal" were not clearly expressed as such and because no attention was paid to how probable the subjects might have thought the sanction was, it provides powerful evidence in favor of a deterrent hypothesis. Still, it suggests that other variables may be more important in some instances than sanctions and that sanction threats may have produced countertendencies.

In 1967, Jai B. P. Sinha required pairs of experimental subjects to perform a difficult task with a financial reward as an incentive to successful completion. One member of each pair was a stooge. The test subjects were told not to help each other in performing the task, but they were allowed to give instructions to each other. Actual aid in response to the pleas of the stooges, therefore, represented

---

[33] See Chambliss, "The Deterrent Influence."

[34] Richard D. Schwartz and Sonya Orleans, "On Legal Sanctions," *The University of Chicago Law Review,* vol. 34 (Winter 1967), pp. 274-300, and Richard D. Schwartz, "Sanctions and Compliance," Paper delivered at the Annual Meeting of the American Sociological Association, San Francisco, 1969.

cheating. In one condition the subjects were threatened with punishment, while in the other, no mention of punishment was made. Significantly less cheating occurred in the threat condition than the free condition. But among those who broke the rules, the number of violations was similar in each of the conditions. These data suggest that deterrence is likely to operate among those who have not transgressed, but that once violation occurs, the threat of sanction is less likely to inhibit further evidence.[35]

These studies were followed by two similar, but independently undertaken, investigations using official statistics. In 1968, Jack P. Gibbs constructed indexes of severity and certainty of punishment for homicide in each of the United States using FBI and prisoner statistics. He then examined the relationship between these indexes and homicide rates. The data showed strong negative associations which suggested that the greater the certainty of imprisonment and the greater the length of time in prison, the lower the homicide rate.[36]

In my own research in 1969, I used official statistics to develop indexes of the certainty of imprisonment and the severity of punishment for seven major offense categories and a category of total felonies.[37] The actual content of the indexes differed from those used by Gibbs, although they employed the same logic. Again the relationship between these indexes and crime rates indicated that low crime rates were likely to be present when there was a high probability of imprisonment for any offense. A negative relationship between the average length of prison time served and the crime rate, however, was present only for the offense of homicide. Other analysis highlighted a complex interaction, in their relationship to crime rate, between certainty of imprisonment and length of time spent in prison. Certainty generally corresponded to lower crime rates regardless of the level of severity, but severity seemed to be associated with lower crime rates only when particular levels of certainty were extant.

The work by Gibbs and myself, described above, immediately led to research and commentary by others. In 1969, Louis N. Gray and J. David Martin reanalyzed Gibbs's data; in 1971 William C. Bailey, working with Martin and Gray, and Charles H. Logan, working separately, reanalyzed my data using more precise and rigorous statistical techniques. In all three instances the original findings were confirmed with the exception that Logan's results suggested a more important influence for severity of punishment than the original analysis.[38] In 1970 Theodore

---

[35] Jai B. P. Sinha, "Ethical Risk and Censure-avoiding Behavior," *Journal of Social Psychology,* vol. 71 (April 1967), pp. 267-75.

[36] Jack P. Gibbs, "Crime, Punishment and Deterrence," *Southwestern Social Science Quarterly,* vol. 48 (March 1968), pp. 515-30.

[37] Tittle, "Crime Rates."

[38] Louis N. Gray and J. David Martin, "Punishment and Deterrence: Another Analysis of Gibbs' Data," *Social Science Quarterly,* vol. 50 (1969), pp. 389-95; William C. Bailey, J. David Martin and Louis N. Gray, "Crime and Deterrence: A Correlation Analysis," mimeographed, 1971; Charles H. Logan, "Legal Sanctions"; and idem, "General Deterrent Effects of Imprisonment," *Social Forces,* vol. 51 (September 1972), pp. 64-73.

G. Chiricos and Gordon P. Waldo, however, employed similar indexes in studying, on the one hand, the association among certainty of imprisonment, severity of punishment and crime rates at different points in time, and, on the other hand, in looking at percentage changes in the indexes from time period to time period. Their analysis suggested to them that the evidence was too inconsistent to be accepted in support of deterrence theory. Furthermore, they challenged the original findings of Gibbs and myself on methodological grounds, with charges that the results were spurious and artificially produced.[39]

Logan, in turn, criticized the Chiricos and Waldo paper, arguing first, that their data concerning certainty of imprisonment were in fact remarkably consistent and even impressive (the authors observed this themselves but dismissed it because they believed it was an artifact); second, that their technique of studying the relationship between percentage change in two indexes was deceptive and unreliable since the base on which the percentages were calculated was so small; third, that it was inappropriate to relate measures of change in indexes selected arbitrarily at widely separated points in time; and fourth, that they maximized the likelihood of finding inconsistent results by using specific offenses only (excluding a category of total offenses), and by considering only small time periods.[40] Bailey, Gray, and Martin in another critique pointed out that much of the data used by Chiricos and Waldo were incomparable and incomplete.[41] Moreover, both critiques demonstrated that the Chiricos and Waldo methodological attack was without merit. Thus, my conclusions and those of Gibbs in support of deterrence theory appear to be well grounded, and some basis has been established for interpreting the Chiricos and Waldo findings concerning certainty of punishment as supportive of the deterrence notion.

In the same research vein, Logan in 1972 used higher order statistical techniques to analyze original arrest data provided by the FBI. The results were consistent with deterrence theory in revealing a generally negative relationship between arrest probability and crime rate for the states of the United States for all offenses except homicide.

Research of a different type was conducted by Richard G. Salem and William J. Bowers. In 1970, they examined the relationship between the severity of sanctioning policy in universities and the frequency of self-reported academic rule breaking by samples of students. In one analysis they found negative relationships which they interpreted as being indirect.[42] Their statistical elaboration suggested that peer disapproval may have intervened as the interpretive link between formal

---

[39] Theodore G. Chiricos and Gordon P. Waldo, "Punishment and Crime: An Examination of Some Empirical Evidence," *Social Problems,* vol. 18 (Fall 1970), pp. 200-17.

[40] Charles H. Logan, "On Punishment and Crime (Chiricos and Waldo, 1970): Some Methodological Commentary," *Social Problems,* vol. 19 (Fall 1971), pp. 280-84.

[41] William C. Bailey, Louis N. Gray, and J. David Martin in ibid., pp. 284-89.

[42] Richard G. Salem and William J. Bowers, "Severity of Formal Sanctions as a Deterrent to Deviant Behavior," *Law and Society Review,* vol. 5 (August 1970), pp. 21-40.

sanctioning policy and rule breaking. But in a later, more careful analysis, they concluded that the sanctioning policy did not have even an indirect effect, but was instead a dependent variable representing response to deviant behavior.[43] If it can be assumed that the later analysis using only one type of deviance is representative of all of the deviances considered in their earlier analysis, the Salem and Bowers data are contrary to deterrence theory. However, had the investigators taken into account the actual or perceived certainty that the university sanctioning policies would have been carried out, the results might have been different. Just as in the case of the capital punishment research, we find that a policy may differ considerably from what is usually done, and perceptions of either or both might be different still.

The importance of perceptions of the probability of experiencing a sanction is shown by two studies. In 1969, Gary F. Jensen examined the relationship between beliefs concerning the likelihood of being caught and punished and delinquency (self-reported and officially recorded). His measure of perceived certainty was quite crude—an expression of agreement with a statement implying high probability of apprehension/punishment for delinquent behavior generally—but the data still revealed negative associations.[44] Although those associations were not overpowering in magnitude, they are especially interesting because they deal with the question of deterrence at the level of cognition. Jensen's work confirms that many people misperceive the actual probability of apprehension and punishment, though delinquency was directly related to perceptions. This is consistent with common sense reasoning that the effectiveness of sanctions actually depends upon perceptions about those sanctions—perceptions which may bear little relationship to reality but which may vary from individual to individual and from social group to social group as a result of other variables.

Further support for this notion is provided by Waldo and Chiricos. In a sample survey of students at a southern university, they found that perceived certainty of apprehension and penalty were negatively related to probability of marijuana use and theft, but more strongly to marijuana use than theft. The authors interpreted the findings as supportive of deterrence ideas but pointed out that such deterrence is most likely for crimes lacking moral endorsement in the population. They argue that for rules rooted in moral imperatives, official sanctions are secondary to informal pressures imposed by peers and others, or to control by internalized inhibitions. The authors found no support, however, for the proposition that perceived severity of sanction had any deterrent effect.[45]

---

[43] William J. Bowers and Richard G. Salem, "Severity of Formal Sanctions as a Repressive Response to Deviant Behavior," *Law and Society Review,* vol. 6 (February 1972), pp. 427-41.
[44] Gary F. Jensen, "'Crime Doesn't Pay': Correlates of a Shared Misunderstanding," *Social Problems,* vol. 17 (Fall 1969), pp. 189-201.
[45] Gordon P. Waldo and Theodore G. Chiricos, "Perceived Penal Sanction and Self-Reported Criminality: A Neglected Approach to Deterrence Research," *Social Problems,* vol. 19 (Spring 1972), pp. 522-40.

Finally, an experimental test of the effect of a sanction threat and a moral appeal demonstrated that while college classroom cheating could be substantially deterred by a threat of detection and punishment, a moral appeal had no effect whatsoever.[46] The study also showed that the sanction threat produced greater deterrence among females than males and also among those who had less need to cheat than among those who had greater need. The evidence was interpreted as strongly supportive of deterrence theory, at least in a situation involving instrumental behavior, low commitment to the deviance, and a norm with little moral support.

Indirect Investigative Evidence. Other recent research is relevant to the deterrence question but is less directly applicable. In one 1963 study, Salomon Rettig and Harve E. Rawson asked students to judge the probability that hypothetical persons would perform unethical behavior in various kinds of situations. The situations varied with regard to the intent of the act, the type of victim, the certainty of apprehension, the severity of punishment, and the value of the behavior to the individual. Of the six variables, the one that most influenced the predictions of the actions of the hypothetical characters was the severity of punishment.[47]

In another piece of research the same questionnaire was answered by students who had participated one year earlier in an experiment. The experimental subjects had been paid to complete an essentially impossible task so that any reported success represented deviance. The results showed that those who had cheated in the experiment were far less sensitive to punishment as a behavioral influence on the hypothetical person than were those who had not cheated. Assuming that the judges were reflecting their own sensitivities in predicting the behavior of the hypothetical individuals, the authors concluded that "the reinforcement value of a censure is the most significant determinant which predicts unethical behavior." [48]

The same approach was used again by Rettig in 1964 when he compared the "ethical risk sensitivity" of reformatory inmates and a sample of college students. In predicting whether a hypothetical bank teller would embezzle funds, the prisoners more often took into account the teller's perception of the severity of censure than his consideration of gain, expectation of discovery, or intention to steal rather than borrow. The students also placed first priority on the severity of censure, but their predictions were more affected by considerations of gain and probability of detection than were the prisoners' predictions.[49]

---

[46] Charles R. Tittle and Alan R. Rowe, "Moral Appeal, Sanction Threat, and Deviance: An Experimental Test," *Social Problems,* vol. 20 (Spring 1973).

[47] Salomon Rettig and Harve E. Rawson, "The Risk Hypothesis in Predictive Judgments of Unethical Behavior," *Journal of Abnormal and Social Psychology,* vol. 66 (March 1963), pp. 243-48.

[48] Salomon Rettig and Benjamin Pasamanick, "Differential Judgment of Ethical Risk by Cheaters and Non-cheaters," *Journal of Abnormal and Social Psychology,* vol. 69 (July 1964), p. 112.

[49] Salomon Rettig, "Ethical Risk Sensitivity in Male Prisoners," *British Journal of Criminology,* vol. 4 (October 1964), pp. 582-90.

In 1968, the original Rawson and Rettig technique was refined by Sinha, who changed the scale and included different ethically dubious behaviors in the hypothetical situations. He concluded that behavioral decisions involve different sets of considerations for various ethical situations and types of deviance. Unlike the previous researchers, he found that expectation for censure was the most important factor taken into account by the respondents, but he concluded that probability of censure and reinforcement value of the censure (severity) were interrelated in such a way that the effect of severity is contingent upon certainty,[50] a conclusion similar to one I reached in 1969 in another kind of study.[51]

In 1967, Daniel S. Claster compared a sample of incarcerated delinquents with a sample of nondelinquents with respect to the accuracy of their knowledge concerning probability of arrest and conviction for different crimes, the self-reported likelihood that they might engage in the various criminal behaviors, and for those who could conceptualize themselves as committing crimes, their perceptions of the probability that they might be arrested and convicted. The data showed no significant differences between the delinquents and nondelinquents in knowledge about the actual general certainty of arrest and conviction, but they did reveal that delinquents who said they might engage in different crimes perceived the likelihood of personal arrest and conviction to be lower than did the nondelinquents who admitted that they might do the deviant things.[52]

Irving M. Piliavin and his associates were concerned with whether potential informal sanctions ("personal costs") differentiated delinquents from nondelinquents [53] and whether concern with informal personal costs was predictive of laboratory cheating.[54] Perceived personal costs were measured by questionnaire responses to items concerning the importance to the individual of favorable opinions from significant others such as parents or teachers. A survey revealed a negative association between perceived personal costs and delinquency, while the experiment demonstrated that "low cost" boys cheated more than "high cost" boys.

There is also a series of studies focusing on the use of sanctions by one person to induce obedience by another individual to commands. In 1969 J. Horai and James T. Tedeschi had college students play an interpersonal game ("prisoner's dilemma") in an experimental situation. One player was allowed to use sanctions

[50] Jai B. P. Sinha, "A Note on Ethical Risk Hypothesis," *Journal of Social Psychology,* vol. 76 (October 1968), pp. 117-22.

[51] Tittle, "Crime Rates."

[52] Daniel S. Claster, "Comparison of Risk Perception Between Delinquents and Nondelinquents," *Journal of Criminal Law, Criminology, and Police Science,* vol. 58 (March 1967), pp. 80-86.

[53] Irving M. Piliavin, Jane Allyn Hardyck, and Arlene C. Vadum, "Constraining Effects of Personal Costs on the Transgressions of Juveniles," *Journal of Personality and Social Psychology,* vol. 10 (1968), pp. 227-31.

[54] Irving M. Piliavin, Arlene C. Vadum, and Jane Allyn Hardyck, "Delinquency, Personal Costs, and Parental Treatment: A Test of a Cost-Reward Model," *Journal of Criminal Law, Criminology, and Police Science,* vol. 60 (July 1969), pp. 165-72.

in an effort to get the other player to act against his self-interest. They varied the credibility of the sanctions (probability of imposition) as well as the severity. Both were observed to be instrumental in generating compliance.[55] The next year Tedeschi repeated the experiment with Thomas Faley using ROTC cadets and varying the status of the threatener as well as the severity and credibility of the threats. Again certainty and severity of the sanction threat were found to influence the degree of compliance, and the results showed greater compliance to threats by high status persons than to threats by low-status individuals.[56] In 1970, James Gahagan and others conducted a similar experiment in which they varied the pattern of punishment as well as the credibility of threat. They were able to confirm the importance of certainty of sanction but found no effect for patterning.[57] All three experiments suggest that compliance with interpersonal commands is affected by sanction threats.

These indirect studies are all consistent with the proposition that negative sanctions bear importantly upon behavior. But the data are too oblique and involve too many dubious assumptions to permit anything more than tenuous suggestions. Rettig and Rawson did not ask their subjects how they would behave in the various situations; they asked them how they thought a hypothetical person would behave. Thus, while they probably measured the variables which the subjects thought were generally operative in behavioral decisions, these might not be the variables which are operative. Similarly Claster failed to examine the relationship between self-assessed likelihood of deviant behavior and perceived probability of personal arrest and conviction. He reported only how the delinquents and nondelinquents who thought they might commit deviant acts differed in perceptions of the probability of personally experiencing sanctions. And the Piliavin studies neglected the subjects' perceptions of the probability of their deviance being found out by others significant to them, perceptions of the probability that "costs" would result from discovery, or even perceptions of the probability of getting caught. They just assumed that all these probabilities were perceived as high, or at least high enough to generate an effect. Finally, the experiments about interpersonal control did not involve real rewards for winning; they also are restricted in applicability because obedience to individual orders may not be comparable to conformity with social norms or laws.

Case Materials. Other evidence comes from contemporary case material. Increases in some types of crimes have been recorded in situations where police were im-

---

[55] J. Horai and James T. Tedeschi, "Effects of Credibility and Magnitude of Punishment on Compliance to Threats," *Journal of Personality and Social Psychology,* vol. 12 (February 1969), pp. 164-69.

[56] Thomas Faley and James T. Tedeschi, "Status and Reactions to Threats," *Journal of Personality and Social Psychology,* vol. 17 (February 1971), pp. 192-99.

[57] James Gahagan, James T. Tedeschi, Thomas Faley and Svenn Lindskold, "Patterns of Punishment and Reactions to Threats," *Journal of Social Psychology,* vol. 80 (February 1970), pp. 115-16.

mobilized,[58] and decreases in crime following greater police surveillance or improvements in police techniques have been registered.[59] Perhaps the best data of this type are those presented by H. Lawrence Ross and his associates in 1970. They employed a time-series design to study the effect of the British breathalyser law of 1967. This legislation made it possible for suspected drinkers or traffic offenders to be tested immediately, and under the law a person who was ultimately convicted would receive a mandatory penalty. If it can be assumed that fewer traffic casualties indicates fewer cases of drinking while driving, then the data clearly demonstrate that the law had a substantial impact. Since the purpose of the law was to increase the probability of detection and penalty for driving while drinking, its effect strongly supports a deterrent interpretation.[60]

Case material concerning situations in which severity of penalty was varied, however, have not supported a deterrent hypothesis. Although most of these studies have equivocal interpretations,[61] one clear-cut investigation was conducted by Barry Schwartz in 1968. He found no basis for concluding that the amount of rape in Philadelphia was significantly affected by increased penalties.[62]

In general, recent case material is consistent with the other research in suggesting that sanctions have some deterrent effect when the probability of imposition is reasonably high, but that the severity of sanctions in the absence of certainty seems to bear little relationship to future deviance.

IV. Synthesis

What, then, can be concluded from the recent research? It seems quite clear from this work that social scientists must at least take the deterrence question seriously. Almost all research since 1960 suggests that the deterrence hypothesis is worth considering, at least as far as certainty of sanction is concerned. Enough suggestive

---

[58] Gerald Clark, "Black Tuesday in Montreal: What Happens when the Police Strike," *New York Times Magazine,* November 16, 1969, p. 45ff.; and Johs Andenaes, "The General Preventive Effects of Punishment," *University of Pennsylvania Law Review,* vol. 114 (1966), pp. 949-83.

[59] See Zimring, *Perspectives,* pp. 68-73; Walker, *Crime and Punishment,* pp. 241-42; John E. Conklin, *Robbery and the Criminal Justice System* (Philadelphia: J. B. Lippincott, 1972), p. 143.

[60] H. Laurence Ross, Donald T. Campbell, and Gene V. Glass, "Determining the Social Effects of a Legal Reform: The British 'Breathalyser' Crackdown of 1967," *American Behavioral Scientist,* vol. 13 (March-April 1970), pp. 493-509.

[61] See Patrik Tornudd, "The Preventive Effect of Fines for Drunkenness," in *Scandinavian Studies in Criminology,* vol. 2 (Oslo: Univereitetsforlaget, 1968), pp. 109-24; Donald T. Campbell and H. Laurence Ross, "The Connecticut Crackdown on Speeding: Time-Series Data in Quasi-Experimental Analysis," *Law and Society Review,* vol. 3 (1968), pp. 33-53; and Gene V. Glass, "Analysis of Data on the Connecticut Speeding Crackdown as a Time-Series Quasi-Experiment," *Law and Society Review,* vol. 3 (1968), pp. 55-76.

[62] Barry Schwartz, "The Effect in Philadelphia of Pennsylvania's Increased Penalties for Rape and Attempted Rape," *Journal of Criminal Law, Criminology, and Police Science,* vol. 59 (December 1968), pp. 509-15.

data have been reported to mandate systematic research efforts and to compel theoretical consideration of sanctions in the search for explanations of human behavior and social organization. But it is equally obvious that the research conducted so far is not definitive. The only safe conclusion it permits is that sanctions probably have some deterrent capability under some circumstances. There are many gaps in our knowledge which must be filled before we can speak with confidence on the subject.

First, we do not know what influence the type of norm has on the degree of deterrence that is possible. Sociological literature suggests that the type of norm ought to make a difference. Some norms are thought to provoke obedience irrespective of sanctions while others seem to invite disobedience despite provisions for sanctions.[63] Research has dealt with a wide variety of norms, from parking regulations and arbitrary rules to serious felonies. Yet so many other variables have been involved and the measurement of the degree of deterrence achieved has been so crude that specifying variation by type of norm is impossible with present data. Adequate data would demonstrate the relative degree of deterrence for norms that vary in specificity, importance, legitimacy, legality, formality, and moral status.

Second, it is presently unknown how much difference the type of behavior makes with respect to effectiveness of deterrence. Some behaviors are intrinsically rewarding while others are rewarding only for purposes of achieving long-range goals. Furthermore, the same behavior may have high utility for one person but low utility for another, or it may have high utility for the same person in one situation but not another. Thus, deterrence may be more or less possible depending upon the strength of motivations involved; it may also be dependent upon the kind of motivations that are operative. It is reasonable to imagine that acts of rebellion, behavior in search of martyrdom, behavior undertaken to reinforce a deviant identity, or deviance in protest of injustice would be less deterrable than deviance undertaken for other purposes. The value of an act to the actors has always been of key importance in deterrence theory. Yet few studies have attempted to take this into account. Most assume that motivation is equal across behaviors and individuals. But without some control of this variable, knowledge of the effects of sanctions will always be incomplete.

The type of behavior may be important in other ways as well. Sanctions may have more influence upon behavior that is subject to reasoned calculation than on emotional or impulsive behavior.[64] Finally, a distinction might have to be made concerning the position of an act in a series of potential deviant acts. Sinha's 1967 experiment and much of the recidivism research suggests that once a sanction

---

[63] See William J. Chambliss, "Types of Deviance and the Effectiveness of Legal Sanctions," *Wisconsin Law Review*, Summer 1967, pp. 703-19; and H. Taylor Buckner, *Deviance, Reality, and Change* (New York: Random House, 1971).

[64] See Chambliss, "Types of Deviance."

threat fails to deter an act, its potency as a deterrent to further deviant acts by that person may be eroded.

Third, evidence is especially lacking concerning the impact of sanction threats upon various types of people. Social class, age, sex, race, social visibility of occupation, personal alienation from the political and social system, and moral commitments to the norms may all be major determinants of the probability that deterrent effects will be possible in various situations. But there are presently no systematic data to assess this possibility or to establish how much relative difference these various social characteristics might make.

Fourth, aspects of the sanctions themselves, no doubt, have a great deal to do with deterrence. Several studies have indicated that the certainty of experiencing a threatened sanction is a key variable, although the importance of severity has been shown to be more problematic. Other dimensions of probable importance include whether the sanction is to be imposed on a formal or an informal level, the status of the sanctioner, the celerity with which the sanction is applied, and the universality of imposition.[65] But again one must rely on theoretical, rather than empirical, guidelines in considering these dimensions. One is especially handicapped in trying to answer questions about the interrelationship of these dimensions in their impact upon conformity. It has been suggested that some sanction characteristics are contingent upon others. Formal sanctions may be generally effective only when reinforced by informal sanctions or when the certainty of punishment is high.[66] Similarly, severity of sanction may come into play only after certain levels of certainty have been achieved.[67]

But beliefs or perceptions about sanctions may be more important than actual sanction characteristics. Ignorance probably constitutes the major component of deterrence. Anxiety probably influences behavior more than raw fear, at least as far as legal norms are concerned. After all, the chance of experiencing a sanction for most crimes is miniscule,[68] and the severity of punishment frequently turns out to be relatively light.[69]

If individual fear of sanction has a bearing on behavior, surely cognitions are key linkages; since cognitions probably vary somewhat independently of reality, then the most useful knowledge is not actual sanction characteristics, but what those characteristics are perceived to be by different categories of people. For instance, the propensity of middle-class people to refrain from ordinary crime may be at

---

[65] Alexander L. Clark and Jack P. Gibbs, "Social Control: A Reformulation," *Social Problems,* vol. 12 (Spring 1965), pp. 398-415.

[66] Jackson Toby, "Is Punishment Necessary?" *Journal of Criminal Law, Criminology, and Police Science,* vol. 55 (September 1964), pp. 332-37, and Ernst W. Puttkammer, *Administration of Criminal Law* (Chicago: University of Chicago Press, 1953).

[67] Tittle, "Crime Rates."

[68] Logan, "Legal Sanctions," pp. 80-81.

[69] See the National Prisoner Statistics, "Prisoners Released from State and Federal Institutions" (Washington, D. C.: Bureau of Prisons, U.S. Justice Department, 1960).

least partly a result of their gross overestimate of the probability that they would be caught, and of their perception of punishment as more severe than it might actually turn out to be. Middle-class people usually have little personal experience with law enforcement processes, and they therefore are in no position to judge accurately. Lower class individuals, however, often have frequent contact with the legal system and consequently know that the probability of being caught and punished is really not great and that being legally sanctioned is not unbearable. But even if objective knowledge about sanctions were available to all, people would still perceive the personal costs differently.

It is important to note that the relationship between perceptions of sanction characteristics and deviance might not be simple or linear. It is possible that some people may be stimulated to engage in deviance by a certain amount of risk,[70] but that this incentive diminishes when the risk becomes so great that it is no longer a gamble. The relationship for such people would be curvilinear, while for others it might be linear or log linear. Unfortunately there are very few data about these matters, so we are left to speculation.

Not only may sanctions influence the amount and kind of deviance, but the relationship is probably reciprocal, at least for legal sanctions. Once we can identify and describe the causal influence of sanctions under various conditions, we will then have to attack the problem of separating the effects of sanctions on deviance from the effects of deviance upon sanction reactions.

Fifth, it is a total mystery how the various factors that have been discussed are interrelated in the generation of conformity. Surely these variables do not operate in a vacuum; they occur in combinations, and the effect of each is probably influenced by the presence of the others. Some evidence already suggests that dimensions of sanctions interact in crucial ways. But when it is recognized that characteristics of norms, of the subject population, and of the behavior may all mesh in endless varieties, it becomes clear that theoretical questions about deterrence have not even been addressed, much less resolved.

Finally, other variables may affect conformity independently or they may combine with sanction variables in influencing behavior. Social scientists have at one time or another attributed significance to biological propensities, internalization of moral standards, beliefs about the amount of deviance that is occurring, imputed legitimacy of the general normative system, peer acceptance or rejection, relative deprivation, self-concepts, and symbolically learned motivations.[71] But we don't know how important each of these is, how important they are relative to sanctions, or how they might influence sanction-related variables. Understanding of conformity/deviance will not be complete until statements can be made about how

---

[70] Carl Werthman, "Delinquency and Moral Character," in *Delinquency, Crime, and Social Process,* ed. Donald R. Cressey and David A. Ward (New York: Harper and Row, 1969), pp. 613-32.

[71] See Albert K. Cohen, *Deviance and Control* (Englewood Cliffs, N. J.: Prentice-Hall, 1966).

each of the factors discussed here is generally and specifically operative in the production of conformity.

V. Conclusion

Despite the confidence expressed by some, it is clear that very little is known about the role of sanctions in generating social order. Enough research evidence has accumulated to justify serious consideration of the question. But this paper has outlined so many gaps in knowledge that need to be filled that closing them would require decades of full-time work by hundreds of social scientists. It is time that we begin in earnest to supply that information, remembering that the task is not an easy one. The job requires many kinds of data gathered in a wide variety of circumstances, with numerous research methods. Productive outcomes will depend upon clearer definitions and conceptual formulations than have been found in the past. In an area so prone to ideological contamination, moreover, we must exercise great effort to generate and preserve a spirit of objective inquiry. Nevertheless, if social order is to be understood and if fundamental assumptions on which so many social institutions rest are to be evaluated, we must turn our attention to this long-neglected problem.

COMMENTS ON THE
PAPERS IN SEMINAR

Gregory Krohm

I would like first to say that the papers of Professors Phillips and Tittle represent what I think is a significant and very desirable change in research on deterrence. The real issue under study is not whether punishment *can* deter. We can easily imagine sufficiently harsh sanctions, given with a consistently high degree of probability, which would deter most rational decision makers from crime. Instead, the object of research should be to identify those behavior patterns which can be most easily controlled and to point out the most effective means of controlling them.

In the past, the efficacy of punishment in deterring crime, as broadly conceived, was made to stand or fall on the slenderest threads of evidence, mostly dealing with murder and recidivism. Both papers presented here have broken down this oversimplified notion of deterrence into more tractable and meaningful statements about the subject of control.

In examining the question of the effectiveness of punishment on murder rates, Phillips separates what he calls deterrent factors from causal, or etiological, factors. Ultimately, crime is "caused" by a set of circumstances which make deviance more desirable than socially approved forms of behavior. The threat of punishment is used, or can be used, to alter this set of conditions so that, in the individual's own decision calculus, the expected costs of deviance outweigh the expected benefits. What Phillips calls deterrent factors are simply those causes or conditions contributing to crime which can be most easily modified by imposing sanctions. Although this approach is quite sensible, I feel that certain logical and technical errors were made which invalidated the findings.

Early in his paper Phillips correctly emphasizes the simultaneous interaction between conviction rates and criminal activity. But he later goes on to dismiss this influence in his model by claiming that conviction rates for murder are merely a function of the number of homicides. Since the deterrent variable—homicides committed with a gun—is such a small fraction of the total number of homicides, the simultaneous nature of the relation was supposedly reduced to insignificance. What I think he failed to recognize is that conviction rates are not only a function of homicides but of all felonious crimes. Punishment may have the effect of decreasing homicide with a gun, while at the same time increasing the rate of aggravated assault or even the rate of murders committed with knives and other weapons. The incidence of these other crimes should affect the conviction rate for murder (equation 8) and thus enter into the decision to commit murder with a gun (equation 7). The simultaneous action-reaction relationship is still present in the model.

The second error is a logical one in the construction of the "probability model" used to separate deterrent from causal factors. He says that the probability of murder with a gun in a nonfelonious crime (hereafter called a "family crime") is the probability of assault, times the probability that the assault will involve a gun, times the probability that the assault with a gun will result in death.

Although Phillips was somewhat careless in defining the usage of his terms, it seems that he made the mistake of using total assaults in the above probability statement. What he should have done is include only assaults arising under non-felonious circumstances.

The final problem I can see in his empirical work involves biases in the data he used. It is widely acknowledged that many, if not most, serious crimes go unreported to the police. The best current data indicate that about one-half of all aggravated assaults go unreported. Now the proportion of guns used in unreported crimes is not likely to be so high as in the reported crimes, but this difference is not so important as the underestimation of family crimes in relation to felonious crimes. Studies indicate that most of the aggravated assaults that went unreported were *between family members or acquaintances*. Thus the independent variables in Phillips's regressions contain some serious biases which attentuate confidence in his estimated coefficients.

When Phillips favorably compares his estimate of the probability of death resulting from a gun assault to the "independent" estimate of Newton and Zimring, he is merely comparing estimates based on inaccurate national data with inaccurate data for Chicago.

My final comment on the Phillips paper regards his conceptual model of crime control. In presenting the model, Phillips emphasizes the functional relationship between physical resources spent on courts and police on the one hand, and the conviction rate on the other. It seems to me, however, that this emphasis is misplaced. The principal factors affecting convictions are not physical inputs but legal institutions and procedures. I believe that pumping more money into the judicial system, given present legal procedures, is likely to have only a mild effect on the conviction rate. The inevitable cost of changing legal institutions to increase the conviction rate is a weakening of safeguards against mistakenly convicting the innocent. The more stringent these safeguards, the higher the percentage of guilty defendants who go free. This type of trade-off is quite analogous to the chance of making "Type I" or "Type II" errors in statistical hypothesis testing. The principal determinant of conviction rates is not dollars spent on courts but legal procedures which set up the "confidence interval" around the correctness of judicial decisions.

Professor Tittle's paper, besides containing an excellent survey of the literature on deterrence, brings to light a new body of literature which is generally ignored in the study of the effectiveness of deterrence. Psychologists have long studied the impact of negative stimuli on modifying behavior, but the results of these investigations both with human beings and with animals were not transferred to the issue of punishment and criminal behavior.

Perhaps it was felt that experiments done with laboratory animals were not helpful in predicting the human response to negative stimuli. Many of these psychological tests, however, used human subjects in a variety of test situations. One may suppose that many people felt that although human beings could be deterred by appropriately designed sanctions, the present penal institutions did not provide the correct type of sanctions. As evidence of this, critics cited the high recidivism rate.

After providing a list of cogent arguments disqualifying the aforementioned recidivism studies as evidence against the deterrence hypothesis, Tittle attempted to show how much of the research done on recidivism *overstated* the true rate at which released prisoners return to jail. Attempting to debunk an FBI study, he showed that of the 65 percent of released prisoners that were arrested during a follow-up period, only 35 percent actually returned to prison. The relevant question, though, is not whether they return to prison, but whether they return to crime. I, for one, am not prepared to assume, as Tittle apparently did, that the 35 percent actually convicted were the only ones who returned to crime. One has to consider the ex-convicts who returned to crime but were never arrested, and those criminals who were arrested but never convicted.

Why be surprised if a high proportion of incarcerated criminals return to crime once again upon release? While in prison, a convict cannot help amassing a great deal of new knowledge about criminal activities. One need talk to prison inmates for only a short while before their wide knowledge of the law and police procedures becomes evident. This period of human capital formation ordinarily makes the convict even more adept at earning easy money in property crimes. If crime was a good occupational choice before prison, in light of these increased skills, it should be even more attractive after prison.

In conclusion I would like to comment on the list of variables Tittle recommended for consideration in future research on deterrence. While I think most of his recommendations were quite proper, some of the things he wished to use as explanatory variables may have the effect of making the theory untestable. Permitting vague or unquantifiable factors as explanatory variables has a debilitating effect on empirical work.

As an illustration of what I am referring to, Tittle berates previous researchers for assuming that all individuals have equal motivation. Unless some quantifiable variable can be found to explain this difference between individuals, then it must be assumed to be equal. Otherwise "differences between individuals" may be used as a crutch to explain all those cases when the test results differ from the results expected by the researcher.

Benjamin Klein

This conference represents part of a renewed effort to apply economic analysis to criminology. I say renewed rather than new, since more than a hundred years ago Bentham explicitly employed an economic framework in analyzing criminal behavior.[1] Professor Tittle's paper, I am sorry to say, however, is inconsistent with the spirit, or at least the title, of this conference. His survey of some of the existing evidence on the deterrent effects of punishment is certainly not undertaken within an economic framework. The terminology he employs is not only not part of the average economist's vocabulary but it is also clearly tendentious. I find particularly disturbing the continued use of the term "deviance," since it suggests thinking of criminal activity in psychological rather than economic (that is, choice-theoretic) terms. Although it may be difficult for academics to imagine themselves ever "voluntarily" deciding to commit the criminal acts being investigated, we must resist the easy temptation to describe the behavior as pathological.[2]

To an economist the question of whether punishment deters seems curious. We are taught from a very young age to draw demand curves sloping downward and supply curves sloping upward. And the presumption is if empirical work does not pick up these price effects, there are most likely some deficiencies in the work. Tittle's paper is clearly not written with this a priori economic bias while, on the other hand, Phillips's paper is obviously that of an economist. (Phillips makes a statement at the end of his first paragraph that those studies which have found a zero or positive correlation between punishment and crime have merely demonstrated that there is more to the explanation of crime than the certainty and severity of punishment.) Although I would not maintain that the partial effect of punishment on crime must *necessarily* be negative, I am extremely hesitant to accept the existence of negatively sloped supply of criminal activity schedules, especially since punishment generally takes the form of imprisonment and thereby reduces the

---

[1] Jeremy Bentham, *The Theory of Legislation* (New York: Harcourt, Brace and Co., 1931).

[2] There is an interesting theoretical question of what, from an economic point of view, a criminal act consists. The assertion that criminal acts refer to "involuntary" transactions is much too naive, since most transactions are fulfilled under the threat of some sanction. Analytically, what is the difference between an individual being "forced" by a theater owner with the help of the police to pay for the right to attend a movie and an individual being "forced" by muggers to pay for the right to walk across the park at night? One may seem to be able to draw a distinction on the basis of the violation of "property rights," but economically the concept of property rights must be meaningfully defined not in terms of written governmental regulations but in terms of the predictability of actual behavior. For example, if it is generally recognized that one will almost certainly be mugged if he crosses Central Park at night, a group of muggers in New York may reasonably be assumed to "own" Central Park after dark. One major difference between "criminal" and "noncriminal" transactions may be the greater variability in the anticipated price that criminals charge. This uncertainty associated with the erratic behavior of criminals is a major cost of crime. All of this is, of course, foreign to the standard economic model where property rights are assumed to be defined and enforced without cost.

number of individuals likely to commit crimes who are present in the population over which the crime rate is defined. Fortunately, much of the evidence inconsistent with the standard economic hypothesis can, I think, be explained.

Tittle cites two major negative pieces of evidence on the deterrent effects of punishment. The first is the supposed ineffectiveness of capital punishment as a deterrent of homicide. Much of this evidence, however, is based solely on a comparison between political units which differ in the presence or absence of the death penalty; it fails to consider the actual probability that the penalty will be imposed or that the other determinants of the homicide rate vary across political units.

Since judicial and police costs can generally be decreased by decreasing the apprehension and conviction rate while increasing the severity of punishment by the same proportion, social optimality implies that in equilibrium criminals should generally be risk preferrers.[3] Hence, on the margin, we should generally expect an increase in the severity of punishment to have less of a deterrent effect than an increase in the certainty of punishment. Becker also proves that the supply of criminal offenses will probably be inelastic with respect to changes in the severity or certainty of punishment. It is important to recognize, however, that this refers to the marginal elasticity at the point of social equilibrium. If, for example, the severity of punishment elasticity were greater than one, society should (and would?) increase the severity of punishment until the elasticity were less than one. It makes no sense to talk about *the* effect of punishment on crime. We are likely to be observing elasticity responses only in the region of social optimality.

There may, in addition, very likely be some minimum threshold or demonstration effect. A severe punishment that is hardly ever used may therefore have little effect. (An interesting analogous argument seems to hold for the optimum design of a lottery. Although lottery tickets are purchased by individuals who are risk preferrers it does not seem to be efficient to have only one very large prize awarded. An increase in the number of prizes, even though they may be of only small or moderate size, may produce a demonstration effect.)

The most nearly complete attempt I know of to standardize for the many other influences on the rate of criminal activity and to isolate a pure deterrent effect of punishment is made by Isaac Ehrlich. Using data across states for 1940, 1950, and 1960 he estimates supply of offense functions for seven felonies (including murder, in addition to rape, aggravated assault, robbery, burglary, larceny, and auto theft) and finds, after correcting for the possible influence of many economic and demographic variables (such as income, income inequality, unemployment rate, education, region, percentages of population nonwhite, urban, young and male) significant and stable negative effects of variations in the probability and severity

---

[3] Gary S. Becker, "Crime and Punishment: An Economic Approach," *Journal of Political Economy,* vol. 76, no. 2 (March-April 1968), pp. 169-217.

of punishment. This highly competent piece of work provides unambiguous evidence in support of the deterrence hypothesis.[4]

The second piece of evidence Tittle cites is the high rate of recidivism for prison releasees. I have great difficulty, however, in understanding the relevance of this. If an individual maximizing his expected utility made a "correct" calculation when deciding to engage in criminal activity and his parameter estimates do not change, we should expect him to make the same choice again when released. If his experience supplied him with information which forces him to increase substantially his estimates of the probability of detection and conviction or of the costs of punishment, we may then expect a low recidivism rate. But there is no reason to believe that individuals generally underestimate the "true" expected costs of crime before they are punished and that such a learning process occurs. In fact, it is often said that it is the fear of prison rather than the actual experience of it which is the primary deterrent. The recidivism rate supplies no evidence on the effectiveness of punishment in deterring crime but solely on whether punishment "rehabilitates" and, as a policy matter, we should be concerned with the recidivism rate only if it affects the crime rate. But, in fact, we should probably expect that an increase in punishment that decreases the crime rate would at the same time increase the recidivism rate, since the decrease in the expected return from crime would leave a noncompeting group of individuals with the greatest comparative advantage and taste for crime as a larger fraction of the remaining industry.[5]

Some of the other evidence cited by Tittle deals with laboratory and questionnaire experiments. Economists are generally hesitant about employing these tools and I also must confess to a severe prejudice against them. I believe it is much more revealing to analyze actual criminal behavior than to ask criminals what they were motivated by or to design interesting games for undergraduate students to play.

The most encouraging aspect of Tittle's framework is his important recognition of the fact that sanctions which motivate human behavior need not be provided solely by governmental bodies, nor need they even be explicit. Most economists can learn something here. We have been extremely slow to recognize, for example, the importance of trust as a regulator of economic transactions. And peer group approval for failing to observe even seemingly minor social and economic "rules of the game" appears to have a strong influence on behavior. In fact, for many business

[4] Isaac Ehrlich, "Participation in Illegitimate Activities: An Economic Analysis" (Ph.D. diss.: Columbia University, 1970).

[5] Under present conditions of punishment the recidivism rate is influenced by the fact that while in prison criminals develop specialized human capital for use in illegal activities and that when released, their criminal record decreases their legal wage rate. On this latter point, there is some advantage therefore in having criminals bear the total cost of punishment before release, so that relative wages in legal and illegal activities are not altered, but then valuable information is destroyed.

We could arbitrarily reduce the recidivism rate by, for example, guaranteeing all prison releasees $50,000 a year for life unless convicted of a crime again. But this would, of course, doubtless increase the crime rate.

crimes, governmental sanctions are so uncertain and so inefficiently administered (e.g., with a very long lag) that individuals generally rely on these private sanctions, most important of which is the depreciation of the individual's reputation.[6]

Although much of the deterrence of crime is rightly supplied privately, individual decisions often have social consequences which may require public interference. An interesting example is when an individual decides to install a burglar alarm system in his house and then prominently advertises this fact by displaying a sign. It is this sign which produces the great deterrent effect of the alarm system, but the sign also increases the robbery rate on the homes without alarms, that is, it produces a negative externality on the individual's neighbors. Clearly, the same expenditure on alarms could be much more effective in reducing the total crime rate if criminals were not supplied the information on the location of the alarms. (But under those circumstances the *incidence* of crime would not be such as to minimize total expected disutility.)

Governmental policy seems most confusing with respect to the most basic type of deterrence: physical resistance. One who lives in New York City is constantly reminded about how far we have strayed as a society from the old American moral and cultural attitude of vigorously defending one's property rights, especially one's person. The confusing thing here is the public encouragement of the new docile behavior. Unless criminals can discriminate, and, without cost, isolate those individuals who are likely to resist, any individual who does resist raises the cost of criminal activity and provides a net positive externality for the rest of society. (But, of course, some individuals would become less well off. The random distribution of knowledge of self-defense across the entire population, for example, would cause brawny young men to lose, relative to women and the old who are now the primary targets of attacks.) But instead of attempting to equate the private and social net benefits of such actions by rewarding individuals who resist, the government has adopted the opposite policy of urging individuals not to resist. The justification, I suspect, rests on the likelihood that although increased private resistance would decrease the number of crimes, it would increase the violence of criminals (a negative externality) and that, on net, it is a generally inefficient form of deterrence.[7]

---

[6] See Stewart Macaulay, "Non-Contractual Relations in Business: A Preliminary Study," *American Sociological Review*, vol. 28 (February 1963), pp. 55-69. The existence of more information on individuals who are members of one's own "group" and the greater possibility of applying social sanctions on such individuals may explain much discrimination in business hiring.

[7] Another explanation for the government's policy is that individuals will generally "irrationally" overreact to protect their interests. But such a commonly held presumption is what deters. The most obvious example is the accepted belief that we would "irrationally" respond to any first strike nuclear attack which destroyed us with a similar attack. It is such a belief that deters the initial attack. A crucial aspect of defense is the setting up of mechanisms which will produce responses that may narrowly seem to be "irrational."

Let us now turn to Phillips's paper. Phillips has the proper intention of attempting to document empirically deterrence effects. The conclusions he reaches, however, although they may very well be true, cannot be derived from his analysis.

Phillips notes at the outset that an empirical analysis of the deterrent effects of punishment must resolve two difficulties: the simultaneous relationship between criminal activity and expected punishment and the necessity to control for causal factors other than the degree of punishment. Phillips first constructs a model, very similar to Becker's more sophisticated model, to demonstrate the first difficulty of simultaneity. But he assumes this problem away in his empirical analysis.

His crude attempt to solve the second problem of standardizing for other causal factors is, unfortunately, based on doubtful assumptions and faulty econometric reasoning. By the use of what Phillips calls a "probability model," but which is essentially just unnecessarily complicated arithmetic, he defines the following tautology:

$$P(M,G) = P(M,G,F) + P(A)P(G/A)P(M/G,A), \tag{1}$$

which relates the rate of murders committed with firearms, $P(M,G)$, to the rate of felonious murders committed with firearms, $P(M,G,F)$ and the rate of murders arising from assaults where no other felony is involved. This latter factor (which he somewhat misleadingly refers to as the rate of murders with firearms committed by "average citizens" or "family and friends") can be broken down into the rate of assaults, $P(A)$, the fraction of assaults involving firearms, $P(G/A)$, and the fraction of assaults involving firearms which result in murder, $P(M/G,A)$. Although data seem to be available only on $P(M,G)$, $P(A)$, and $P(G/A)$, Phillips attempts to show that the nearly 150 percent increase in $P(M,G)$ over the 1961-70 period cannot be attributed at all to $P(M,G,F)$. He asserts that this is demonstrated by comparing two regressions, which are equivalent to his equations (29) and (30):

$$P(M,G) = a_0 + a_1 P(G,A), \tag{2}$$

and

$$P(M,G) = a_0^* + a_1^* P(G,A) + a_2^* t, \tag{3}$$

where $P(G,A)$ is the rate of assaults involving firearms which equals $P(A)P(G/A)$ and t is a time trend. Because t in equation (3) is insignificant, Phillips claims that $P(M,G,F)$ can be assumed to be approximately constant (and equal to a_0) and the increase in $P(M,G)$ can be attributed solely to nonfelonious assaults with firearms, $P(G,A)$. This conclusion is incorrect. First of all, Phillips assumes that $P(M/G,A)$ is constant (and equal to a_1). He states that this is a reasonable assumption and that his estimate of $P(M/G,A)$, (.0927), "compares favorably" with an estimate from an independent study (.122). But, although $P(M/G,A)$ may be assumed constant over this period, it is likely to be a function of any policy alterations which seem to be implied by this study (for example, it is negatively related to an increase in the penalty for gun use in assaults). In addition, his

110

estimate of $P(M/G,A)$ is nearly 10 standard deviations less than the independent estimate he cites. If he has confidence in this independent estimate, why not simply use it in addition to his other data to obtain an estimate of $P(M,G,F)$ without going through all this trouble?

Secondly, Phillips is implicitly assuming that $P(M,G,F)$ and $P(G,A)$ are not closely related. Otherwise from the insignificance of t one cannot infer that $P(M,G,F)$ was constant over time. If $P(G/A)$ and $P(M,G,F)$ are highly correlated [8] (and, for example, both are determined by some additional variable such as the availability of guns), then $P(M,G,F)$ could trend moderately, but adding t would yield nothing not already in $P(G/A)$. The insignificance of t would then merely prove that t is no better a proxy for $P(M,G,F)$ than $P(G/A)$.

Phillips defines a similar relationship for the rate of murders with weapons other than guns (called knives), $P(M,K)$; he breaks it down into the rate of felonious knife murders, $P(M,K,F)$, the assault rate, $P(A)$, the fraction of assaults involving knives, $P(K/A)$, and the fraction of assaults involving knives which result in murder, $P(M/K,A)$:

$$P(M,K) = P(M,K,F) + P(A)P(K/A)P(M/K,A). \tag{4}$$

He then runs similar regressions to "prove" that the increase in $P(M,K)$ can also be attributed solely to $P(A)$ and $P(K/A)$.

In the last section of the paper Phillips finally estimates a behavioral (rather than a tautological) relationship which seeks to determine the effectiveness of punishment as a deterrent. Using data across states, he attempts to explain $P(G/A)$ or, equivalently, $P(K/A)$,[9] by the certainty and severity of imprisonment for criminal homicide and by the rate of fatal firearm accidents (as an index of gun ownership within a state). To sum up, he uses $P(G/A)$, rather than the total murder rate (the sum of equations [1] and [4]), as the relevant dependent variable because (a) he assumes $P(M/G,A)$ and $P(M/K,A)$ are both constant, although any change in punishment for gun use would result in some substitution between weapons; (b) he mistakenly thinks he has "demonstrated" that $P(M,G,F)$ and $P(M,K,F)$ are constant; and (c) he makes the additional assumption, based on his view that fights seem to "erupt" spontaneously, that $P(A)$ is independent of deterrence factors. This last assumption, however, is inconsistent with Ehrlich's results which show a highly significant, if partial, effect of certainty and severity of punishment on the rate of assault. In addition, the relatively low $\overline{R}^2$ (Ehrlich gen-

---

[8] Since the reported data on $P(M,G,A)$ may actually include a fraction of $P(G,F)$, that is, the fraction of attempted felonies that were entirely unsuccessful, we should certainly expect a positive correlation between $P(M,G,F)$ and $P(M,G,A)$. Entering a variable such as the rate of robberies may then help to explain $P(M,G)$.

[9] Although $P(G/A)$ has the statistical defect of only varying from zero to one, the particular functional form specification chosen, $\ln[1 - P(G/A)] - \ln P(G/A)$ or $\ln P(K/A) - \ln P(G/A)$, remains a mystery to me.

erally gets $\overline{R}^2$s of about .8) indicates that the rate of fatal firearm accidents certainly does not standardize for all the other causal factors on the murder rate.[10]

Finally, both papers reach the controversial conclusion that more research is called for. (Tittle even suggests that full-time work by hundreds of social scientists for decades is necessary.) Now of course we could get almost everyone working in a field to agree that more research (and especially more research money) is required. But this is all too easy to say. Although I think I also fit fairly closely into the ivory tower academic stereotype, I believe in this particular field especially we owe the public at least some tentative conclusions and some cautious policy discussion.[11]

Jack P. Gibbs

Research on the deterrence question is haunted by so many problems that social scientists should receive medals for working on the subject. Hence, I cannot bring myself to be truly critical of the work of Professors Tittle or Phillips. My bias, however, does not reflect a law and order ideology, or even a conviction that punishment does deter. Rather, I simply admire the audacity of those who do research on the deterrence question. They must be audacious, because the problems involved in such research defy exaggeration. Accordingly, my comments on the two papers will focus on those problems.

The Deterrence Notion

Professors Tittle and Phillips do not speak seriously of a theory of deterrence, and rightly so, for the deterrence idea is a vague notion, not a systematic theory. I am sure that both men are aware of the point, but they do *not* emphasize its significance. I consider the vagueness of the deterrence idea to be the paramount consideration, for most of the problems in research design cannot be solved satisfactorily without reference to a systematic theory.

The deterrence idea is both vague and ancient. Specifically, conventional versions of the deterrence idea scarcely make use of the concepts or principles of

---

[10] Although these results are therefore meaningless, I would also like to correct one interpretation Phillips places on them. A coefficient less than one does not imply that punishment deters at a decreasing rate, but merely that on the margin the effect on the criminal activity with respect to changes in punishment is inelastic, that is, a one percent increase in punishment will decrease the crime less than one percent. As one continues to increase punishment there is no presumption that the elasticity declines. In fact his whole estimation procedure (1n-1n functional form) assumes a constant elasticity response.

[11] When such discussion occurs we should explicitly recognize that society not only chooses the quantity of resources devoted to deterrence, but also the rules of the judicial process. "Justice," for example, the probability that an innocent individual will not be convicted, is an economic good like any other, with resource costs of supply and a finite social demand.

contemporary social science. Consider one consequence of that condition, starting with a question: Does the deterrence idea assume reliable knowledge on the part of the public as to the certainty and severity of legal penalties for each type of crime? It may be that the deterrence idea necessarily entails some such assumption, but that recognition introduces a dilemma. As an illustration of that dilemma, my own findings indicate that the certainty of imprisonment for criminal homicide is about four times greater in Utah than in South Carolina. Consistent with the deterrence idea, the criminal homicide rate is much greater in South Carolina. But is it reasonable to suppose that even a majority of Utah residents know that the certainty of imprisonment for criminal homicide in that state is between 80 and 90 percent? Surely it is not reasonable, but what is the alternative if one is to take the deterrence idea seriously? I submit that it is difficult to state a plausible assumption about the cognitive basis of deterrence, and I am convinced that such an assumption cannot be stated without using the terminology and principles of contemporary social psychology. Certainly the language and psychology of Bentham are not adequate.

A statement of the deterrence idea as a systematic theory should do more than clarify underlying assumptions. It should also speak to objections by critics to that idea. In that connection I sense that Tittle's paper may create a dubious impression. Some of his comments suggest that research evidence has led critics to dismiss the deterrence idea. To the contrary, I believe that most critics object to the deterrence idea either because they find it ideologically distasteful or because they question some of the ostensible, underlying assumptions. The problem is that one can read questionable assumptions into the deterrence idea as one sees fit, and that problem can be solved only by a statement of the idea as a systematic theory.

Problems of Interpretation

Professor Tittle's paper is a real contribution to the literature if only in that it offers a concise and fair assessment of research evidence on the deterrence question. His assessment comes down to one painful point—the evidence is inconclusive. I do not question Tittle's assessment, but I will chide him about a related consideration. Tittle may have created the impression that conclusive evidence is possible, but there are so many problems in the interpretation of research findings that the very idea of conclusive evidence is incredible.

As the first step in a brief consideration of the interpretation problems, contemplate a hypothetical research finding. Suppose that someone finds the correlation between the robbery rate and the certainty of imprisonment for that crime to be $-.25$ among states. Suppose further that the same kind of correlation is $-.20$ in the case of length of prison sentence for robbery. Now, critics of the deterrence idea would point out that such coefficients are hardly compelling evidence. The reply would be, of course, that it is unrealistic to expect greater coefficients, since etiological conditions other than legal reactions have not been controlled. That reply is realistic because, as stressed by Phillips and Tittle, the deterrence idea does not assume that legal reactions alone determine the crime rate. But the argument virtually precludes evidence against the deterrence idea. Thus, even if the correlation between the robbery rate and certainty of imprisonment is .00, it could still be true that imprisonment deters some individuals. In other words, deterrence is not reflected in the correlation because the states differ sharply as to unidentified extra-legal conditions that are conducive to robbery. Certainly that possibility is plausible, but note again that the argument creates a major problem. Unless etiological conditions are controlled in conducting research on the deterrence question, any interpretation of the findings will be most debatable.

Therein lies the significance of Phillips's research. I view his research as an imaginative attempt to control for etiological conditions. By considering homicides as a class of assaults and by focusing on the homicidal use of firearms, Phillips presumably has controlled for extra-legal conditions that are conducive to homicide, even though those conditions are unknown.

My critical comments will be limited to three brief points. First, ingenious though it is, I do not see how Phillips's procedure can be applied to all types of crime. Second, more seriously, I have doubts about a purely statistical control of etiological conditions without a theory that purports to identify those conditions. We need a theory not only to identify the relevant conditions but also to suggest the appropriate kind of control. Contemplate one illustrative possibility in the case of homicide. Suppose that political units differ as to their cultural approval of violence, and suppose further that cultural approval is the only etiological factor in homicide apart from legal reactions. If that cultural approval or emphasis on violence is diffuse, then it will be reflected in nonfatal assaults as well as homicides, and Phillips's control procedure would be defensible. But it could be that some social units differ not only as to the cultural approval of violence but also as to the means of expressing aggression, including the use of firearms. The custom of dueling with pistols is a case in point, and I doubt if such a cultural factor would be controlled by considering homicides as a class of assaults.

Do not construe my observations as a condemnation of Phillips's procedure. I have not had the time to assess the procedure thoroughly, so all I am expressing is an intuitive doubt and one that may not be relevant for the United States today.

My third criticism is less conjectural. Since Phillips ostensibly controlled for etiological conditions, I am surprised that the relation among states between Phillips's special assault rate and the certainty or the severity of imprisonment is not closer. In any case, what are we to make of the fact that among states a great deal of variance in Phillips's special rate remains unexplained?

All of my previous comments on the need for theory amount to a tacit criticism of Tittle's paper and Phillips's paper. Both are aware of the interpretation problems, but they fail to stress the role of theory in contemplating solutions. For example, a truly sophisticated statement of the deterrence idea would recognize the possibility of more than two determinants of the crime rate, that is, more than etiological conditions and deterrence.

The point is not just that some legal reactions to crime may generate more crimes. Tittle recognizes the point, but he does not stress that deterrence is only one mechanism by which legal reactions may prevent criminal acts. I take deterrence to be an instance where an individual refrains from committing an act out of fear of detection and punishment. As such, deterrence cannot be observed or measured directly, and therein lies a major problem. But there is still another problem. Some kinds of legal reactions may prevent criminal acts independently of specific or general deterrence. Contemplate one possibility: Assume that in each state there is a hard core of professional criminals who are responsible for virtually all bank robberies in the state. As each of them is arrested, convicted, and incarcerated for long periods, they are deprived of an opportunity to rob banks, and the bank robbery rate would fall if the number of such criminals remains more or less constant. So an inverse relation among states between the certainty or severity and a crime rate could reflect not deterrence but, rather, a deprivation of opportunities for criminal activities (incapacitation).

Now consider just one other possible preventive consequence of legal reactions apart from deterrence. Numerous social scientists seem to argue that internalization of norms promotes conformity independently of legal or official punishment of deviation. The argument may or may not be correct, but it ignores a very important possibility. The consistent and severe punishment of individuals who violate a norm may serve to validate that norm in the eyes of the public. So while a citizen may conform to a norm not out of fear of punishment but of respect for the norm, it could be that the norm is respected at least in part because those who violate it are punished. My hunch is that severe punishment validates a norm more than does certain punishment. In any case, the possibility of a "validation effect" is just one more problem in interpreting what purports to be evidence in favor of the deterrence argument.

The Problems of Policy

I am surprised that Professor Tittle did not devote more attention to policy issues. Ordinarily, we think of theory and research as having an impact on policy, but in this case the reverse is true. My hunch is that neither governmental nor non-governmental policy encourages work on the deterrence question. Judges, policemen, and even lawyers have expressed puzzlement over my research on the deterrence question; they apparently view it as a needless demonstration of the painfully obvious. But some of my social science colleagues seem to view my research as an attempt to resurrect a discredited and reactionary idea. So we have two camps on the deterrence issue, and neither one appears to press for research on the subject.

Given that situation, I fear that Tittle is whistling in the dark when he calls for more research.

To be sure, support of research would be important, as criminal law is based in large part on the questionable assumption of deterrence. Nonetheless, support of research is debatable. Given all of the problems that haunt such research, anything approaching conclusive evidence is a remote possibility at best, and even conclusive evidence against the deterrence idea would not settle the policy issue. Criminologists commonly assert that vengeance is the only rationale for conventional penal practices, and they constantly allege that criminal law is alien to the principles of rehabilitation. Such critics of the penal system persistently ignore one consideration—the real or imagined functions of legal reactions to crime are not limited to vengeance or rehabilitation. Consider again the deprivation of opportunities for criminal acts, validation of norms, and the possibility of general deterrence. Note especially that even if legal penalties do not deter, they may have other preventive consequences. So, while deterrence may be the central question in contemplating penal policy, it is by no means the only consideration.

If social scientists are to undertake research on the deterrence question with a view to policy, they must abandon conventional strategies. For one thing, the deterrence question has not been stated properly. The question should not be: "Do legal penalties deter?" Rather, as suggested by Tittle, it should be: "Under what conditions will a given type of legal penalty deter a given type of crime and to what extent?" The question is more realistic, and it is more consistent with policy concerns. After all, policy makers are not likely to recommend just any kind of penalty for the sake of deterrence. Moreover, if a condition of maximum deterrence can be identified, then we arrive at the three ultimate policy questions. First, is it possible to create such a condition? Second, how much would it cost? And, third, would it be worth it?

Observations by Tittle and Phillips are especially important in connection with my version of the deterrence question. Recall that Tittle emphasized the need to consider the relative deterrent efficacy of different legal penalties, a subject that is grossly neglected in conventional research. Tittle also has indicated that the conditions of deterrence include far more than what we loosely call etiological factors. It also includes the type of law in question, the intrinsic properties of conformity to or deviation from that law, and the social or personal characteristics of individuals who are threatened with punishment.

Finally, recall that my version of the deterrence question focuses on the extent of deterrence, and in that connection Phillips's paper has a policy implication. He postulates a diminishing return in increasing the certainty or severity of punishment. The idea is important because it may be that research can show the limits of punishment in reducing the volume of crime. Attempts to estimate those limits might have much more impact on policy than does conventional evidence for or against the deterrence idea.

PART THREE:
ORGANIZED CRIME

A DEFENSE OF
ORGANIZED CRIME?*

James M. Buchanan

... we should try to make the self-interest of cads a little more coincident
with that of decent people.

Samuel Butler

I. Organized Crime as Monopoly Enterprise

Monopoly in the sale of ordinary goods and services is socially inefficient because
it restricts output or supply. The monopolist uses restriction as the means to increase
market price which, in turn, provides a possible source of monopoly profit. This
elementary argument provides the foundation for collective or governmental efforts
to enforce competition. Somewhat surprisingly, the elementary argument has rarely
been turned on its head. If monopoly in the supply of "goods" is socially undesirable, monopoly in the supply of "bads" should be socially desirable, precisely
because of the output restriction.

Consider prostitution. Presumably this is an activity that is a "bad" in some
social sense, as witness the almost universal legal prohibitions. (Whether or not
particular individuals consider this to be an ill-advised social judgment is neither
here nor there.) For many potential buyers, however, the services of prostitutes
are "goods" in the strict, economic sense of this term; these buyers are willing to
pay for these services in ordinary market transactions. From this it follows that
monopoly organization is socially preferable to competitive organization precisely
because of the restriction on total output that it fosters. It is perhaps no institutional accident that we observe organized or syndicated controls of that set of illegal
activities that most closely fits this pattern (prostitution, gambling, smuggling,
drug traffic). In journalistic discussion, the concentration of organized crime's
entrepreneurs in these activities is explained by the relatively high profit potential.
The supplementary hypothesis suggested here is that monopoly is socially desirable
and that this may be recognized implicitly by enforcement agencies who may
encourage, or at least may not overtly and actively discourage, the organization of
such industries.

The monopolization thesis can be extended and developed. Significantly,
elements of the analysis can be applied to those criminal activities that involve

---

* I am indebted to Thomas Borcherding for helpful comments.

Figure 1

RELATIONSHIP OF RESOURCES DEVOTED TO
CRIMINAL ACTIVITY AND LAW ENFORCEMENT

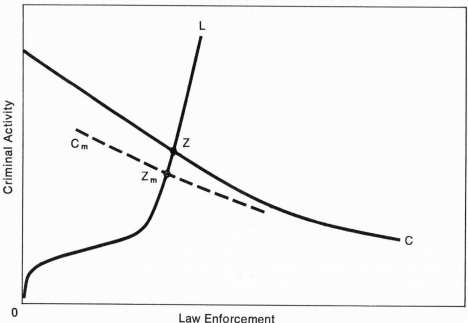

nonvoluntary transfers. In this paper, I shall present first the simple geometry of the relationships between law enforcement and criminal effort. This allows me to discuss, in abstract and general terms, the social advantages that may be secured from effective monopolization of criminal activities. Following this, I shall discuss some of the possible objections to implications of the simple economic argument.

II. The Geometry of Crime and Law Enforcement

The geometry of crime and law enforcement may be presented in a model that is familiar to economists. We may apply a reaction curve construction quite similar to those that have been developed in several applications such as international trade theory, duopoly theory, voting theory, or public-goods theory.[1] Consider Figure 1. On the horizontal axis we measure resources devoted to the enforcement of law. On the vertical axis we measure resources devoted to criminal activities. We want to develop two separate and independent functional relationships between these two variables. If there were no criminals, if no resources were devoted to

---

[1] For an application that perhaps comes closest to this paper, see my "Violence, Law, and Equilibrium in the University," *Public Policy,* vol. 19 (Winter 1971), pp. 1-18. Also see Gordon Tullock, "The Welfare Costs of Tariffs, Monopolies, and Theft," *Western Economic Journal,* vol. 5 (June 1967), pp. 224-232.

criminal activities, society would not find it useful or advantageous to apply resources that might be used to produce goods of value in wasteful law enforcement effort. If no one breaks the law, there is no need for policemen, who could be trained instead as plumbers or carpenters.[2] This establishes the origin as the base point for one of the two functional relationships, the one that we may call the "enforcement response" or reaction curve. As resources are observed to be applied in criminal activity, society—that is, the collectivity of citizens acting through organized political units, governments—will find it advantageous to invest resources in law enforcement. Passive acquiescence to crime is rarely advocated, even among Quakers.[3] Furthermore, there are acknowledged to be major advantages from organizing law enforcement publicly rather than through private and independent action.[4] We should, therefore, expect to find the enforcement response curve sloping upward and to the right from the origin in geometrical representation, as indicated by the curve L in Figure 1. The precise shape of this curve or relationship need not concern us at this point. The general upward slope indicates only that the public will desire to devote more resources to law enforcement as the observed input of resources into criminality increases.

A second relationship, independent of the first, exists between criminal activity and law enforcement effort, with the first now being the dependent and the second the independent variable. To derive the L curve, we made the enforcement response depend upon the observed level of resources in criminality. To develop the separate "criminal response" relationship, drawn as the C curve in Figure 1, we make criminal resource input depend on the level of law enforcement that is observed. It is reasonable to hypothesize that the C curve slopes downward and to the right throughout the range of enforcement effort. If no resources were devoted to enforcement, if there were no policemen, we should predict a relatively large investment in criminal activity. This locates the left-hand intercept high on the vertical axis. As more resources enter enforcement, investment in crime becomes less and less profitable.[5] At some relatively high enforcement levels, it

---

[2] For a generalized account of the "social dilemma" that law enforcement represents, along with numerous applications, see Gordon Tullock, *The Social Dilemma* (forthcoming).

[3] At minimal levels of criminal activity, acquiescence may be the efficient course of action. The formal properties of an efficient or optimal position will take into account both the amounts of criminal activity and the costs of enforcement activity. See Winston Bush, *Income Distribution in Anarchy* (forthcoming) for an attempt to specify these formal properties.

[4] Law enforcement qualifies as a genuine "public good" in that there are major efficiency gains from joint, as opposed to individual, provision. All persons secure benefits from the same policeman on the beat simultaneously. This need not, of course, imply that private supplements to public law enforcement may not also be advantageous. And there is nothing in the argument for public organization of law enforcement that suggests explicit governmental production. A collectivity may well secure efficiency gains from hiring the services of a private policing firm, as opposed to hiring its own municipal policemen.

[5] For those who adopt a pathological interpretation and explanation of crime, the C curve would be horizontal. This would indicate that the number of criminals and the amount of criminal effort are not influenced by enforcement at all.

seems reasonable to think that a minimal level of criminality would be realized and that further enforcement would have little or no effect. This is indicated by the flattened portion of the C curve in its rightward extremities in Figure 1.

Some care must be taken to define just what the C curve represents. For any observed level of law enforcement effort, a level of investment in criminality will be generated. This will be the result or outcome of the private and independent behavior of many persons, potential criminals all, and there is no implication that the response is deliberately controlled by anyone or by any group. Hence, we may qualify or restrict the C curve by the adjective "competitive" if we assume that entry into criminality is open and that the industry is not centrally controlled, not cartelized or monopolized.

Given the two independent relationships as depicted, we can readily demonstrate convergence of the system to a stable equilibrium position at Z, provided that the L curve exhibits a steeper absolute slope value over relevant adjustment ranges than the C curve.[6] Given any starting point, under these conditions the two response or reaction patterns will lead through a succession of adjustments to Z. At such point, no further responses will be forthcoming unless the system is shocked by external forces. At Z, the public demand for inputs into law enforcement is adjusted properly to the level of input into criminality that is being observed, while at the same time, the criminal industry finds itself in equilibrium under the law enforcement effort that it confronts. There is no observed net entry into or net egress of resources from either criminality or law enforcement. Furthermore, as noted, the equilibrium is stable; if an external force shifts the system from Z, a response mechanism will come into play to return the system to a new equilibrium.

III. The Predicted Effects of Criminal Monopoly

We may now move beyond this elementary adjustment model and consider the effects to be predicted from the effective replacement of a fully competitive criminal industry by a monopolized industry. For this purpose, it will be necessary to distinguish two types of activity. The first, referred to initially in the introduction, covers those activities that are deemed "socially bad," but which involve the sale of goods and services that are considered to be economic "goods" by some potential buyers. Prostitution is the example used before, and it may be taken as a typical case. In the absence of legal prohibition, activities of this sort would amount to nothing more than ordinary exchange or trade, with mutual agreement among contracting

---

[6] If the society's law enforcement reaction to changes in the level of criminality should be highly elastic relative to the converse reaction of criminal effort to enforcement, the simple system depicted in Figure 1 would generate an explosive cycle. One implication of this suggests that the enforcement response, that which is under society's collective control, should not be overly sensitive. On this, see my paper, "Violence, Law, and Equilibrium in the University."

parties. Journalistic discussion often labels these as "victimless crimes," although this terminology seems misleading.

The second type of criminal activity involves no such mutual agreement, even in the complete absence of legal prohibition. We may think of burglary as an example of these so-called "crimes with victims." Here the legal structure proscribes involuntary transfers of "goods" among persons rather than the voluntary transfers proscribed under activities of the first type. As the analysis below will indicate, there are three possible sources of an argument for monopolization or cartelization of criminal industries fitting the first category, but only two of these remain applicable to those criminal industries falling within the second category.

Consider a "Type I" industry, exemplified here by prostitution. Initially, we may assume that inputs are available to this industry at an invariant supply price that is determined by the resource returns in alternative employment. Under competitive organization of the industry, there will be a tendency for each productive service to be employed so long as this exogenously fixed input price (or wage) falls below marginal value product, MVP, of this input. The necessary condition for competitive equilibrium in the employment of a particular input, I, is:

$$W_I = MVP_I = MPP_I \cdot P_O. \qquad (1)$$

As noted in equation (1), the marginal value product is made up of two components, the value of the output, represented by the price, P_O, and the actual change in total quantity of output consequent on the change in the supply of inputs, MPP_I. Elementary price theory suggests that when we replace competition by monopoly, the necessary conditions become:

$$W_I = MVP_I = MPP_I \cdot MR_O. \qquad (2)$$

Marginal revenue replaces output price as a component of marginal value product of input. The reason for the change is that, under monopoly, rational decision-making (profit-maximizing behavior) will take into account the fact that price varies with total output placed on the market. Even if the monopolist acts as a pure price-taker in the market for inputs, as he does under our assumptions, he cannot assume the role of price-taker in the output market. In setting output, he also sets price. Hence, he will take into account not only the actual price that an incremental unit of output can command but also the effects that this addition to supply will exert on the potential selling price of all inframarginal units. Total revenues are a multiple of price times quantity, and it is the change in this total that is relevant to the monopolist's decisions.

From this element alone it is clear that a monopolist will find it profitable to reduce total output in the industry to some level below that which would be observed under competition. This straightforward, price-induced output effect may be identified as the first of the three parts of an argument for the effective monopolization or cartelization of a Type I criminal industry,[7] provided, of course, that the legal prohibition of this type of activity is itself a welfare-increasing policy rule.[8]

This effect is not directly applicable to industries embodying the second type of criminal activity, that which involves no potential contractual agreements or arrangements among willing buyers and sellers. Monopoly control in these "Type II" industries, exemplified by burglary, could not exploit a price-induced, output effect. This requires us to look more carefully at the basic economic model for a Type II activity, again taking burglary as our example.

Output here is presumably measured by the value of the loot that is stolen. Since, however, this material is not different in kind from that which remains in the possession of legal owners, modifications in the rate of supply of loot by the burglary industry will not affect price significantly. In this respect, a potential monopolist of this industry would remain in the same position as the single member among the many members in an openly competitive structure. This point can be seen clearly if we treat the theft of money as an illustration. Units of money are indistinguishable, and the price of a dollar is invariant at a dollar.[9]

In this initial model, there is no incentive for the monopolist to restrict output in a Type II activity because of the effects on output price. But there may exist an *input-price effect,* applicable for both Type I and Type II activities, that would offer the monopolist an incentive to restrict total supply below that which would be observed under open competition. Initially, we assumed that resource inputs were available to the industry in question at constant supply prices. This amounts to assuming that the resources are unspecialized, that criminality generates no

---

[7] The argument holds so long as anything less than perfect discrimination is available to the monopolist. If perfect discrimination were possible, the output under monopoly would be identical to that under competition. Note particularly that the complete absence of discrimination is not required for the argument, and, in fact, some less-than-perfect discrimination might be expected to take place in industries of Type I. Buyers' information about alternatives would presumably be less than with noncriminal industries, and transaction costs involved in retrading would probably be significantly higher.

[8] The welfare of participants in the voluntary exchanges, considered as a subset of the total population, would be maximized by an absence of legal prohibitions. In the presence of such proscriptive rules, furthermore, restrictions on industry output would be welfare-reducing. Hence, for this subset of the population, monopoly control is less desirable than competition. For the inclusive community, this welfare-decreasing effect of monopolization must be more than offset by welfare gains of nonparticipants if the legal proscriptions are, themselves, socially desirable. There is, of course, no means of determining by simple observation whether or not this condition is fulfilled. For purposes of analysis here, I shall assume that it is.

[9] When we consider the theft of real goods, such as items of clothing, jewelry, plate, and automobiles, some elements identified as characteristic of Type I industries may enter. The value of stolen items here is determined by the ability to market them through indirect and illegal channels. To the extent that the supply of "fence" services is not, itself, highly elastic, the monopolist might face a downsloping curve of effective "demand price." In this case, the argument developed above would, of course, hold and marginal revenue would fall below price. My purpose is not to deny the real-world relevance of this situation, but to develop a pure Type II-model in which, by assumption, final purchasers do not distinguish stolen from nonstolen goods and in which there are no institutional or supply barriers to resale.

differential rents. If we drop this assumption and allow for this possibility, then an expansion in output of the industry may increase the prices of inputs. If a monopolist (monopsonist) is unable to discriminate among different owners of specialized inputs, he will have an incentive to reduce total inputs hired (and hence total output produced) below that generated under competitive organization.[10]

There remains the third source of the argument for monopolization, and this part also carries over for both Type I and Type II criminal activities. Note that in our discussion of either the output-price or input-price effect, we did not find it necessary to introduce law enforcement effort or investment as a determining variable. Regardless of the public's attitudes toward law enforcement and the total investment in enforcement determined by such attitudes, if the conditions described are present, monopolization will tend to reduce total social investment in criminality below that which would be forthcoming under competitive structure. This conclusion holds when society does nothing at all toward law enforcement as well as when society expends a major share of its annual treasure to this end. Furthermore, the shape of the relationship between law enforcement and the level of criminal activity, the enforcement response, or L curve, in Figure 1, is not relevant. Indeed, we could have dispensed entirely with any L curve to this point in the analysis.

Things become different when we examine the third part of the monopolization argument. Here the ability of a potential monopolist to observe the *shape* of the enforcement-response relationship distinguishes the monopoly outcome from the competitive one. If the L curve should be vertical, indicating that there is no enforcement response to changes in the level of investment in criminality, the monopoly situation becomes identical to the competitive. For almost all other configurations, however, strategic behavior by the monopolist in recognition of anticipated enforcement response will generate lower levels of criminality than those predicted under competitive organization.

In order to isolate this effect, which we may call the "internalization of externality" effect, we shall assume that the output of the criminal industry is marketed in a fully competitive setting, and, furthermore, that inputs are available to the industry at constant supply prices.[11] This means that producers must remain price-takers in both output and input markets whether the industry is organized along competitive or monopolistic lines. Despite the invariance in input prices, however, average costs of engaging in criminality would increase with an expansion in the output of the industry. This increase in the costs would be directly caused by the shape of the L curve in Figure 1, that is, by society's expressed response

---

[10] Discrimination among suppliers of inputs may be considerably easier to accomplish than discrimination among purchasers of outputs. See Footnote 7 above.

[11] These assumptions are not fully consistent with a general equilibrium setting. They may be made plausible by assuming that the industry is small relative to the total economy. They are made here, however, solely for purposes of exposition.

to the aggregate level of criminality. The effect is to increase the average cost of a unit of criminal output, or, to state the same thing differently, to decrease the marginal (and average) productivity of an input into criminality. The supply curve for the criminal industry would slope upward, despite our assumption that input prices are invariant.

The individual firms in a competitive organization of the industry will not recognize the effects of expanded industry output on average costs. The enforcement response generated by expanded industry output acts to place such firms in a position of imposing reciprocal external diseconomies, one on the other. In considering its own output decisions, the individual firm will act as if it has no influence on total industry output and, hence, on the change in costs as industry expands. In making a decision to produce an additional unit, the competitive firm will impose costs on other firms in the industry.

It is precisely the existence of this enforcement-induced external diseconomy that provides the third argument for monopolization. The replacement of competition by monopoly has the effect of internalizing the diseconomy. The monopolist can take into account the relationship between aggregate industry output and the predicted enforcement response, and he can control total industry output so as to increase profits above those forthcoming under competition.

Both the price-induced and the enforcement-induced effects work in the same direction; both provide opportunities for the rational monopolist to secure gains from reducing output below competitive levels. For any given enforcement level, we could, therefore, predict that monopoly output would fall short of the competitive. We may return to Figure 1 and depict monopoly output as a function of enforcement effort, as indicated by the curve C_m in the diagram. This curve falls below C at all points. The equilibrium toward which the system converges under monopoly or cartel control of the industry is shown at Z_m.

If the enforcement-response depicted in Figure 1 is assumed to be socially efficient, then a position at Z_m is clearly preferable to one at Z. The level of criminality is lower, and this must be evaluated positively unless crime itself is somehow considered to be "good." Furthermore, at Z_m, the total amount of enforcement effort is lower than that at Z. Resources involved in enforcement may be freed for the production of alternative goods and services that are positively valued; the taxpayer has additional funds that he may spend on alternative publicly provided or privately marketed goods and services.

IV. Possible Objections to Criminal Monopolies

We should examine possible counterarguments or objections to the monopolistic organization of criminal industries. Are there effects of monopolization that are socially undesirable and which have been obscured or neglected in our analysis?

126

Distributional objections may be considered at the outset. Monopolization offers opportunities for profits in crime over and above those forthcoming under competition, and this, in itself, may be deemed socially "bad." It must be noted, however, that profits are made possible only because of the reduction in total criminal activity below fully competitive levels. Furthermore, the possible monopoly profits do not represent transfers from "poor deserving criminals." Under open competition, in the absence of specialization, owners of inputs into crime secure returns that are roughly equivalent to those that could be earned in legitimate, noncriminal activities. Monopolization has the effect of shifting a somewhat larger share of these inputs into noncriminal pursuits. For some of these services, transfer rents may be reduced, but these reductions are offset by increased transfer rents received by other owners of services. It seems difficult to adduce strictly distributional objections to the monopolization of crime.

A second possible objection may be based on the presumed interdependence of the several types of criminal activities. In the analysis above, I have implicitly assumed that the separate criminal industries are independent one from another. If we should assume that potential criminals constitute a noncompeting group of persons, distinct and apart from the rest of society, monopolization of one or a few areas of criminality may actually increase the supply of resources going into remaining and nonorganized activities. This sort of supply interdependence provides an argument for the extension of monopolization to all criminal activities. It does not, however, offer an argument against monopolization per se. Under full monopolization or effective cartelization, the allocation of resources among the separate criminal activities may not be equivalent, in the proportional sense, to that which would prevail under competition. The crime syndicate that effectively controls all criminal activities will equalize the marginal return on its resources in all categories, but the returns captured will include portions of "buyers' surplus" not capturable under effective competition. The mix among crimes will probably be different in the two cases; there may be more burglars relative to bank robbers under one model than under the other. There will, however, be fewer of both under monopoly except under exceptional circumstances.

A third possible objection to the whole analysis must be considered more seriously and discussed in more detail. To this point, I have implicitly assumed that resource inputs are transformed into criminal output with equal efficiency in competitive organization and in monopoly. This assumption may not be empirically appropriate. It seems plausible to argue, at least under some circumstances, that a monopolized or cartelized criminal industry can be more efficient than competition. For any given output, the monopoly may require fewer resource inputs. If this is the case, the C curve of Figure 1 cannot be allowed to represent resource input and/or criminal output interchangeably as we have implicitly done in the discussion. The nonstrategic monopoly-response curve will not be coincident with the competitive C curve if the former is defined in terms of output. The nonstrategic monopoly-response curve will lie above that which describes competitive criminal response. The strategic monopoly-response function will lie below the nonstrategic function, as depicted, but there is no assurance that it need lie below the competitive-response function as shown in Figure 1. To the extent that there are significant economies of large scale in crime, monopoly organization will tend to be relatively more efficient. Even if this hypothesis is accepted, however, the advantages of competitive criminal organization are not clear. Consider an example in which a fully strategic monopoly response, given a predicted enforcement-response function, generates a criminal output valued at X dollars, which is the same as the output that would be generated under competition. Assume, however, that the latter industrial organization uses resources valued at X dollars in alternative uses, whereas the monopoly uses up only X/2 dollars in generating X. The social "bad" represented by crime is identical in the two forms; law enforcement investment is the same. But resources valued at X/2 are freed for the production of valued "goods" under monopoly whereas these "goods" cannot be produced under competition.[12]

A possible misunderstanding of the whole analysis rather than an explicit objection to it may well emerge. Emotions may be aroused by the thought that one implication of the whole analysis is that governments should "deal with the syndicate," that law enforcement agencies should work out "accommodations" or "arrangements" with those who might organize central control over criminal effort. I should emphasize that there is nothing of this sort implied in the analysis to this point. In its strictest interpretation, the analysis carries no policy implications at all. It merely suggests that there may be social benefits from the monopoly organization of crime. Policy implications emerge only when we go beyond this with a suggestion that governments adopt a passive role when they observe attempts made by entrepreneurs to reduce the effective competitiveness of criminal industries. In practice, this suggestion reduces to an admonition against the much-publicized crusades against organized crime at the expense of enforcement effort aimed at ordinary, competitive criminality.

I do not propose that explicit "arrangements" be made with existing or potential criminal syndicates. If this approach were taken, the solution to the system depicted in Figure 1 would not be at Z_m, but would, instead, be located to the southwest of Z_m, embodying even less criminal output and less enforcement effort. At Z_m, "gains from trade" between a monopoly syndicate and the com-

---

[12] The media sometimes become confused in assessing the comparative efficiency of organized and unorganized crime. In June 1971, attention was focused on the theft of stock certificates from brokerages. On consecutive evening news broadcasts, one TV network reported (1) organized crime *exploits* the actual thieves by giving them only 5 percent of the face value of the stolen certificates, and (2) the increase in theft is facilitated because organized crime provides a *ready market* for the securities.

munity may be exploited only by moves in the general southwesterly direction.[13] There are compelling arguments against this approach. In the first place, even if the persons in potential control of criminal activity could be identified in advance and a bargain struck with them, the governmental agency involved would find that the "trading" solution lies off the community's enforcement response, or L, curve. This would bring pressure on politicians to break the agreement. A government agency, precisely because it acts on behalf of, and is thereby subject to review by, the whole community, cannot readily behave monolithically, whether this behavior is unilateral strategic response to, or explicit bilateral dealing with, a syndicate. The community enforcement-response function necessarily describes outcomes generated by the interaction of many behavioral components; in many respects such responses are more closely analogous to competitive, than to monopoly, behavior.

Perhaps an equally important technical difficulty with this approach involves the question of identification itself. Even if the enforcement agencies could act monolithically, independent from community political pressures, the question would remain: If the criminal syndicate could be identified with sufficient predictability to allow bargains to be struck, why should "trade" be necessary? The community's preferred position is the reduction of criminal activity to zero, allowing for a comparable reduction in enforcement effort. The enforcement-response function, shown by the L curve in Figure 1, is based on the implicit assumption that there are technological limits to the productivity of police effort. These limits may rule out the full identification of the organizers of crime, even if monopoly is known to exist and to be effective. Passive acquiescence in the syndication of crime is a wholly different policy stance from active negotiations with identified leaders.

If "arrangements" are ruled out on technological, ethical, or contractual bases, however, a subsidiary question arises concerning appropriate policy norms to be followed when and if positive identification of the monopolists becomes possible, either fortuitously or as a result of search effort. Suppose, for example, that a municipality that is initially in a Z_m equilibrium finds it possible to identify leaders of the local syndicate. Should the community prosecute these leaders and break up the monopoly? Failure to prosecute here is quite different from the arrangement of explicit trades or deals. Breakdown of an existing control group may loose a flood of entrants and the competitive adjustment process might converge toward a new equilibrium at Z. If such a pattern is predicted, attempts at breaking up even those criminal monopolies whose leaders are positively identified should be made with caution.

---

[13] Economists familiar with ridge-line or reaction-curve constructions will recognize that the C_m curve depicts the locus of vertical points on the series of indifference contours representing the preferences of the monopolist. Similarly, the L curve is the locus of horizontal positions on the community's set of indifference curves, assuming away all difficulties in interpersonal amalgamation. The preferred position of the monopolist lies high along the ordinate, and the preferred position of the community lies at the origin.

The law enforcement response that this analysis implies is no different in detail from that which might be followed under competitive organization of the criminal industries. Enforcement units and agencies are presumed to make normal efforts to apprehend criminals of all sorts, and community or public pressures will insure that these efforts are bounded from both sides. Indeed, the monopolist's response function has been presumed to be based on the expectation that community response would be as noted. The analysis does nothing toward suggesting that enforcement agencies should not take maximum advantage of all technological developments in crime prevention, detection, and control. To the extent that new technology increases the cost of criminal output, the relevant C curve, competitive or monopolistic, is shifted downward. To the extent that court rulings increase the expected productivity of investment in criminality and/or reduce the productivity of enforcement effort, the relevant C curve is shifted upward. The whole analysis has been presented on the assumption that the public's "tastes" for enforcement remain unchanged. This is merely a convenient expository device, and there is no difficulty in incorporating shifts toward the right or left in the L function.[14]

V. Criminal Self-interest as a Social "Good"

The genius of the eighteenth century social philosophers, notably Bernard Mandeville, David Hume, and Adam Smith, is to be found in their recognition that the self-interests of men can be made to serve social purpose under the appropriate institutional arrangements. The sought reform in the organization or the institutions of society as an instrumental means of accomplishing more specific social objectives. The philosophical foundations of competitive economic organization are contained in Adam Smith's famous statement about the butcher whose self-interest, rather than benevolence, puts meat on the consumer's supper table. So long as attention is confined to the production, supply, and marketing of pure "goods," both as evaluated by direct purchasers, and by the members of the community in their "public" capacities, competition among freely contracting traders, with entry into and egress from industry open, furthers the "public interest" in a meaningful sense of this term. There is no argument for monopolistic restriction in this setting, whether this be done via governmental agencies, as in Smith's era (and, alas, all too commonly in our own) or by profit-seeking private entrepreneurs. The preservation of free entry and egress, the prohibition of output-restricting, price-increasing agreements among sellers, the control of industries or groups of industries by one or a small number of persons and/or firms—all of these are genuinely "public goods" and, as such, their provision warrants the possible investment of governmental resources.

---

[14] The situation in the United States in the early 1970s may be interpreted in terms of the analysis of this paper. Adverse court rulings since the middle 1950s have continually shifted the relevant C curves upward. This has created a disequilibrium in the whole system that is reflected in the observed increases in enforcement effort.

Things become somewhat different, however, when it is recognized that "goods," which individuals value positively in their private capacities, may be mixed variously with "bads," which individuals value negatively in their capacities as members of the community. To the extent that the "goods" element is isolated, restrictions on competitive supply are socially undesirable. If the "bads" necessarily accompany the production-sale of the "goods," however, some balance must be struck and some reductions in the output of "goods" below openly competitive levels may be in the social interest. If the "bads" are internal to an industry, monopolization will cause these to be internalized and taken into account in decision making. In this case, profit-seeking behavior of the monopolist will reduce the output of "goods" below socially optimal levels. In this case, it becomes impossible to determine, a priori, which of the two organizational forms, competition or monopoly, is socially more efficient. If the "bads" are external to an industry, wholly or partially, monopolization will at least shift the total supply of "goods" in the direction indicated by social optimality criteria, but profit-induced restriction may fall short of or overshoot the mark. Aside from this, there may also be highly undesirable distributional consequences of monopolization. In general, no straightforward organizational or institutional principles can be deduced for the cases where "goods" and "bads" are mixed. The choice between competitive and monopoly organization, if these are the only effective alternatives, must be made on the basis of pragmatic considerations in each case.[15]

Unambiguous organizational-institutional guidelines re-emerge, however, when we examine activities that are unambiguously "bads" in the social or public sense. Here the argument advanced by Mandeville and Smith becomes applicable in reverse. If it lies within the self-interest of men to produce "bads" without accompanying and compensating "goods," this same self-interest may be channeled in a socially desired direction by encouraging the exploitation of the additional private profit opportunities offered in explicit restraint of trade. Freedom of entry, the hallmark of competition, is of negative social value here, and competitiveness is to be discouraged rather than encouraged. These principles become self-evident once we recognize, with the eighteenth century philosophers, that institutional structures are variables that may be used as instruments for achieving social purpose,

---

[15] Economists, in their roles as social reformers, constantly search for alternatives that will accomplish the explicit objectives more directly, without basic modifications in organizational structure. For example, witness the current popularity of schemes to correct for "public bads" exemplified in air and water pollution by placing charges or fees on the production and sale of marketable goods and services, while maintaining competitive structure as the organizational form.

It will be recognized that the content of this paragraph covers, in extremely brief form, many parts of modern welfare economics. Earlier works of my own have discussed some of the points made. See my "Private Ownership and Common Usage: The Road Case Re-examined," *Southern Economic Journal,* vol. 22 (January 1956), pp. 305-16; "External Diseconomies, Corrective Taxes, and Market Structure," *American Economic Review,* vol. 59 (March 1969), pp. 174-76; and "Public Goods and Public Bads," in *Financing the Metropolis,* ed. John P. Crecine (Beverly Hills: Sage Publications, 1970), pp. 51-71.

in this case, the reduction in the aggregate level of criminality along with the reduction in resource commitment to law enforcement. It is not from the public-spiritedness of the leaders of the Cosa Nostra that we should expect to get a reduction in the crime rate but from their regard for their own self-interests.[16]

---

[16] Only upon reading another paper delivered at the conference did I see the reference to the paper by Thomas Schelling on the economics of organized crime. Upon subsequent examination, I find that Schelling explored some of the issues touched on in my paper, but that he did not explicitly discuss the central principle that I have emphasized. See Thomas C. Schelling, "Economic Analysis of Organized Crime," Appendix D in *Task Force Report: Organized Crime,* Annotations and Consultants' Papers, Task Force on Organized Crime, The President's Commission on Law Enforcement and the Administration of Justice (Washington, D. C.: Government Printing Office, 1967).

AUTHORITY, POWER AND RESPECT
The Interplay of Control Systems in an Organized Crime "Family"

Francis A. J. Ianni

Ever since the hearings of the Kefauver committee in 1951, and increasingly since the 1963 appearance of Joseph Valachi before the McClellan committee, government law enforcement agencies and their consultants have been trying to uncover the organizational structure of the nationwide Italo-American criminal syndicate known as the "Mafia" or "Cosa Nostra." Their approach has mainly focused on a formal organization model of analysis. That is, the criminal organization has not been studied as a social system with its own set of rules, but rather as a business empire deliberately designed to achieve specific goals. Elaborate charts have been made showing the organization of model criminal "families" staffed by a hierarchy of members whose titles and functions are sometimes borrowed from the overseas Mafia (*capo, sottocapo, consigliere,* et cetera) and sometimes analogized to positions in an American business corporation (*sottocapo* = vice-president; *caporegima* = plant supervisor, et cetera).

The organization they describe seems, in its bureaucratic character, not much different from the Bell Telephone System. Like Bell, it is called "a nationwide . . . cartel . . . dedicated to amassing millions of dollars through the provision of services" to the public. Like Bell, this cartel is a confederation of local syndicates or companies which function with some independence at their own level, but are subject to corporate policy decisions by a "national commission" which structurally at least resembles a board of directors. Like any large corporation, this organization "continues to function regardless of personnel changes," because its local organizations are "rationally designed with an integrated set of positions geared to maximize profits." And, like the Bell System, Cosa Nostra maintains contact with its counterparts overseas.[1]

While such a structuralist approach to organizational analysis has its uses, it also has major drawbacks. For one thing, in this approach the criminal organization is viewed primarily as a hierarchy of jobs to be filled and carried out, a blueprint which can be used to construct and reconstruct organizations everywhere. But as three years of field study here and in Italy have shown us, secret societies,

---

[1] All exemplary quotations in this paragraph are taken from *Task Force Report: Organized Crime,* The President's Commission on Law Enforcement and the Administration of Justice (Washington, D. C.: Government Printing Office, 1967), pp. 7-8.

such as the Sicilian Mafia and Italo-American criminal families, are not really formal organizations, rationally designed and consciously constructed. Rather, they are traditional social systems, products of culture, and responsive to cultural change. Far from being hierarchies of organizational positions which can be diagramed and then changed by recasting the organization chart, they are patterns of relationship among individuals which have the force of kinship, and which can be changed only by drastic, often fatal, action.

Another problem with the attempt to analogize the structure of Italo-American criminal syndicates to the organizational structure of an American bureaucracy is that those making the analogy try to describe these same positions in terms of equivalents in the Sicilian Mafia when, in fact, such equivalents do not exist. For example, the position of *capo* in the Sicilian Mafia does not correspond to that of president of an American company, for the authority of the *capo* is far less subject to controls than is that of even the most autocratic of corporate leaders. While the role of a military commander is closer in power to that of the *capo,* the closest comparison would be with the leader of a paramilitary guerrilla band. Consequently, lifting this term from its place in Sicilian Mafia, using it to describe a role in Italo-American criminal syndicates, and then explaining that role as comparable to one in corporate business creates a serious distortion.

In my own research, I have attempted to define organizational "roles" in criminal families not by borrowing from other systems, but by observing the complex, real-life behavior of the families themselves. I have had the opportunity to make such observations for the last two years, as part of a field study of patterns of behavior and relationship in an organized crime "family" in the New York area.[2] Basically, our approach has been to view the family not as a formal organization, but as an integrated social system. We have attempted to learn the rules which structure and motivate behavior by observing how people behave. We have seen our task as one of formulating the implicit rules shared by the members of Italo-American criminal syndicates by examining how members apply these rules.

In the following pages I will present some of our findings on role relationships within the Lupollo "family"—an Italo-American organized crime syndicate which controls the numbers and loan sharking in one section of Brooklyn and which has large legitimate business interests as well.[3] By a role, I mean that constellation of behaviors which defines an individual's relationship with others when they interact with him in that role. Thus the role defines both how he will interact with other individuals and how they will interact with him. Within a social system, roles are social norms which define how specified categories of members will

[2] The study was financed by the Russell Sage Foundation. Dr. Francesco Cerase, now of the Institute of Social Research in the University of Rome, and Elizabeth Reuss-Ianni, now of the Institute for Social Analysis, Newfoundland, New Jersey, were associates in the study.

[3] Lupollo is a pseudonym, as are all other names used in this paper.

interact with each other. The focus here is on dynamic relationships rather than on static positions. If we use this approach, there would seem to be two important considerations for the empirical study of role phenomena which dictate the study and analysis of roles. First, since role behavior is interactional, it has to be observed in interpersonal relationships rather than in observations of single action. Second, identifying and describing roles can come only from studying the regularities in behavior in interpersonal relationships between the role-actor and other individuals. After observing these behaviors and the frequency with which they occur, we can then describe some distinctive, integrative patterns of behavior and behavior expectations which seem to characterize a particular role. Having observed one such pattern, the field worker must then observe others behaving in the same role (or seek out other studies which have done so); he then attempts to identify those patterns of interpersonal relationship which seem indeed to characterize a particular role in many settings, and to factor out those which are idiosyncratic to a particular role-actor. Finally, following our general principle of looking for the rules which regulate behavior, we looked for the social norms which define roles.

In studying the Lupollo family, we were looking for patterns of social relationship which would establish who related to whom, how, and under what conditions. In particular, we were interested in discovering a network of relationships which would define some members as more powerful than others, some who command, and some who follow. For example, we asked whether there was someone in the family who, under all circumstances, is always "the boss." If there is, what are the techniques of control, the sanctions and the communications network he uses to exercise his authority within the 15-member family executive group, and how does he relate to others inside and outside the family?

In looking for a network of power relationships, however, we soon discovered that we were dealing not with one but with several behavioral structures which tie the Lupollo family members together. The first of these is the legitimated system of role-prescribed relationships which establishes power in a hierarchy of authority. In this system, the authority of the individual is largely inherent in the role itself; the individual is powerful because of the status he occupies. But within the Lupollo family, as elsewhere, authority and power are not always the same. Accordingly, our observations led us to a second behavioral structure—a network of alliances based on power which is not role-related but is an attribute of the individual himself, or more exactly, a property of his social relationships with others. Power, in this sense, is an individual's capacity to exert influence. Authority is associated with one form of power—legitimated power.

By distinguishing between the family's authority structure and its power structure, we were able to give a more nearly complete picture of the family's stratification pattern than we would have in concentrating on one system. Still, there were some factors which were unaccounted for in our description. For example, it became obvious to us that certain forms of control behavior, such as the operation of "deference," were not fully explained by either the concept of power or that of authority.

We therefore turned to another ranking dimension, that of "prestige." By prestige we mean the hierarchical ordering of the esteem in which a person is held by others in the social system they share. In the Lupollo family and within Italian and Italo-American culture generally, there is an accepted term which combines all the meanings of prestige in one ranking device: "respect" (*rispetto*). In the Lupollo family, respect is a constant characteristic of an individual, though it is modified by age. Old Giuseppe, the family's founder, was *respettato* because of his power and authority, but as he grew older, he earned even more *rispetto* because age carries with it respect in Italian culture. However, his partner and underling, Cosimo Salemi, who was feared because of his personal power, did not have high respect because he always had to defer to Giuseppe. As Cosimo grew older he accrued more respect, but that again was associated with age.

In this paper, then, I will describe the role networks within the Lupollo family which are based on the three criteria of authority, power, and prestige-respect. I will show, in the process, that conflict inevitably arises within the family when the three structures do not coincide—where, for example, different authority and power roles are held by the same person—but that when the three structures do coincide, the same system produces a high degree of stability and cohesion.

I. Methodology

In our attempt to obtain data on power, authority, and prestige-respect, we used several techniques. The main one was that of participant-observation. My original contacts with the Lupollo family were through personal friendship with one of the members, who introduced me to other family members. Hence, in a sense, I had commenced observing family patterns before the study began, and what was principally required was that I begin to record the data I observed, and to discipline and sharpen my techniques in accordance with procedures I had employed in previous anthropological field work. Over a two-year period I was present and able to observe behavior in settings which varied from large-scale family events, like weddings and christenings, to more intimate situations such as dinners with one or more family members in their homes, or in the social clubs to which we all belonged. I should add that members of the family were aware of my role as an anthropologist.

In my observations of role behavior, I followed my usual practice of recording who initiated the action I observed, who showed deference to whom, what were the forms of address, and other modifications of behavior which indicate the recognition by the actors that they are not equals. We developed a "map" showing patterns of deference within the family based on repeated observations in a variety of situations. Once I had a map in hand, I tested it through further observations.

As a check on our map, I also used an interview technique for determining how the family members estimated each other in terms of power, authority, and respect-prestige. I did this by introducing into our conversation questions about who has the most power in the family and so on. Since I did not want to create any tension with family members over these questions, I took a period of over a year in order to introduce the questions when they came up naturally in the conversation. I was able to get responses from only nine of the fifteen members of the family executive group, since in some cases the occasion for asking the questions never came up and in others, my relationship with the family members was such that I could not ask the question naturally. We also asked people outside the family who they thought held power, authority, and respect.

Since information gained from interviewing was one step removed from my own direct observations, a problem of validity was created. In effect, there were two closely related, but separable, questions in assessing the interview data: first, how to assess the reliability of the source of a particular piece of datum; second, how much validity to assign to the information itself. For example, it is possible that an individual informant who has always proved reliable in the past may provide information which he is passing on from someone else, and about which the analyst must make a separate judgment. Or, in another case, an informant who is usually unreliable may pass on a piece of information which can be checked against factual data such as ownership of a business.

To look at the questions of informant reliability and data validity separately, we set up a two-dimensional system for evaluating interview data. With regard to data validity, we assigned the highest validity score (a score of "A") to data gathered by *direct* participant observation; a lower score of "B" to data gathered by observation where we were not involved as direct participants. Scores of "C," "D," and "E" were assigned to interview data according to how carefully the data could be checked. Similarly, five categories for informant reliability, ranging from a "1" for "always reliable" to a "5" for "unreliable," were created by constantly comparing data from our major informants.

In presenting the data in this paper, I rely primarily on those summary data with a validity score of at least "C" and a reliability score of at least "2." Specific notation is made for any data falling below "C-2," indicating the probable validity and the reliability of our source.

Before proceeding to describe the authority, power, and prestige systems in the Lupollo family, it will be worthwhile to provide some background on the family's history.

II. The Lupollo "Family"

Italo-American criminal syndicates are justly called families because the relationships established within them produce kinship-like ties among members, ties which are given greater power when they are legitimated through marriage or godparenthood. Every family member knows that every other member has some duties toward him and some claim on him. Whether the relationships are based on blood or marriage as they often are, or whether they are fictive as in the intricate pattern of ritual alliances through godparenthood, it is kinship which ties generations together and allies lineages and families. It is this feature which sets Italo-American crime families apart from gangs in ethnic groups similarly involved in organized crime.

In this and most other respects, the Lupollo family is no different from any other Italo-American criminal syndicate. In it, as in others, the association of members as a kinship group and their alliance as a business organization are one and inseparable. Functional roles in the family's business enterprises—whether legal or illegal—are almost always determined by kinship relationships, and the power hierarchy usually parallels generational position. A member of the Lupollo family may have other "outside" business activities and even a profession of his own, but these are completely separate and have little or no effect on his functional role within the Lupollo family business.

The patriarch and founder of the family empire, Giuseppe Lupollo, was born of peasant parents in the district of Corleone in western Sicily. Coming to New York's Lower East Side in 1902, he began the family business by using his nest egg to set up two small enterprises. One of these, a grocery-importing business was legitimate; the other, a private storefront "Italian bank," was also apparently legitimate but seems related, by the interest charged and the methods used to collect, to the family's future loan-sharking activities.

Soon thereafter, by shrewd management of these original enterprises, Giuseppe established himself as partial or complete owner of an ice delivery service, an Italian bakery and confectionery store, an importing and retail grocery store, and a small combination bar and card parlor. He also began the family gambling interest by setting up a branch of the "Italian lottery," the precursor of the policy or numbers racket.

By 1915, Giuseppe Lupollo was an established and feared "man of respect" in the Italo-American community. He had achieved considerable financial success, and while his loan shark and gambling activities were well known in the community, his status there was that of a banker and businessman.

Over subsequent decades, the family business continued to expand. On the legitimate side, such businesses as real estate, garbage and refuse hauling and disposal were added. The original ice and coal delivery company was transformed into a fuel delivery enterprise which has since expanded to include a limousine-leasing

138

business in Brooklyn, and a trucking firm. By the beginning of World War II, the grocery, bakery, and importing business had been consolidated into one major bakery chain and a nationally known food products firm. On the illicit side, family ventures included bootlegging during the Prohibition era and the continuance of the loan shark and gambling operations.

In addition, the family itself expanded. Through marriage and other kinship ties, three other lineages—the Alcamos, the Salemis, and the Tuccis—entered the family businesses. While members of these lineages today hold some important positions (the Salemis mainly in illegal, the Alcamos and Tuccis mainly in legal, businesses), the Lupollos continue to dominate family decision making. Around 1940, when he was 68 years old, Giuseppe relinquished active control of the family enterprises to his son Joe, who remains today the "head" of the family. Closest to him in power is his brother Calogero (Charley). Originally chosen by Giuseppe to manage the family's legitimate operations, Charley's main functions now are in the fields of politics and public relations, where he uses his contacts in local, city, and state politics to advance the family's interests. Almost as important in the family, and performing a similar function, is Philip Alcamo, whose main contacts are in Washington.

Other members of the family's executive group include Joe's and Charley's sons (Joey, Tony, Marky, and Patsy) and grandsons (Paulie, Bobby, Tommy, and Freddy); Phil Alcamo's son Basil; Vito Salemi and his son Vic, who manage the family's numbers and loan shark operations; and Pete Tucci, who directs one of the family's largest legitimate businesses.

A noteworthy feature of the family's history is the movement toward legitimization. As the family's legitimate businesses have increasingly moved into the mainstream of American enterprise, their financial and organizational structure has been changed. Legal and illegal activities have been increasingly segregated from each other, both in terms of the personnel involved and in terms of cash flow.

Even more important, with each generation of the Lupollo family, fewer members have gone into the family business. Though most of the third-generation males do work in the family enterprises, only four of the ten fourth-generation male members of the Lupollo-Alcamo-Salemi-Tucci lineages are similarly involved. The rest are lawyers, teachers, and doctors. This gradual but increasing movement away from criminal activity—and even from involvement in the crime family's legitimate activities—seems to support the idea held by some that for the Italo-Americans, as for other ethnic groups previously involved in organized crime, crime has been the first rung on a "queer ladder of social mobility," leading up and out of the ghetto and into respectable roles in the wider American community.[4]

---

[4] Daniel Bell, *The End of Ideology* (New York: The Free Press, 1969), p. 19. Bell, by the way, was not convinced otherwise even after the Valachi affair, as he indicated in a subsequent article entitled "The Myth of Cosa Nostra" in *The New Leader,* December 23, 1963.

III. Role Relationships in the Lupollo "Family": The Authority Structure

Against this background, we can return to our examination of the three behavioral structures which underlie the Lupollo family's organization as a social and business unit. The first, and most obvious, of these is the structure of authority roles.

It may seem somewhat strange to talk about authority—or legitimated power—within an organized crime family, but it does exist there. There is a sense of legitimacy that permits the family to organize power and its use into a hierarchical pattern so that some members hold roles of authority and others do not. Those who hold authority are able to commit the family's resources to the pursuit of goals and to command members to action in that pursuit. Those who have little or no authority act with all the deference to the authority figure that one would expect to find in any hierarchically structured social system.

The most obvious rule which regulates the authority structure is that roles within it are distributed on the basis of generational affiliation within the various lineages. In every case, the older the generation, the greater the authority. The second feature which stands out is that the various lineages—the Lupollos, the Alcamos, the Salemis and the Tuccis—enjoy differential status within the family so that generally, but not universally, a Lupollo will have more authority than a Salemi of the same generation. There are exceptions to this rule of ranking which we shall point out later, but they are special cases which result from the operation of the third rule of ranking. This third rule is actually not so much a rule as a principle which has the force of a rule. Within the family, some members now achieve authority on the basis of specialization or expertise—they are lawyers or accountants whose skills become more valuable as the family business expands.

Joe Lupollo is the undisputed head of the family both as a business empire and a social organization. Members of the family acknowledge his leadership, and their behavior toward him is always deferential. This deference is manifested in many ways. Whenever there is an important business decision to be made he makes it, even in those business enterprises with which he has no direct contact. In the business operations, one hears such comments as, "Patsy wants to go into building suburban shopping centers but his father nixed the deal," or, "Charley represents his brother Joe's interests on the docks," or, most frequently, "Check it with Joe."

Throughout the Italo-American community in New York, Joe is recognized as the "head" of the Lupollo family. This means more than being the patriarch of his family. It means also that he is the accepted leader of the "business family" as well. Thus, someone wanting to make an important business deal with one of the companies in the family business begins by contacting the member of the family executive group who is nominally in charge of the business; but he knows that if the decision is big enough, eventually Joe will have to make it.

140

Joe also commands authority within the social structure of the Lupollo lineage and within the associated lineages as well. At all social events he sets the tone by his own mood and actions. If there is a baptism or a wedding in any of the lineages or even in the family of some distant relative or employee, Joe is expected to send the most expensive gift and he seldom disappoints. When several members of the family agree to have dinner out together whether for business or social reasons, it is always Joe who chooses the restaurant (always from among the same two or three) and then picks up the check. And on the few occasions when the Lupollo family is approached as a group—at religious gatherings or benefits in the Italo-American community, for example—it is always through Joe.

In addition to Joe, his brother Charley and Phil Alcamo also hold important roles in the authority structure. Charley is the family surrogate for Joe and, in his absence, the decision-making role is his both in the business and the social life of the family. All that we have said of Joe is true of Charley when Joe is not present; in no case, however, does Charley enjoy this deference when Joe is present. Since Joe dislikes traveling, Charley usually handles any business dealings out of town which require decisions at Joe's level. When Joe and Charley are together at family gatherings or at family meetings, Charley shows deference to Joe and usually advances no new ideas or even suggestions unless Joe asks for them. (The family meetings which I attended were, of course, not formally called ones but ad hoc situations where some items of business came up during a social gathering. Whether this deferential behavior holds true in formal meetings, assuming there are formal meetings, we do not know.)

In addition to his surrogate role, Charley has another informal role in the family organization. The younger members of the family consider Joe difficult to approach. He is far from garrulous and when he does speak, he is usually peremptory. He is also ultraconservative; he views most ventures with suspicion and seldom asks for advice. He seldom loses his temper, but when he does, he becomes violent and abusive. The younger members of the family, wanting some decision or favor, usually find Joe a forbidding person to approach. Charley, on the other hand, is more approachable, has close relationships with many of the junior members of the family, and is a good listener. Thus, another role for Charley is to present new ideas, advance petitions or relay unfavorable business data and, generally, to intercede for other family members. He does this with considerable sensitivity and no little skill. The other side of this role has Charley carrying decisions back from Joe to other family members. Rather interestingly, Charley seems to perform this same role even for Joe's sons Tony and Marky.

These two roles, Joe as "boss" and Charley in a role which seems to combine elements of the *sottocappo* and *consiglieri* described by experts as hierarchical roles in Cosa Nostra, are the only offices we observed. There is also a role on which we do not have enough data to do more than suggest its existence; the role

Figure 1

STRUCTURE OF AUTHORITY IN THE LUPOLLO "FAMILY"

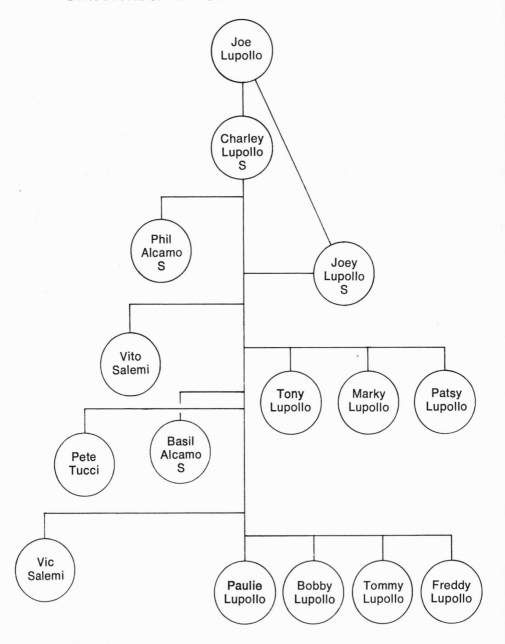

Rules of Ranking:

1. The earlier the generation, the higher the rank.
2. Within generations, the Lupollo lineage takes precedence over others.
3. Specialists (S) are ranked higher than generalists.

is that of "heir apparent" and it is held by Joey Lupollo, who seems to have been selected to take eventual control of the family from his father. This is generally accepted within the family and is obvious in some of the behavior relationships we saw. Joey, for example, does not use his Uncle Charley as a go-between with his father but approaches him directly while his two brothers do not. When Charley is unable to represent Joe at business meetings or to travel out of town, it seems to be Joey who goes instead. Most important, however, is the fact that Joey spends a great deal of time with his father, more than any other member except Charley.

There are a number of functional roles—roles which develop as a result of the particular expertise of the individual within the family as well. For example, Charley shares with Phil Alcamo the role of political contact for the family. Basil Alcamo, who is a certified public accountant, and Joey Lupollo are considered to have the two best business minds in the family, and their advice is often sought on investments and business problems. Phil Alcamo is also considered to have good business sense, and generally he is the arbiter and interpreter of national and international events and their probable effects on the world of the Lupollos.

There are any number of other functional roles in the family, but they are more social than business specialties. Nevertheless, since the family is so much an integrated social and business unit, these roles have some effect on the family as a business unit also. Bobby Lupollo, for example, is considered the sharpest dresser in the family, although the older members consider his dress somewhat extreme. Yet not only does he set the style for the younger family members, but his views carry considerable weight in the family-related "Danny Boy" clothing line.

The pattern of roles which describes the authority structure in the family is diagramed in Figure 1. What this diagram shows is the operation of the three rules of ranking which we extracted from our observations and from interview data. What it cannot show, however, is that this pattern is not a fixed one, and that slowly but surely it is changing because the traditional placement of power in the authority roles we have described is now being challenged by new sources of power developed within the family.

IV. The Changing Bases of Power in the Lupollo "Family"

Power is often defined as an individual's ability to compel or influence another to do his bidding. This definition implies that power is an attribute of the individual. But we insist again that power does not reside in the individual, any more than authority rests in some position. Power is a property of a social relationship; it is an individual's capacity to influence someone or some group. We feel that the term "network" captures this sense of relationship far better than a term like "power structure," and so in our analyses of the flow of power within the Lupollo family, we use this term to describe the pattern of power relationships.

Within the Lupollo family, we saw three main power networks. The first and most obvious of these centered around Joe. As traditional head of the family, he is by far the most influential in deciding such power-based matters as the allocation of resources, the selection of goals, and the ordering of social and business life; his younger brother Charley is second most powerful. The exercise of Joe's power is based on the fear which other family members feel for him in his role as traditional authority—a fear expressed as reticence in initiating any new idea or social action, and as reluctance to try to challenge the existing locus of decision making. I most often heard this described as an unwillingness of family members to "step out of line."

But if Joe is a control figure with complete authority within the family, the basis of his power seems to be shifting. He is boss precisely because he is the traditional head of the family, and this role, based on kinship, necessarily carries with it a conservative approach to control over the family empire. Joe's personality seems to have fitted him well for this role, and his experiences certainly did little to alter that fit. After leaving school at an early age to work for his father, he worked first with the Salemis in the gambling enterprise, then with his father in the legitimate businesses as they grew and prospered. Toward the end of his life, old Giuseppe designated Joe as his successor, and the two worked closely together during a transition period in which Joe learned from his father both the tasks and the role of family head. It was undoubtedly from his close association with his father that Joe gained his sense of family-oriented, kinship-based responsibility for holding the business-social unit together. Like his father, too, he operates entirely within the Italo-American community, where his contacts and associations are restricted to a relatively small group of family members, *paesani,* and other Italo-Americans involved in legitimate and illegitimate businesses.

While Joe maintains control over the family's businesses on the basis of his traditional authority, his brother Charley and Phil Alcamo compete with him for that power. Unlike Joe, both these men operate outside the social-business milieu of the Italo-American community. Charley, better educated than Joe both in formal schooling and in self-education, is interested and involved in city politics, and it is here that he seeks friends and contacts. He is joined in this quest by Phil Alcamo, and the two literally compete for new alliances within the "American" business and political establishments. Neither Charley nor Phil is by any means "liberal" or "progressive" in politics or social attitudes, but compared to Joe they are both far less conservative and dogmatic. Joe is more "Italian" than "American" not only in his affiliations but also in his outlook on life; the reverse is true of Charley and Phil.

These differences in world view and affiliation are producing power tensions within the Lupollo family. As the family moves more and more into the legitimate business establishment, the contacts that Charley and Phil have there become more and more crucial; without them, in fact, even the illegal activities probably could not survive. In their roles as power connections for the family, Charley and Phil must inevitably challenge the supremacy of Joe's authority.

Faced with this challenge—implicit but seldom acted out—Joe has turned back into his own world of power for support rather than seeking political and business connections of his own. Two sources of his own power within the family are the Salemis and Pete Tucci. Vito and Vic Salemi operate the family's illegal activities. Through them, Joe has connections in the underworld of Italo-American criminal syndicates as well as his own associations there, and the potential of this power is an important asset to Joe as he must struggle in the future to retain his control over the family. Pete Tucci, who heads one of the family's largest legitimate businesses, is, like Joe and Vito, more conservative than Charley and Phil, and more oriented toward the Italo-American community. To him as to Joe, the kinship bonds of the family are important and valued, and he sees the social unity of the group as critical to its survival. With these allies, Joe fortifies his position as a conservative, traditional family head.

Joe was seventy-five years old in 1970, and the undercurrents of the power struggle going on in the Lupollo family must soon become someone else's problem. Here, the power networks come into play and provide some important insights into the family's future. In the third generation of the family—the children of Joe and Charley Lupollo and of Vito Salemi and Phil Alcamo—more members affiliate with Joe than with Charley and Phil. Tony and Marky Lupollo exhibit complete filial deference to their father and, moreover, really seem to believe that Joe can and should use his traditional authority to hold the family together. Vic Salemi is also allied with Joe; he seems distrustful of Phil Alcamo and even more so of Basil Alcamo. Basil, on the other hand, is closely allied with his father, and through him with Charley. While he is publicly deferential towards Joe, privately he is often critical of Joe's "old-fashioned ideas" and stubbornness. He is not so circumspect in his open hostility to the Salemis and his contempt for Pete Tucci. Patsy Lupollo is his father's man and allies himself with Charlie and Phil.

The key figure in the third generation, and indeed the key actor in the latent power struggle, is Joey Lupollo. All of Joey's inclinations and values would logically lead to an affiliation with his uncles Charley and Phil. Like them, he is connected in the "American" establishments, and sees the future of the family as dependent on nurturing and expanding these contacts. His tastes and styles, like theirs, have climbed beyond the baroque attitudes and ostentatious life styles of his brothers Tony and Marky.

Yet in every observable act and social relationship, Joey allies himself with his father. There are, of course, obvious reasons why Joey would side with his father in the developing struggle for power in the family. As the heir apparent, he is slated to take over his father's traditional role as family head, and the challenges from Basil, Charley and Phil call into question the legitimate authority of that role. Also, his ties of kin with his father are strong ones, and family loyalty may be important to him. Finally, he may simply be waiting for his father to step down before showing where his true allegiances stand in the family.

In the fourth generation, all of the family members save one tend to align themselves with Charley and Phil. Bobby, Freddy, and Tommy Lupollo all understand access to the establishments of the larger society to be far more potent than the traditional control of some piece or pieces of territory. All well-educated and quite comfortable in "American" society, they see little future in the old world of organized crime. They look to Charley and Phil for that future rather than to Joe or to Vito Salemi. The one exception here is Paulie Lupollo, whose mother, Yolanda Salemi, ties him to that lineage as well as to the Lupollos. Paulie allies himself with his uncle Vic Salemi, and through him with Joe.

All four of the fourth generation members of the family are also allied with Joey Lupollo, and it is to him they relate most easily. Some of this comes about because of a greater congruence of life styles and tastes between Joey and the younger family members. Their attachment to Joey also comes from the fact that he has sought their allegiance in a way which his father and uncles have not. All of the leading members of the family—Joe, Charley, Phil, and Joey—know that a network of supporters is crucial to anyone interested in gaining or maintaining power. Joey, however, is most successful in building that network because of his direct access to his father, which enables him to extend special help or favors to younger members. And so he establishes a reciprocity relationship with them in which his assistance is repaid by their loyalty.

Whether Joe is a confederate with his son in developing this new channel of communication which bypasses Charley and so strengthens both Joe and Joey we do not know. There is no question that he tacitly approves of it because it could not work without his knowledge, since the favors must come from him or at least be approved by him. Whether Charley and Phil are unaware of this (which seems unlikely) or whether they too have an understanding with Joey, we also do not know, but once again, the only visible opposition comes from Basil Alcamo:

> Joey is like a cute politician; he promises Freddy one thing and Tommy something else, and keeps them both happy. Sometime he's going to promise more than he can deliver, or he's going to promise the same thing to different people, and then watch out.

While these networks of power alliances are visible within the family, it is important to remember that they do not, as yet, create enough static in the normal system of power flow to generate tension or dysfunction. Rather they point to the effects of changing expectations and attitudes of family members. New power alliances are forming both within the family and between family members and the outside world. Rather than being based on kinship, these new alliances are based

146

Figure 2

POWER ALLIANCES IN THE LUPOLLO "FAMILY"

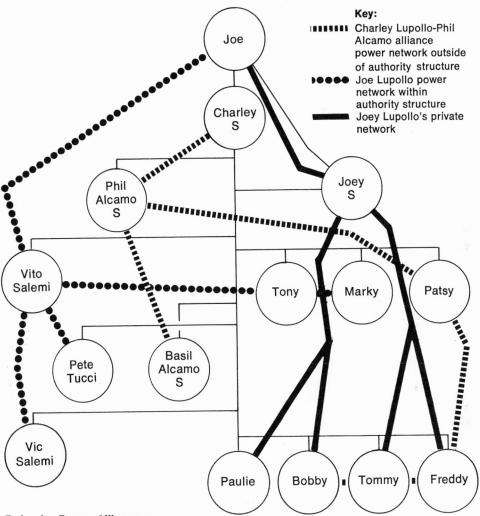

Rules for Power Alliances:

1. Kinship remains the most important basis for power alliances and forms the basis for legitimating power into authority.

2. In addition to blood and marriage ties, power alliances are formed through ritual kinship in the tradition of *compareggio* (godparenthood) which allies generations and lineages together as well as individuals.

3. While *consanquine*, affinal and ritual kinship are important bonds for the formation of power alliances, a system of reciprocal obligations within the family also operates to link individuals to each other and into power alliances.

4. Finally, where none of the above rules of alliance for power are compelling, mutuality of interests, friendships and self-interest also provide motivations for new alliances.

on associational ties and the "reciprocity of service and return service." Increasingly, these associational and reciprocal ties are with the power establishments of the larger society, and so those members of the family who relate to that society—especially Charley, Phil, and Joey—are enjoying new possibilities of power within the family.

The rules by which power alliances are established in the Lupollo family are demonstrated in Figure 2.

V. Prestige-Respect Rankings in the Lupollo "Family"

While lines of authority and alliances of power are beginning to conflict in the Lupollo family, there is a third type of ranking which differentiates members with some consistency. That ranking is one of "respect." As we noted earlier, respect in Italian and Italo-American culture is a major dimension of what is normally called "prestige" in studies of social stratification. In Italo-American society, *rispetto* is traditionally meted out as it is in Italy, according to age, kinship (generational membership), authority and power.[5]

Today, under the pressure of acculturation, the relative weight of these factors in ranking an individual is changing in Italo-American society. While age and kinship are still important factors, authority and particularly power are increasingly important and probably outweigh age and kinship. A successful young physician or politician earns as much *rispetto* among his fellow Italo-Americans as an older, less successful colleague and, among younger Italo-Americans at least, more respect than an older nonprofessional. It is not just how successful he is in his role but the relative importance of the role which wins respect.

In the Lupollo family, respect is expressed in many different ways. It is the basis for protocol in both business and social interaction, and it determines who will make decisions for a group, no matter how important or how insignificant the matter to be decided. It even establishes the relative social power of the wives whose husbands have more or less of it. At a family social gathering, positions at the table, service of food, and even who serves and who is waited upon, are signs of the respect accorded each man. In "business" matters, the right to initiate ideas and make suggestions is a function of how much respect an individual commands. Within the family, we found it to be the single most important dimension for differentiating members hierarchically.

Once we had noticed how important it was as a means of stratifying the family, we decided to assess systematically how it was allocated within the group and then, as always, to look for the rules which determine this allocation. About one-third of the way through the study, I began asking family members how much respect other members had within the group. Their responses are presented in Figure 3. I would have liked to have carried out this part of the study with

---

[5] Donald Cressey, *Theft of the Nation* (New York: Harper and Row, 1969), p. 229.

Figure 3
RESPECT RATINGS BY LUPOLLO "FAMILY" MEMBERS

	Rater														
Rated	Joe	Charley	Phil	Vito	Joey	Tony	Marky	Patsy	Pete	Vic	Basil	Bobby	Freddy	Paulie	Tommy
Joe		+	+	+	+	+	+	0	+	+	−	+	+	0	+
Charley	+		+	0	+	+	+	0	+	+	+	−	+	0	+
Phil	+	−		−	+	−	−	0	0	−	+	+	+	0	+
Vito	+	+	+		+	+	−	0	+	+	−	−	−	0	−
Joey	+	−	+	0		+	−	0	+	−	+	+	+	0	+
Tony	0	−	−	+	−		+	0	0	−	−	−	−	0	+
Marky	+	−	−	+	−	+		0	−	−	−	+	−	0	+
Patsy	−	+	−	0	−	+	−		−	−	−	−	+	0	+
Pete	+	−	−	+	−	−	−	0		−	−	−	−	0	−
Vic	+	+	+	+	+	+	−	0	+		−	+	−	0	−
Basil	−	+	+	−	+	+	−	0	+	+		+	+	0	+
Bobby	+	+	+	+	+	+	−	0	+	−	−		+	0	+
Freddy	0	+	−	+	+	−	+	0	+	−	+	+		0	−
Paulie	−	−	0	+	+	−	−	0	−	−	−	+	−		−
Tommy	+	+	−	−	+	+	−	0	−	−	−	−	−	0	

Key: + High − Low 0 Did not rate

149

greater precision, but the nature of the group I was studying and the field conditions simply did not allow it.

We had to be fairly arbitrary in ranking the responses. Thus "high" includes such responses as "a lot," "the most," and "more than X" (if X was rated low). I was also unable to get responses from two members of the family core group. I never felt close enough to Patsy Lupollo to ask the question, and Paulie Lupollo insisted that he "respected" everybody in the family equally. Despite these disclaimers, we think these data do allow for some beginning assessment of how prestige is allocated in the Lupollo family.

We also talked with seven people outside of the family: three first generation residents of the Brooklyn area where the family operates, a police officer from the same area, Nick Miraglia of the East Harlem De Maio family, Nunzio Passalaqua from a New Jersey family, and James Parone, who is Phil Alcamo's nephew. Here again the nature of the study made it impossible to use a consistent approach or any sorting technique so that the data from each respondent are only roughly comparable with those from others. Generally, however, there was congruence in the following ratings given by nonfamily members:

1. Joe Lupollo was rated highest by all respondents except James Parone, who rated him second.

2. Charley Lupollo was rated second highest by all respondents except James Parone, who rated him first.

3. Phil Alcamo was rated third highest by four respondents, fourth highest by two respondents and fifth highest by one respondent.

4. Joey Lupollo was rated fourth highest by four respondents, third highest by three respondents.

5. Patsy Lupollo was rated fifth highest by four respondents, third highest by one respondent (James Parone), not rated by two respondents.

6. Tony Lupollo was rated sixth highest by four respondents, fifth highest by two respondents, and not rated by one.

7. Marky Lupollo was rated seventh highest by three respondents, sixth highest by one respondent, and not rated by three.

8. Basil Alcamo was rated sixth highest by one respondent, seventh highest by two respondents, and not rated by four.

Remaining family members were either not rated, or were mentioned by only one respondent.

Considering both family and nonfamily sources of data three rules seem to emerge:

1. *Respect is highest where power and authority are linked in one person.* Not only does Joe Lupollo have the highest estimates of respect, but some of

150

the comments made by family members and others indicate that this respect is associated more with his position than with any personal attributes. A police officer we interviewed, for example, presented a less than impressive description of the respect commanded by Joe:

> I've seen him make a jackass out of himself a couple of times. Once when he was in Brooklyn to see one of his *paisans* buried he got his car stuck behind a big trailer truck and sent his chauffeur up to raise hell with the driver. The truck driver either didn't know or didn't give a shit about his being a big man and told the chauffeur to get off his back and he would move the truck as soon as he could. Joe got wild and had the chauffeur try to go around the truck and smashed hell out of his fender. Joe got out of the car and started raising hell with the chauffeur but didn't say beans to the truck driver. He treats the people who work for him like dirt but they're all afraid of him because he's boss and they respect that position.

In several of the interviews inside and outside the family, it was pointed out that old Giuseppe had the higheset respect of anyone in the family when he was alive because he had complete, unchallenged control over all aspects of the family's functioning. He was, in a phrase, a "man of respect" because he combined traditional authority with utilitarian power in a way which his successors can no longer manage.

2. *Where authority and power are not associated with the same role, the role with the highest power wins the most respect.* Thus within the family Phil Alcamo is rated as having more respect than Charley, despite the fact that Charley has more authority as second in command. In the interview materials, comments such as, "Phil knows Senator X," or, "Phil is connected in Washington," suggest that his access to national politics gives him greater power in the eyes of family members than is true of Charley. Outside the family, however, it seems that the traditional authority of Charley is viewed as giving him greater respect and so higher prestige.

3. *The more recent the generation, the higher respect given to power rather than authority.* The defections from Joe as the most respected are most consistent in the younger members of the family just as the highest respect is reserved for Phil and Charley and especially for Joey. It could be argued that at least some of the respect for Joey comes from his authority as heir apparent, but once again the comments made by these younger members indicate that it is his "connections" and ability to "get things done" which lead to his high ranking.

VI. Summary: Authority, Power and Respect—The Interplay of Control Systems

An important function of social structure is to provide everyone with a personal community within which he can interact with other members of that community with some certainty of reciprocity. Thus within a social system, each role is

151

connected with another or others in patterned ways which define how they interact with each other. In the Lupollo family we found three behavioral structures which relate roles to one another: the structure of authority roles, the network of alliances for power, and the ranking systems through which respect (prestige) is awarded to various roles and so to role players. The authority structure is based on the traditional, legitimated system of role relationships which fixes power in the head of the family. Old Giuseppe Lupollo named his son Joe as head of the business family as well as of the extended social family. The values of the southern Italian culture which still illuminate behavior in the family imply that Joe should have undisputed power in the group. But as the relationship between the family and the larger society changes, it is the utilitarian power of access to establishments in that society which define the new power centers in the family.

Joe's associations are with the Italo-American community while Charley and Phil, younger, better educated, and more "American," are connected in power establishments of the larger society. In this situation there is inevitably conflict between authority and power. In fact, this represents a value conflict in the family as well, because Joe's traditional coercive power comes from conservative, southern Italian, kinship-oriented, Mafia-like values, while the new power for Charley and Phil grows out of progressive, American, bureaucratic, efficiency-oriented values. Thus Joe's authority comes from the articulation of generations in a vertical structure based on kinship, while Charley and Phil are part of a horizontal contemporary set of power alliances which keeps them "tied in" with power establishments in the larger society. While this conflict is still fairly latent within the family, it is increasingly obvious and could be destructive to cohesion and control.

In the Lupollo family, the congruence between the vertical, kinship-oriented authority structure and the horizontal, utilitarian network of power alliances is the surest sign of group cohesion and control we have found. The rules regarding this congruence seem to be two: where there is integration of the authority and power roles, there is the high degree of cohesion and solidarity in the family; where there is no integration of authority and power roles, there is conflict.

The conflict generated by the growing separation of authority and power in the Lupollo family is leading to some new alliances of power. While Joe becomes more and more dependent on the power networks which Charley and Phil have created in American establishments, he senses his growing loss of power and so turns to Vito Salemi for support of his legitimate authority. Vito, who controls the illegal activities of the family, holds the balance of power for Joe, but only so long as the illegal activities continue to be profitable and so long as they represent a source of power. Joe and Vito thus depend for power on their associations in the Italo-American community and on alliances with other families in organized crime. Yet, as the family movement into legitimate business areas continues, the balance of power will shift more and more towards Charley and Phil and their associations in the larger society. And so a new factor is added to the power equation. Authority in the family is based on traditional values of kinship-oriented relationships within Italo-American culture and Italo-American syndicates in organized crime, while the new power grows out of utilitarian values associated with legitimate American power establishments.

Within the family, as within Italian and Italo-American culture, the social ranking of individual members is based upon the amount of respect accorded to their role in the family. Respect, which is one dimension of prestige, is highest when a role combines traditional authority with *utilitarian power,* but when the two are not joined it is power which commands the greater respect. In each new generation of the family there is even more respect awarded to power, and the younger members of the family look up to Charley and Phil because these members identify their own values and tastes with the life styles and power alliances which Charley and Phil have developed. Of all the family members, Joey Lupollo seems in the most secure position, for his role as heir apparent to the traditional authority of his father coincides with the power he enjoys from alliances with the younger members of the family and from his own contacts in power establishments. Today, he is a boundary runner, connecting the authority and power systems skillfully, and creating few obvious antagonisms by this balancing act. Unless there is some violent upheaval in the family from internal or external forces, his ascent to power and authority seem assured.

The effects of acculturation seem to have come very slowly to the Lupollo family and to its component lineages, but they can be seen increasingly today. Slowly but surely, the younger generations of Lupollos, Salemis, Tuccis, and Alcamos are disengaging themselves from the family business. In the fourth genera-tion, as we have seen, only four out of ten males are involved in the family organization. The movement of the younger generation into mainstream careers would seem to support the thesis that for Italo-Americans, as for other ethnic groups, organized crime has been a way station to ultimately respectable roles in American society. If the Lupollo family is a fair example, it is predictable that fewer and fewer young Italo-Americans will be recruited for membership in criminal syndicates in the future. Instead, like the Irish and the Jews before them, they will continue to advance into mainstream politics, professions, and corporate businesses. Only one obstacle would seem to stand in the way of this trend; with public interest in the infiltration of organized crime into business and politics at its height, it is possible that the younger generation of Italo-Americans will be penalized for the sins of some of their elders, and that the Mafia stigma will act, temporarily at least, as a brake on this natural movement.

THE ECONOMIC THEORY
OF THE CRIMINAL FIRM

Paul H. Rubin *

Economists have recently begun studying organized crime.[1] However, we do not yet know what factors determine which crimes will be organized. (We consider a crime to be "organized" if criminals in that line have some market power.) It is the contention of this paper that the traditional analysis of vertical integration can shed much light on this subject.

It is generally recognized that much criminal activity involves selling goods and services which people want to buy but which are illegal; it is not so generally recognized that much criminal activity involves provision of goods and services *to criminals;* that is, criminal firms which sell directly to the public may themselves need to buy some goods and services from other criminals.

Thus, the market for illegal activities can be divided into two parts: illegal goods and services provided to criminals, and illegal activities carried out with the public (noncriminals) as final consumers (or victims). We can identify three goods and services which criminals might use: capital, violence, and police inaction (achieved through bribery). In addition to these generalized goods, criminal enterprises may need specialized services. It is our argument that these items— capital, violence, nonenforcement, and specialized services—will be provided to criminals by organized crime, that is, by firms with some market power.

In any industry, some activities show increasing returns to scale, some constant returns, and some decreasing. As the industry expands, those functions which exhibit increasing returns will tend to be organized in separate firms, which will then sell to those firms which perform the constant or decreasing returns functions.[2] There will be fewer firms providing the increasing returns activities, so these will be

* The author would like to thank Professors Harold A. Cohen, Albert L. Danielsen, and Francis W. Rushing for helpful comments on an earlier draft of this paper. All remaining mistakes are the author's responsibility.

[1] Thomas C. Schelling, "Economic Analysis of Organized Crime," Appendix D in *Task Force Report: Organized Crime,* Annotations and Consultants' Papers, Task Force on Organized Crime, The President's Commission on Law Enforcement and the Administration of Justice (Washington, D. C.: Government Printing Office, 1967); hereafter cited as *Task Force Report.* Also, Simon Rottenberg, "The Clandestine Distribution of Heroin, Its Discovery and Suppression," *Journal of Political Economy,* January 1968, pp. 79-80.

[2] George Stigler, "The Division of Labor is Limited by the Extent of the Market," reprinted in *The Organization of Industry* (Homewood, Ill.: Richard D. Irwin, Inc., 1968).

more easily monopolized. It is argued that the activities mentioned above show increasing returns; these are the major items provided by organized crime.

There are three relevant sources of increasing returns: indivisibilities, internalization of externalities, and pooling of risks. As will be shown, risk pooling is the major source of increasing returns to capital (especially in gambling). Violence shows increasing returns because of indivisibilities (small operators may not be able to provide full-time employment to an enforcer); and, as Thomas C. Schelling has pointed out, centralized provision of violence may serve to internalize the external cost to all criminals of excessive violence. If there are increasing returns in nonenforcement, they are probably due to indivisibilities: an official bribed to ignore gambling will be more easily bribed to ignore prostitution as well.

Schelling agrees that organized crime earns its profits by dealing with other criminal firms, but he feels that these profits are earned by extortion.[3] I disagree. If there is a chain of vertically connected firms, a monopolist at any stage in the chain is able to appropriate for himself all of the profit in the industry;[4] therefore, a criminal monopoly can, by suitably pricing its services, obtain all of the profit in that activity. It need not rely on extortion or violence except as necessary to maintain its position as a monopoly.

In section I, we consider some illegal businesses dealing with the public, with particular reference to the degree to which these businesses use the services provided by organized crime. In section II we examine in more detail the role of organized crime, and in the last section we discuss the policy implications of the analysis.

I. Criminal Activities Dealing with the Public

We are primarily concerned with the extent to which this class of criminal activity requires the services mentioned above, and hence with the degree to which they are subject to organization. We consider in turn gambling, drugs, extortion and racketeering, loan sharking, and other crimes.

Gambling. Three main types of illegal gambling may be distinguished: betting on athletic events (including horse-racing), lotteries (mainly numbers), and casino-type operations (dice, roulette, et cetera). These have two requirements in common: a need for some way of collecting bets, and a need for some capital stock for reserves. They differ primarily in the actual method of collecting bets.

Bookmaking involves relatively few large bets, and does not require the physical presence of the bettor. For this type of betting, the telephone is a useful instrument. But one problem with using the telephone is that it may be difficult to

---

[3] Schelling, "Economic Analysis of Organized Crime," p. 119.

[4] Douglas Needham, *Economic Analysis and Industrial Structure* (New York: Holt, Rinehart, and Winston, 1969), p. 118.

collect debts incurred in this way. Lotteries involve many small bets collected before winners are selected; there is no collection problem. Casino operations require the actual presence of the bettors.

There are definite economies involved in telephone betting. One function or organization is the provision of a central clearing bureau for telephoned bets.[5] Numbers runners do not show the same sort of economies; each additional runner is merely a duplicated facility. There are economies in tabulating bets, calculating payoffs, and other accounting functions; hence, one accountant can serve several runners. There do not seem to be such economies involved in operating casino-type betting, except perhaps economies of information (that is, notifying potential customers of the location of the casino). Since casinos must be physically visited by the customer, risks are high, and unless police are bribed, these risks would seem to outweigh the benefits of such information. Thus, we would expect casino operations, such as "floating crap games," to be relatively small operations.

All types of gambling require rather large amounts of capital. A small operator can be wiped out by one or two large winners. Thus, proprietors of gambling operations require some sort of pooling of resources. This pooling is probably the major source of economies in gambling.

Pooling can be done in two ways. First, it is possible for small operators to "lay off" large bets with larger operators, that is, to place bets themselves with such large operators. Second, small operators can merge or become absorbed by large enterprises, and hence have a larger stock of capital for reserves. This usually requires payment of some proportion of profits to the large firm.[6]

Functionally, there does not seem to be much difference between the two methods. In one case, the small bookies are employees of the large organization, paid on a commission basis; in the other, they are independent contractors buying security (in the form of capital reserves) from the large firm. If gambling were legal, we would expect more vertical integration, for this would lead to lower transactions costs, but since gambling is illegal, the greater risks of detection lead to less integration and more lay-off betting.[7] Vertical integration would probably require more bookkeeping than an independent operation does, and this would lead to greater risks. Thus, unless police are adequately bribed, we would expect more independent operators than might be optimal.

---

[5] Daniel Bell, *The End of Ideology* (Glencoe, Ill.: Free Press, 1960), p. 124.

[6] It has been reported that in one case where the syndicate moved in and demanded 50 percent of the profits of bookie operations, profits actually increased for the independent operator, largely because of the additional capital provided by the syndicate. *Task Force Report,* p. 3, note 25.

[7] *Time* magazine reports that Ladbrookes, the largest bookmaker in England, operates 450 betting shops (*Time,* April 20, 1970, pp. 29-30); The New York State Commission on Investigations, in *Syndicated Gambling in New York State* (New York, 1961), p. 22, reports that bookies will employ 10 to 20 bet collectors.

In any type of gambling operation, if there are economics of scale, firms must balance extra profits from larger operations with increased costs and risks of capture. (Larger operators deal with more customers, and hence are operating as a greater risk; if they are caught, more money is confiscated and more bets are lost, so their costs are greater.) If demand for gambling is independent of enforcement effort, as seems plausible, we would expect that more rigorous enforcement would lead to formation of many small firms, and that less rigorous enforcement would result in fewer and larger firms in any given market.

Bookmakers also need certain specialized services. In horse-race betting, a wire service for quick information about race outcomes is needed. This can best be provided by one centralized firm; in fact, the original horse wire was provided by a firm entirely separate from organized crime. It was only later that organized crime took over the operation.[8] Numbers operators need some specialized documents which are provided by organized crime.[9]

Some gambling operations (especially those involving telephone betting) on occasion require violence for the collection of debts. A small criminal firm will have only occasional need of force; therefore, it will not pay for such firms to hire full-time specialists. Organized crime can serve as a provider of such force when needed.

It may also be worthwhile for gamblers to pay bribes. Bribes will be paid to the point where the marginal cost of the bribe is just equal to the (expected) marginal cost of arrest and conviction. As penalties for gambling become larger, bribes become more desirable strategies for criminals; hence, we would expect that larger penalties might actually be associated with lower arrest and conviction rates.

Drugs. There are many illegal drugs, and most are sold and distributed by small independent dealers. The only apparently organized drug market is that for heroin distribution, and this is organized primarily on the East Coast; in California, heroin is handled mostly by independents.[10]

Heroin distribution on the East Coast is the narcotics market which uses the most capital. Other drugs can be manufactured domestically or imported easily from Mexico. California heroin also seems to come from Mexico. Heroin in New York is imported from Europe. Because of the illegal nature of the traffic,

---

[8] Bell, *The End of Ideology*, p. 121.

[9] In a raid on an "independent" numbers bank in Detroit, it was found that the operators bought "dream books" and numbers pads from the Mafia. U.S. Congress, Senate, Committee on Government Operations, Permanent Subcommittee on Investigations, *Organized Crime and Illicit Traffic in Narcotics, Hearings Pursuant to Senate Resolution 17*, 88th Congress, 1st session, 1963, p. 412; hereafter cited as *Hearings*.

[10] John Storer, chief of the California State Bureau of Narcotics Enforcement, has testified: "In California we don't have a syndicate operation in the narcotic traffic. . . . Anyone who has an automobile and ambition to be a narcotic peddler can drive to Mexico and pick up narcotics. These people who peddle in California are private entrepreneurs." Ibid., p. 745.

purchase arrangements are usually made by dealers through personal visits. This practice increases the costs of the transactions and as a result large shipments are imported. Because of the unenforceability of illegal contracts, payment is usually made with or before delivery. Since relatively large amounts of capital are required, it appears that organized crime is involved primarily in the provision of this capital at interest rates high enough to appropriate a large share of the profits.[11]

The main reason for having a large operation in gambling, which involves great risk is to provide for a big enough operation to spread the risk. This would be true even if gambling were legal. In the distribution of heroin, the advantage of large size is mainly artificial; there is no reason to believe that heroin would be provided by monopolistic firms if it were legal. If we want to reduce the degree of organization in heroin distribution (as opposed to the amount of heroin imported), there are some policy measures which can be taken. In particular, the way to reduce organization would be to reduce capital requirements. The way to do this would be to reduce the optimal size of each shipment. The average cost (AC) per pound of imported heroin can be expressed as:

$$AC = \frac{T + Aq + p(F + Aq) + r(Aq)}{q},$$

where T = transactions cost, A = price per pound of heroin in Europe, q = number of pounds in the shipment, p = probability of capture, F = cost to the criminal of penalties (that is, jail) if he is caught, and r = interest rate on illegal funds. (The confiscation of heroin if the smuggler is caught is included in the equation.)

The variables which society (that is, the narcotics agents) controls are p and F. If it is desired to reduce the average shipment, we need only make F, the penalty, an increasing quadratic function of q. This will then make smaller shipments cheaper in relation to large shipments, and thus reduce the need for capital and the dependence on organized crime. (Of course, to do this would require lowering some penalties, and this might as a consequence increase the amount of heroin imported; less *organized* crime is not the same as less crime. This point will be discussed again in section III.)

As to the other services provided by organized crime, narcotics selling does not seem to require violence. If criminals have bribed police and other officials, it is likely that narcotics, because of public disapproval of them, might actually inhibit external *diseconomies:* Police are less likely to accept a bribe from a bookie if he is also a narcotics peddler.[12] Therefore, the only organized service required by narcotics sellers would seem to be capital.

---

[11] The informer Joseph Valachi was involved in narcotics importing, but primarily in the role of financier; he in turn borrowed from his superiors in the Cosa Nostra. Ibid., pp. 630-640.

[12] Valachi reported that Cosa Nostra members were ordered not to engage in narcotics smuggling. (This ban was, however, ineffective.) The order may have originated in external costs of having criminals engage in this crime. Ibid., p. 317.

Extortion and Racketeering. Let us consider the case of a criminal who attempts to extort money from a legitimate business, as in the selling of "protection." How much profit can the criminal make?

Assume first that the potential victim is in a competitive industry. If the criminal can extort money from all firms in the industry, the extortion is equivalent to a tax. The purpose of the tax is to maximize revenue for the criminal. In this case, the extorter would set industry marginal revenue equal to supply, and determine industry price from the demand curve. In other words, the industry price would be the monopoly price. He would then charge a lump sum tax equal to the monopoly profit in the industry.

If the extorting firm decided to monopolize some service (say, linen rental to bars) and sell this service to the victims, the analysis would be the same: He would charge the bars such a price for the service that they would charge customers the monopoly price. The criminal firm would then gain the difference between the competitive price and the monopoly price.

Note that this will be profitable for a criminal firm only if it can extort money from all firms in the industry. If it extorts money from only one competitive firm, that firm will cease operations. In Sicily, and in this country earlier in our history, the Mafia evidently was able to make money by extortion. But today, with the increasing mobility of consumers because of the automobile, it is more difficult to succeed in extorting money from all firms in a market. Therefore, this type of crime now seems to be less prevalent than it was in the past.

There is one exception to the above statement: If all firms in the industry already deal with some monopoly, and if the criminal can gain control of this monopoly, then he can make large profits. This is why much racketeering seems to involve labor unions. A union is a government-sanctioned monopoly, and hence all firms in the industry must deal with this monopoly.

If the potential victims of extortion have some monopoly power, then it is possible for a criminal firm, by extortion, to divert to itself some of the profits, even without extorting money from all firms in the industry. This would explain the fact that currently the chief victims of extortion seem to be establishments serving liquor. State licensing of liquor establishments (and the concurrent limitation of their number) leads to monopoly profits in the liquor industry, and hence the possibility of profitable extortion.

In terms of the services provided by organized crime, extortion does not need capital, and it is an industry which would exhibit external diseconomies to bribery. It does rely on violence, but protection gangs would seem to be able to give full-time employment to specialists in violence. Therefore, while extortion itself must be organized to function, it need not be connected with other lines of criminal behavior, and it does not appear to be so connected.

160

Usury. Loan sharking depends on organized crime for capital—both initial working capital and bad debt reserves. Apparently, many of the customers of loan sharks are other members of the underworld, for example, bookies who have been hit for large winnings and need working capital.[13] It is thus at least in part through loan sharking that organized crime diverts profits of other criminal firms to itself.

To the extent that customers of usurers are other criminals, figures on profits from these operations overstate profits in crime, for profits would be counted twice: If a bookie makes $100, but must use $50 to pay off an illegal debt, then the profit to organized crime is only $100; the $50 paid to the usurer is organized crime's cut of the bookie's profit.

It is sometimes reported that the underworld becomes involved in legitimate businesses by foreclosing on them when they are unable to pay off debts to usurers. These businesses sometimes go bankrupt.[14] This is not surprising, for the advantage of owning a business which was forced to borrow at 200 percent interest from a loan shark is not immediately obvious.

Loan sharking is connected with other organized crime primarily through its reliance on capital. It might also need violence on occasion. Because of the nature of the transactions involved, it does not seem likely that this operation would have much use for bribery.

Other Criminal Enterprises. The crimes mentioned above are the main areas in which organized crime operates today. This is not to say that criminals who are members of organized gangs do not participate in other crimes, but they are participating as individuals, rather than as members of monopolistic organizations.

At one time, alcohol was the major source of revenue to criminals, but this is no longer so. It is so easy for anyone to engage in bootlegging that it does not pay for organized crime to become involved. It would not be able to enforce a monopoly position. (In fact, bootlegging does not appear to require any of the services mentioned above, which might imply that it cannot be monopolized. This may be why, even during Prohibition, it was not successfully monopolized. The gang wars of this era could thus be explained by this failure in monopolization. The lack of such wars today is probably due to the ability of existing syndicates to bar entry into activities in which they engage; this will be discussed in section II below.)

Prostitution seems to be relatively unorganized.[15] Again, there does not seem to be any easy way for organized crime to monopolize this activity; hence, monopoly profits would be impossible. After Prohibition's repeal, organized crime

---

[13] Valachi reports that he loaned money to bookies, among other customers, and he himself borrowed from other loan sharks. Ibid., pp. 267-268.

[14] Ibid., p. 265.

[15] ". . . as an *organized* business, . . . prostitution has disappeared from American life." Bell, *The End of Ideology*, p. 151. (Italics in original.)

apparently became involved in prostitution, for reasons which we will discuss below, but they seem to have since left it.

II. The Nature of Organized Crime

We have argued that what is called "organized crime" is essentially a criminal firm whose function is the selling of goods and services to other criminal firms. It is these secondary firms which actually deal with the public. We have identified three possible services which organized crime might provide to other crime: capital, bribery, and violence. It appears that capital is currently the most important of these services, for in our discussion of particular crimes, it became apparent that those usually thought of as organized (gambling, loan sharking and parts of the drug trade) required large amounts of capital. Criminal activities which did not require such capital (for example, prostitution, racketeering, other parts of the narcotics trade) are less organized.

We must now consider the use of violence by criminal firms. Violence is used essentially for the maintenance of monopoly power, that is, for the prevention of entry. Entry is not prevented into the "retail" end of criminal activities; anyone who so desires can set up his own handbook. Rather, entry is prevented into the wholesale side of the business. If someone attempted to set up a wire service for bookies, or a lay-off betting operation, they would undoubtedly be stopped.

Restriction of entry at levels removed from ultimate consumers is much easier than restriction of entry at lower levels. There are economies of scale at higher levels, so that the optimal number of, say, lay-off bookies might only be two or three. As we have mentioned above, it is possible for a monopoly at any stage to appropriate for itself all of the profits in the business; hence, by monopolizing capital, for example, the criminal firm can make as much profit as if it ran all bookie parlors.

This view of organized crime can be used to shed light on some areas which are not fully understood. For example, the geographic scope of the syndicate is an open question. Some authorities feel that the American organization is merely a branch of the Sicilian Mafia,[16] some believe that all American crime is controlled by one organization,[17] and still others feel that most crime is controlled locally.[18] If criminals are rational profit maximizers (as we have been assuming), then there

---

[16] In his testimony, George Edwards, police commissioner for Detroit, speaks of ". . . a conspiracy nationally and internationally organized . . ." and of ". . . a small group of families of Sicilian extraction." *Hearings,* p. 399.

[17] Donald Cressey asserts that "in the United States, criminals have managed to organize a nationwide illicit cartel and confederation." See "The Functions and Structure of Criminal Syndicates," Appendix A to *Task Force Report,* p. 25.

[18] J. Edgar Hoover, writing in the January 1962 *Law Enforcement Bulletin,* said, "No single individual or coalition of racketeers dominates organized crime across the nation. There are, however, loose connections among controlling groups in various areas. . . ." Quoted in Earl Johnson, "Organized Crime: Challenge to the American Legal System," *Journal of Criminal Law, Criminology, and Police Science,* vol. 53, no. 4 (December 1962), p. 400.

would be no more organization than would be economically desirable: Drug traffic requires some international connections; certain aspects of gambling require national information services and perhaps national pools of capital. Other than this, there does not seem to be any particular need for national coordination, and even those functions which do require national coordination can be handled by market relationships among local organizations. Therefore, it is at least plausible to argue that there is relatively little national or international coordination.

Joseph Valachi, a well-known informer, reported that "the books were closed" from 1931 to 1954.[19] That is, the organization of which he was a member did not take in any new members in this period. This organization apparently consolidated its power, that is, set itself up as a monopoly, in the thirties. Once this was done, the syndicate had little need of manpower. In fact, Valachi himself seems to have had relatively little to do for the organization after the thirties. A large number of persons would have been needed to establish a monopoly, but fewer would be needed to run it once it was organized. (Valachi seems to have benefited some from the organization when he was doing nothing for it. It was apparently willing to pay to have some men available if another challenge arose.)

The question we have so far asked about organized crime could have been asked, with slight modification, about noncriminal firms. There are two aspects of crime, however, which differ radically from lawful enterprise: criminal firms must avoid detection, and they cannot use the courts to enforce contracts. Many aspects of criminal behavior which are obscure in conventional analysis can be understood once we introduce these problems.

Let us first consider the need for secrecy. We shall use heroin distribution as an example. Rottenberg has pointed out some of the implications of secrecy in this activity: first, the length of the system may be longer than that indicated by efficiency criteria, and second, prices at each stage will be determined by relative risk of apprehension at that point.[20]

Rottenberg's analysis is based on the assumption of a monopolistic importer selling through a chain of intermediaries to the final consumer. He is not sure if the successive levels are themselves complementary monopolists, employees of the original monopolist, or competitive firms. Our analysis indicates that *all* dealers in narcotics are in fact competitive firms. The only monopolist involved is the supplier of the capital, and as such the monopolist is able to make large profits while reducing greatly his risk of detection. Police are concerned with buyers and sellers of narcotics. They seem less concerned with who lends money for such purchases and sales.

The length of the chain of buyers and sellers is thus not determined by the "organizer" of the enterprise, as Rottenberg indicates. Rather, market forces will

---

[19] *Hearings,* p. 239.
[20] Rottenberg, *Clandestine Distribution of Heroin,* pp. 79-80.

determine the number of stages and the profit at each stage. Consider a particular criminal who has a certain stock of heroin to sell. (We do not care if he obtained this heroin by direct importation or by purchase from the importer.) If he has one kilogram, he can presumably split this into lots of various sizes and sell these. If he sells in smaller lots, he makes higher profits, but risks of apprehension increase as the number of transactions increases. Thus, the dealer would need to balance *for himself* the increased revenue against increased risks. The number of links in the chain would vary with the preferences of particular individuals; for example, one wholesaler might sell in lots of ¼-kilogram for a total of $32,000, while another might sell the entire kilogram for $18,000.[21]

We can predict that as we move closer to the final consumer, sellers will have less fear of apprehension or stronger preferences for money. Thus, lower-level dealers are likely to be young persons with shorter criminal records and correspondingly lower sentences if convicted. Less experienced criminals, moreover, would have less opportunity cost than more highly trained criminals, and it is known that many or most sellers to final consumers are themselves addicts, with a correspondingly high desire for money.

This same analysis can be applied to loan sharking and gambling, the other two main activities of organized crime. In each case, we would expect different patterns of integration from one firm to another depending on the risk preferences of the individuals involved, and in each case, we would expect younger, less experienced criminals at lower levels.

The need for secrecy combines with the lack of enforceable contracts to influence the labor market for criminals. Criminals must trust each other to a much greater extent than ordinary businessmen, both to carry out agreements and not to talk. This explains the seemingly irrational reliance on family relationships,[22] past history, and so forth. It can also explain some other aspects of criminal behavior.

All businesses have some value as a "going concern" which is greater than the market value of their assets. A good part of this value is due to the mutual experience which employees have within the organization.[23] It is this value which is responsible for much diversification of firms.

Criminal firms would also have such a going concern value, but this would be relatively greater for criminal firms than for other firms because of the additional value created by trust. Thus, if one activity is removed from the criminal firm, we

[21] The price figures are from *Hearings,* p. 753. It is reported that a kilogram of heroin sells for $18,000 in New York; by the time it is adulterated and sold, it may bring $225,000.

[22] We find intermarriage between families of high-level members of the Mafia mentioned in several places. See, for example, Gus Tyler, *Organized Crime in America* (Ann Arbor, Mich.: University of Michigan Press, 1962), pp. 29-30. This would also explain the emphasis within criminal organizations on "respect," that is, strong status-based relationships.

[23] Paul H. Rubin, "The Expansion of Firms," *Journal of Political Economy,* vol. 81, no. 41 (July 1973), forthcoming, has a discussion of this point.

would expect the firm to seek vigorously other activities, which might not be sufficiently profitable to warrant organizing a firm. This would explain the entry of organized crime into prostitution and into some forms of labor racketeering after Prohibition's repeal,[24] and this would also explain the current diversification of criminal firms.

III. Policy Implications

In discussing policy towards organized crime, we must determine what we want to do. Do we want to reduce the amount of *organization* or the amount of *crime*? As Schelling has pointed out, these goals are not the same. It is possible, in fact, that more organization will actually lead to less crime. For example, organization can lead to the internalization of the costs of violence, so that organization may lead to *less* violence.[25] In what follows, we shall attempt to point out the implications of various policy recommendations on both the amount of organization and on the amount of crime.[26]

Our basic premise is that crime becomes organized, or monopolized, when there is some service which all criminal firms in a particular activity need and which can be monopolized. In most operations, entry at the retail end is too easy for efficient monopolization to occur; attempts to reduce the amount of organization in criminal activities should, therefore, focus on monopolized services. Apparently, the most important service required by criminal firms is capital. Anything which reduces the use of capital in production of a particular illegal good will tend to reduce the market power of providers of that good, and hence reduce the amount of "organization."

We have already pointed out the implications of this for heroin importation: that is, a sliding scale of penalties would reduce the optimal shipment size and thus the need for capital. On the other hand, policies aimed at decreasing the amount of drugs available from Mexico would tend to increase the costs of transactions (since European supplies would be substituted) and so increase the optimal shipment size and the role of organized crime.

There do not seem to be any comparable policies involving gambling. Here, large scale enterprise is due, at least partially, to economies which exist independently of the illegality of the enterprise. Part of the advantage from organization in horse-race betting comes from the wire service. It would be possible for radio stations to broadcast race results (as is done in Canada), and thus reduce the

---

[24] Tyler, among others, refers to the search for new activities after repeal. See his *Organized Crime*, p. 152.

[25] Schelling, "Economic Analysis of Organized Crime," p. 122.

[26] The recommendations listed here are based on society's value judgments as reflected in current laws; they do not reflect the author's belief about which activities should or should not be illegal.

dependence of small operators on the race wire. This might well serve to increase the number of such independent operators, and they would still be forced to rely on organized crime for capital pools. It is at least possible, though, that there would be more syndicates supplying capital in these circumstances than there are now.

Usury obviously needs capital. Moreover, this activity would tend to persist as an illegal activity even if anti-usury laws were repealed. This is because so many of the customers of loan sharks are themselves engaged in illegal operations, and thus need illegal funds.

There is one final recommendation which we can make. Police seem to concentrate on finding providers of illegal goods and services. At the same time they lament their inability to convict criminals who are known to be high in the organized crime hierarchy. If our analysis is correct, this is not surprising, for these criminals do not commit the crimes which the police attempt to solve. If the police searched for the financiers of illegal transactions, rather than for the parties to the transaction, they might have more success in convicting leaders of organized crime. A fruitful area for lawyers and law enforcement agencies to explore might be the applicability of conspiracy or accessory statutes to the financing of criminal activities.

COMMENTS ON THE
PAPERS IN SEMINAR

Annelise Anderson

Professor Buchanan has demonstrated in his paper that monopoly in criminal enterprises can have the effect of reducing output in the particular criminal industry or activity that is monopolized, and therefore also can reduce the resources used in the production of criminal output and in law enforcement.

Professor Rubin has explored the sources of monopoly or market power in certain criminal industries, specifically the supply of certain goods and services to criminals at the retail level; he has noted that reducing the amount of crime is not the same thing as reducing the amount of organization. Rubin has also acknowledged agreement with Thomas Schelling that organized crime is in the business of providing goods and services to other criminals, but he disagrees with Schelling's hypothesis that this organized criminal activity is extortionate.[1]

Professor Ianni has approached the question of organized crime from the viewpoint of a discipline other than economics, and in so doing he has challenged the view that the Italian organized criminal groups with which we are familiar through the media are formal organizations comparable, for example, to corporations or business firms.

Because the subject of the economic organization of criminal enterprise is a broad one, I have chosen to limit my remarks to what is conventionally viewed as organized crime—the large criminal organizations involved in the supply of illegal goods and services, specifically gambling and loan sharking, to voluntary consumers. I would like to explore further some of the ideas in Professor Rubin's paper for the purpose of suggesting that the market power of criminal organizations in gambling and loan sharking would not exist if these goods and services were legal, that the existence of market power is based on criminal activity beyond the sale of illegal goods and services to voluntary consumers, and that the quantity of crime that is reduced through this market power is therefore only one factor, and probably not the most important one, to be considered in evaluating alternative public policies with respect to organized crime.

Before discussing the papers, I would like to explain my own research on organized crime. In connection with my doctoral dissertation, I have studied in

---

[1] See Thomas C. Schelling, "What is the Business of Organized Crime?" *The American Scholar,* vol. 40, no. 4 (Autumn 1971), pp. 643-652.

depth the activities of one organized criminal group operating in one of the 20 largest cities in the United States. With the assistance of government agencies, I collected information on both the illegal and legitimate activities of all members of this group and some of their close associates. The group is one of the 24 or so Italian organized criminal groups considered by the federal government to be "the core of organized crime in the United States." [2]

This group's main illegal market activities are numbers gambling and loan sharking. The group controls entry into numbers gambling in one section of the city, both the entry of its own members and the entry of independents. Thus there are several firms in the numbers business, some owned and operated by members and a few by independents. Several leaders of the group own a numbers lay-off operation, the services of which are used on a voluntary basis by member firms and independents in other parts of the city as well as in the section controlled by the group. Member-operated retail numbers firms also provide lay-off services to some smaller firms. Bribery appears to be handled centrally, even with respect to local police, for which the member firms and independents may pay a percentage of total amounts bet.

The group also has within it several loan shark firms, some of which are also in the numbers business. There is no indication that entry of members into loan sharking is limited. Some loan sharks lend their own funds and also handle, for a percentage, the funds of one or more other members of the group. Although quoted interest rates suggest an absence of competition, it is also possible that rates are negotiable and that rates actually paid are lower than those negotiated because of failures to pay in full.

Although most of the loan shark firms do their own collecting, several members of the group and their associates are known as strong-arm men. Law enforcement officials familiar with the group claim that the group's enforcers provide enforcement services to all loan sharks in the city. Those members who finance loan sharking may employ salesmen or arrange for another loan shark to handle their funds, but they nevertheless approve all "large" loans, which sometimes means all loans larger than a few hundred dollars. There is a loose network for checking out potential borrowers with other members of the group and other organized criminal groups in the city and elsewhere.

Members of the group also operate occasional casino-type gambling enterprises—card and dice games—that operate for short periods of time, that is, from a few days to several months. Within its section of the city, the group can apparently control entry of independents as well as its own members into casino

---

[2] *Task Force Report: Organized Crime,* publication of The President's Commission on Law Enforcement and the Administration of Justice (Washington, D. C.: Government Printing Office, 1967), p. 6.

gambling. From independents, it may require a percentage of profits and employment of its own members as conditions for operation.

This brief descriptive summary of the illegal market activities of this group shows that the group, through its top members, does provide goods and services—capital, corruption, violence, the evaluation of credit risks—to criminals in retail markets. However, it provides these goods and services primarily to its own members, who are the retailers dealing with the public. Management decisions and many day-to-day operating decisions are made by members of the group who own and operate the individual numbers and loan sharking firms. There is no indication that the leadership of the group, which handles corruption, the numbers layoff, and the use of violence, is extorting from members of the group in return for these services.

The group is not involved in bookmaking or betting on sports to any great extent. This is the industry Thomas Schelling uses as an example in developing his hypothesis that organized crime is in the business of extorting from criminals at the retail level.[3] For the particular organized criminal group that I have studied, there appears to be no extortion of member retail firms in loan sharking and the numbers business.

I would now like to comment further on those goods and services that Professor Rubin has suggested are provided by organized crime to criminals at the retail level.

The first of these is violence. Since an organized criminal group is characterized by some relationship to the provision of illegal goods and services, it does not have available to it the services provided to legitimate business by government: legislation such as the Uniform Commercial Code to define relationships among different parties, the courts to adjudicate disputes, and the executive power to enforce the outcome of the decision process. It must provide its own rules and enforce them. Violence, or the fear of violence that results from its occasional use, therefore appears to be a necessary characteristic of organized crime.

Professor Rubin has suggested that organized crime provides violence because of economies of scale, specifically because small operators in illegal markets cannot provide full-time employment to an enforcer. I think it is unlikely, however, that organized crime possesses its market power because of economies of scale in violence. The widespread capability for violence and willingness to use violence coupled with the absence of any economies of scale in the performance of the service itself suggest that providing full-time employment should be unnecessary.

What is likely, however, is that there are economies of scale not in providing the service but in establishing a reputation for effectiveness. Economies of scale in establishing a reputation for violence is consistent, like Rubin's hypothesis, with the provision of enforcement services to outsiders. The organized criminal group

---

[3] Schelling, "Business of Organized Crime."

which I have studied has several members and close associates who provide enforcement services not only to member firms but also to outsiders. None of these enforcers however is engaged more than occasionally in enforcing.

The second activity Rubin identifies as a decreasing cost activity is that of corruption, because of indivisibilities—that is, an official bribed to overlook one criminal activity may be easily bribed to overlook others. Economies of scale in corruption may well be more important in the establishment and maintenance of organized criminal groups with market power than this comment implies. Some economies of scale in corruption arise from the complexities in the criminal justice system—police, courts, and corrections. These complexities are of two types: overlapping jurisdiction, and the existence of stages in the criminal justice system—arrest, indictment, prosecution, conviction, sentencing, parole. The result is that there are a great many individuals or organizations who present a danger to the criminals, and a great many levels at which such individuals or organizations can intervene to subvert the process of criminal justice. Thus effective protection from law enforcement requires a considerable investment of funds as well as extensive opportunity for carrying out the process of corruption. These are resources not available to the small entrepreneur in illegal markets, and even if they were available, the small operator is unlikely to have sufficient need for the resulting potential services to make the investment worthwhile.

Corruption itself is, of course, illegal for both the corruptor and the corruptee. The risk of getting caught, and the transaction costs, can be reduced through centralized management of corruption by the organized criminal group and through centralized management of corruption by law enforcement units that are corrupted, such as a local police precinct or a gambling squad. This centralization also probably improves the effectiveness of corruption, as individual policemen are not faced with the problem of trying to protect different operators.

The corrupt unit—a gambling squad or a judge—is not a monopolist with regard to enforcement of the law; yet, because of overlapping jurisdictions, it will be a monopolist with respect to nonenforcement, since the nonenforcement provided by that particular unit cannot be purchased elsewhere, and since the unit retains its enforcement potential. The unit is then in a position where it might, by properly pricing its services, appropriate any existing monopoly profits in the industry. Increased public pressure for law enforcement action may provide a justification for raising prices, whether or not these increased pressures increase the risk to the police of providing nonenforcement. If the seller of the services to the public is a monopolist, the increased costs may be passed along to the consumer through higher prices, with some loss, of course, in volume of business. The complete appropriation of monopoly profits is possible only in the unlikely event that the police know how to price their services. There is, instead, usually a bilateral trade situation with a range of possible prices between the maximum the criminals will

170

pay and the minimum the police will accept. The same situation is likely to be the case at higher levels of the criminal justice system.

Although violence rather than the use of a corrupt police force has historically been the means by which competing organized criminal groups or firms have resolved their disputes, corruption may be a means of perpetuating monopoly power once it is established. The police must produce some arrests, but the number and spectacular character of these may be a function of public demand. These arrests will come from those without police protection or they will be arranged by the corrupting group; thus corruption provides the means of using the police, either directly or through their concentration on the remaining potential arrestees, as a method for controlling the entry of independents into an illegal market.

As Professor Rubin has pointed out, there are economies of scale in providing capital for gambling through the pooling of risks. However, in numbers gambling and casino-type gambling, these economies are apparently not so great as to allow for only one firm in a given market area. Most large cities have several financially independent numbers operations large enough not to need lay-off services. As I have mentioned, the group I have studied has one large lay-off firm, but other large retail firms are also able to provide lay-off services.

Another activity that may show increasing returns to scale—this time from economies in the gathering and disseminating of information—is that of evaluating credit risks. This may be as true in the underworld as it is elsewhere. Thus one service an organized criminal group may perform, in conjunction with other organized criminal groups, is to provide information on potential borrowers, especially those, such as gamblers, who may have other illegal loans outstanding.

In summary, market power in retail illegal markets such as loan sharking, bookmaking, the numbers racket, and casino-type gambling seems to arise not from economies of scale in retail markets but from the provision of services needed by firms in retail markets. Some of these services are needed because of the illegality of the retail markets and, like violence and corruption, they involve further crimes.

The question whether monopoly prices in retail markets, with their attendant reduction in output, are desirable must therefore be answered not only with reference to the amount of crime in terms of output of the illegal good or service, but also with reference to the crimes committed in the establishment and maintenance of monopoly power in such markets—crimes that may be far more serious than voluntary, but illegal, market transactions.

Thomas R. Ireland

The primary disadvantage of the presentations by Professors Buchanan and Rubin is that both approach organized crime from a purely economic standpoint. Both conceived the criminal firm as a predominantly profit-maximizing enterprise similar to an economic enterprise. While this concept is partly true, it is also partly misleading.

The contrast presented by Professor Ianni is striking. While he confines himself to Italo-American organized crime, the "organization" of organized crime is seen more as a social system, with economic elements submerged in the background. Between the Buchanan and Rubin papers and the Ianni paper, there is an obvious gap of disciplines. Each offers much, but all three are in an important sense myopic. None of them really handles the political organization of organized crime. Ianni comes closest, but his approach is too specific for a general application. My comments here will be devoted to the Buchanan and Rubin papers.

The organization of organized crime is in many respects more political than economic. There is not a pyramidal decision-making apparatus, but rather a coalition of like, but not identical, interested parties who cooperate more as elements within a political party than as parts of the corporate structure of an American firm.[1] In a sense, organized crime is a hybrid form of organization which combines elements of an economic enterprise with elements of a political party structure, especially of the variety found in one-party dictatorial states.

Government is traditionally defined as "the monopoly of force within a given area." This classic definition is very seldom realized in practice because of the multi-level nature of governmental structures, but since the jurisdictions of "legitimate" governments normally determine power priorities among governments without major conflict (with notable exceptions), this definition is deemed generally operational. For most purposes, this definition is conceptually inadequate because no government or hierarchical set of governments has ever had such a monopoly. There have always been alternative pockets of force within any society and these must at least be called quasi-governments. In purpose and practice, organized crime holds *some* of the force within its given area of operations. In this respect, organized crime is truly a subsidiary government designed to provide certain goods that are "public" to those who come under its governance. It is a government "of criminals, by criminals and for criminals," albeit not on an equalitarian basis.

Organized crime as a government is instrumental in creating a market structure for illegal goods and services in which "charters of privilege" are routinely issued to citizens who are more equal than others. It is only in this latter capacity that Professor Buchanan analyzes the socioeconomic implications of organized crime. When both the political and economic aspects of organized crime are taken into account, the analyses made by both Buchanan and Rubin must be altered. This, however, does no great damage to the conclusions of either paper. Accounting for political as well as economic factors in organized crime strengthens

---

[1] See my "The Structure of Political Party Organization," *Business and Society,* vol. 2, no. 2 (1971).

Buchanan's intellectual defense of organized crime and puts into a common framework some of the loose pieces in Rubin's paper.

Professor Rubin hints at the basic political framework of organized crime early in his paper with his observation that "centralized provision of violence may serve to internalize the external cost to all criminals of excessive violence." More accurately, the point he is driving at is that disorganized crime has the disadvantage of imposing too much of the costs of crime on criminals themselves. Criminals, of course, exist by violating some of the laws of noncriminal society; for that reason they cannot turn to the policing mechanisms of organized society. This makes criminals especially vulnerable to the depredations of their fellows. When their ill-gotten gains are stolen from them or their contracts violated, they cannot turn to the legitimate police authorities for protection or recovery—at least not in most cases.

Most criminals do not favor anarchy nor even an overthrow of the established government of legitimate society. Anyone who has seen the movie of Truman Capote's *In Cold Blood* can hardly fail to be impressed by the fact that most of the men on death row in that movie actually favored capital punishment as a way of keeping down murders in society as a whole. They, of course, did not want to be executed, but felt that they had been accidentally caught in a system whose rules were rational enough for the purposes intended. Whether they were right in their assumptions about the deterrent value of the death penalty is not at issue. The example, however, is the clearest possible indication of the disposition of many criminals toward social order. Even the Cosa Nostra is by reputation politically conservative. The advantages of crime derive from breaking some of the rules of society to one's own benefit, not from the destruction of social order itself.

Because the normal apparatus for the maintenance of social order does not provide for an orderly disposition of illegally obtained economic benefits from crime, criminals face a void in the political system. Organized crime exists to fill this void by providing order for the criminal industries. For criminals, it provides a decision-making process that is more certain than the anarchy of disorganized crime. That is the public good referred to earlier.

That it is not a democratic system of government is not surprising. From a normative bias, the noncriminal observer in a democratic society is likely to expect no better than a totalitarian form of government from professional criminals. But it is also worth noting that the costs of democratic procedure become extremely high for criminal society. A confiscated list of registered criminal voters would be a disaster for the profession. That some individuals are killed in competition for power is common to the form of government actually selected.

The advantages of some amount of order among criminals are not confined to criminals alone. One cannot challenge on economic grounds Buchanan's basic argument that organized crime as a monopoly results in restricted output of criminal activity. As a political instrument, it also provides some amount of order in the delivery of criminal "bads." In this sense, the honest citizen, if there is such a creature, is a resource to the potential criminal, both in the cases of "victimless crimes" and "crimes with victims." In a disorganized crime situation, the honest citizen as a resource is a free good and not subject to conservation by the average criminal with whom he comes into contact. This means that the criminal will not limit his "take" and may even beat or kill his victim.

But where crime is organized, the victim may be seen as a long-term producer of income for the organization. A rational and monopolistic criminal organization looks upon its victims as long-term sources of revenue rather than a one-time benefit source. This will lead to a greater consideration of the basic needs of the victim and to less purely destructive behavior. It will also lead to more certainty in the costs of crime, in that organized crime will extract benefits from the public more as a predictable tax than as an unpredictable catastrophe. Extortion and shark loans are preferred by organized criminals to burglaries, and even in the case of burglaries, organized crime deals with efficient house men and not homicidal maniacs. Efficient house men do not randomly destroy what they do not take, nor do they take things of little value in criminal resale markets, such as clothing, which may have great replacement cost to victims.

One even finds that the policing personnel of organized crime cooperate occasionally with legitimate policing authorities to eliminate randomly destructive, disorganized criminals. The purpose of both policing mechanisms is to provide order because order has value to the members of the unit it governs.

In this respect, Buchanan understates his own argument. He says organized crime is to be preferred to the disorganized variety because it restricts output in order to extract a monopoly profit. But organized crime can also be said to be preferable because organization leads to a more certain cost of crime, and one less randomly destructive. The political-economic rather than purely economic model of organized crime, then, complements rather than contradicts the Buchanan paper.

This same model provides a broader framework within which Professor Rubin's basic distinctions among markets for criminal services must be somewhat revised. Rubin conceives of organized crime as an intermediary which supplies services to independent criminal firms. Characterizing organized crime in this fashion is no more accurate than it would be to characterize a political party as an intermediary which supplies services to political office seekers. The organizational ties of operational criminal units to organized crime itself are much looser perhaps than those within parts of the hierarchy of an economic firm, but they are certainly stronger than the customer-seller relationships between economic firms in legitimate markets. The closest legitimate economic parallel would be franchise arrangements in which the franchise advantage is an inclusion within a known judicial system for property right determination.

174

Still, Rubin's discussion of special market factors is useful. It would be even more useful if he would rethink his factors in terms of whether they are factors increasing the value of some special subsystem of providing order—the government of organized crime—or factors leading to the efficiency of one type of property arrangement over another within particular markets.

One final observation concerning a minor aspect of the Rubin paper should be made in reference to the character of "juice" or shark loans—"usury" in Rubin's paper. There is a special market inefficiency here that does not apply to other forms of crime. If these loans were simply a matter of collecting an illegally high rate of interest, as Rubin implies, they would not be different in character from violating any other type of price ceiling by black marketeering. The difference, however, is that no legitimate firm would make loans to many of the clients involved at any finite interest rate, even given the removal of usury laws. The likelihood that these borrowers would pay back such loans without the threat of violence is vanishingly small. What really happens here is that organized crime allows these people to put up their very lives as collateral. The Romans solved the same problem by allowing human capital itself to be put up as collateral. Those who did not make payment were foreclosed and sold into slavery.

Dagobert L. Brito

I have been asked to comment on papers by Professors Buchanan, Ianni and Rubin on organized crime. I shall preface my remarks by admitting that I am an economic theorist by trade and know very little about crime or sociology.

Professor Ianni's investigation of authority and the power structure in an organized crime family is an interesting and enjoyable paper. From his study Mr. Ianni concludes: (1) position and power within the organization may differ, (2) when position and power are not integrated, there will be conflict within the organization, and (3) acculturation is occurring within the family. The first two conclusions seem very general and one would expect that they are true of most large organizations. Certainly such phenomena can be observed in the U.S. Army and most academic departments.

Professor Rubin's paper, "The Economic Theory of the Criminal Firm," unfortunately does not fulfill the promise of the title. Instead of theory the paper consists mostly of statements about the technology of the criminal firm which are taken from hearings and the popular press, or which are unsupported. What theory there is in the paper is often sloppy or wrong.

Early in his discussion Professor Rubin states, "If gambling were legal, we would expect more vertical integration, for this would lead to lower transaction costs; but since gambling is illegal, the greater risks of detection lead to less integration and more lay-off betting. Vertical integration would probably require more bookkeeping than an independent operation does, and this would lead to greater risks. Thus, unless police are adequately bribed, we would expect more independent operators than might be optimal."

This analysis has several problems. First, it is unclear what Mr. Rubin means by "more independent operators than might be optimal." Does he mean that independent operators would lose money (and still remain in business!) or that many small, independent bookmakers would charge a higher fee than a single monopoly bookmaker? To answer this question, and the question Professor Rubin appears to be addressing, requires that we understand the technology of book-making. What are the economies and diseconomies of scale; which of these are dominant? If vertical integration "probably requires more bookkeeping than independent operations," why does vertical integration result in lower transaction costs? If a larger firm is able to internalize risk, why would increased risk result in smaller firms? Is there any evidence that the risks are not independent? These are not easy questions and deserve more than a paragraph.

Another example of Professor Rubin's loose reasoning is in his discussion of the optimal size of a heroin shipment. He states,

> The average cost per pound of imported heroin can be expressed as:
> $$AC = \frac{T + Aq + p(F + Aq) + r(Aq)}{q},$$
> where T = transactions cost (per trip), A = price per pound of heroin in Europe, q = number of pounds in the shipment, p = probability of capture, F = cost to the criminal of penalties (i.e., jail) if he is caught, and r = interest rate on illegal funds. (The confiscation of heroin if the smuggler is caught is included in the equation.)
>
> The variables which society (i.e., the narcotics agents) controls are p and F. If it is desired to reduce the average shipment, we *need* [my italics] only make F, the penalty, an increasing function of q; this will then make smaller shipments cheaper in relation to large shipments, and thus reduce the need for capital and the dependence on organized crime.

This need not be true. In the context of this problem a criminal firm dealing in heroin has two choice variables, the total amount of heroin it wishes to import and the size of each shipment. Let us redefine the variables, let x be the number of pounds per shipment and n be the number of shipments. For any desired level of heroin, q, it wishes to import, the criminal firm will solve the dual problem. The firm will want to minimize the total cost of importing the heroin subject to the constraint that q pounds of heroin are imported. Mathematically the problem can be written as: [1]

$$\min_{n,x} TC = nT + Anx + np[Fx + Ax] + rAnx, \tag{1}$$

---

[1] In my initial presentation I assumed that the transactions cost was a linear function of the size of the shipment. Professor Rubin objected to that assumption. The interested reader may amuse himself by working out that case.

subject to

$$q = nx. \tag{2}$$

If we manipulate equations (1) and (2), we have:

$$\min_{n,x} TC = nT + Aq + p[Fq + Aq] + rAq. \tag{3}$$

If we examine equation (3) it is clear that the criminal firm will choose to import the heroin in one shipment. This result is independent of the amount of heroin the firm wishes to import. Professor Rubin's statement that "we need only make F, the penalty, an increasing function of q" is clearly wrong. It may be possible to develop a penalty structure which will reduce the average size of heroin shipments. To obtain this goal, however, it is not sufficient to make the penalty an increasing function of the size of the shipment.

It should also be noted that even if society succeeds in creating a penalty structure which will reduce the average size of a heroin shipment, it need not follow that this will reduce the amount of capital required by a criminal importer. Just as one would not argue that the optimal size of an oil company is determined by the optimal size of an oil tanker, one should not argue, in the absence of empirical evidence, that the optimal size of a heroin shipment determines the optimal size of a heroin-importing firm. The size of the firm may be determined by other activities, for example, purchasing, refining and distribution. If the size of the firm is not determined by the optimal size of a heroin shipment, then decreasing the size of the optimal heroin shipment may increase the firm's capital requirements and thus increase the involvement of organized crime in financing heroin traffic. This is not the desired result.

I believe Professor Rubin has some interesting ideas. If he is willing to devote more time and work to the subject of organized crime, he should be able to write several papers that will be valuable to policy makers. In its present state his work is superficial and potentially misleading.

Professor Buchanan's paper is an ingenious and careful analysis of the effects of increased monopoly in crime on the output of "bads" to society. He argues: "If monopoly in the supply of 'goods' is socially undesirable, monopoly in the supply of 'bads' should be socially desirable, precisely because of the output restrictions."

The first criticism I have of Professor Buchanan's paper is that he does not give enough emphasis to the second-best aspects of the problem. For example, permitting the importation of marijuana to become monopolized may reduce the supply of marijuana, a "bad"; however, it may also increase the consumption of heroin, an even worse "bad." While he is not guilty of a logical error, he does avoid the problem in a subtle way. He states:

> In the analysis above, I have implicitly assumed that the separate criminal
> industries are independent one from another. If we should assume that
> potential criminals constitute a noncompeting group of persons, distinct

and apart from the rest of society, monopolization of one or a few areas of criminality may actually increase the supply of resources going into remaining and nonorganized activities. This sort of supply interdependence provides an argument for the extension of monopolization to all criminal activities. It does not, however, offer an argument against monopolization per se.

This assumption of independence excludes second-best problems; however, the argument is complex. Twice in recent years attempts by the federal government to reduce the consumption of marijuana (in this country "Operation Intercept," and in Vietnam) have resulted in an increased consumption of heroin. Since one can not expect that officials in the Department of the Army or the Department of Justice will always appreciate the importance of a subtle assumption in an economic argument, more emphasis should be placed on the second-best aspect of the problem.

The other point is more technical. Professor Buchanan states:

> Given the two independent relationships as depicted, we can readily demonstrate convergence of the system to a stable equilibrium position at E, provided that the L curve exhibits a steeper absolute slope value over relevant adjustment ranges than the C curve.

This statement is insufficient. Propositions about stability require explicit statements about the disequilibrium dynamics of the system. If Professor Buchanan is implicitly assuming a discrete time adjustment model and a Cournot-type assumption of myopic behavior, his statement is correct. This is a minor point.

PART FOUR:
FOREIGN CRIMINAL PROCEDURE

POSSIBLE LESSONS FROM CONTINENTAL CRIMINAL PROCEDURE

Jan Štěpán

American and European legal scholars share a mutually negative evaluation of the criminal process established on each other's continent. To a large extent this may be caused by lack of knowledge.[1]

An American lawyer has been brought up with the general notion that the procedure in continental Europe is inquisitorial (which, as we shall see, is not the whole truth today); ergo, he believes, it must be inferior to the Anglo-American adversary process.

On the other hand, some students of criminal procedure in Germany, France, or the Soviet Union demonstrate their antipathy to, even abhorrence of, the English and especially the American procedure, even with respect to its adversary basis or to some characteristically noninquisitorial features. Gustav Radbruch maintained that this procedure still was a judicial battle, fought in our times with words instead of battleaxes,[2] while Walter Sachs claims that the principle of establishing truth "does not exist" in England and America.[3] Even if these views do not

---

[1] In selecting the features which may be considered as typical of the criminal procedure in the continent of Europe, I have concentrated mainly on the West German, French, and Soviet systems. For further condensed information in English on the process in these and some other European countries, the following fairly recent materials may be recommended: John A. Coutts, ed., *The Accused: A Comparative Study* (London: Stevens & Sons, 1966); Gerhard O. W. Mueller and Fré Le Poole-Griffiths, *Comparative Criminal Procedure* (New York: New York University Press, 1969); Hans-Heinrich Jescheck, "Principles of German Criminal Procedure in Comparison with American Law," *Virginia Law Review,* vol. 56 (1970), pp. 239-53; Gerald L. Kock, "Introduction" to *The French Code of Criminal Procedure,* in the American Series of Foreign Penal Codes, No. 7 (South Hackensack, N.J.: Rothman & Co., 1964), pp. 1-13; Stephen Hrones, "Interrogation Abuses by the Police in France: A Comparative Solution," *Criminal Law Quarterly,* vol. 12 (1969), pp. 68-90; Harold J. Berman, *Soviet Criminal Law and Procedure: The RSFSR Codes* (Cambridge, Mass.: Harvard University Press, 1966); Arthur Rosett, "Trial and Discretion in Dutch Criminal Justice," *UCLA Law Review,* vol. 19 (1972), pp. 353-90; Mirjan J. Damaska, "Comparative Reflections on Reading the Amended Yugoslav Code: Interrogation of Defendants in Yugoslav Criminal Procedure," *Journal of Criminal Law, Criminology, and Police Science,* vol. 61 (1970), pp. 168-80. Sybille Bedford's *The Faces of Justice* (New York: Simon & Schuster, 1961) is an interesting description of the atmosphere of Continental courts by a lay author from a common law country. Adhémar Esmein's classic treatise on the history of French criminal process, published in English translation under the misleading title, *A History of Continental Criminal Procedure* (Boston: Little, Brown, and Co., 1913), is still an unsurpassed source of information on the historic roots and the origin of the reformed French procedure.

[2] Gustav Radbruch, *Der Geist des englischen Rechts* (Heidelberg: A. Rausch, 1946), p. 22.

[3] Walter Sachs, in a foreword to Karl M. Newman, *Das englisch-amerikanische Beweisrecht* (Heidelberg: L. Schneider, 1949), p. 18.

represent the majority, such attitudes must seem surprising once we realize the undeniable historic reality that for two centuries most progressive reforms of European criminal process have been inspired, directly or indirectly, by some concepts or basic institutions of the Anglo-American procedure. This is not an overstatement, if we understand progress to encompass humanization of criminal procedure by gradual repeal of various remnants of torture and forcible inducement of confessions.

The need for some major changes in the American criminal procedure seems to be evident at the present time. Thus this question arises: If the continent of Europe has profited from the influence of the other system for 200 years, could not an exchange of experience operate in the opposite direction now? The answer, in my opinion, may largely depend on what kind of European institutions should be considered for possible transplantation: the traditionally inquisitorial ones (sometimes surviving in rejuvenated forms), or some newly developed kinds and elements of procedure.

The contemporary form of the Continental process has been characterized since the time of Napoleon's Code as mixed, that is, inquisitorially adversary. As we shall see, the initial, still predominantly inquisitorial phase (the "investigation") is followed by an oral judicial trial in adversary form with some inquisitorial elements. On the very similar structural basis, but with some modifications, this French model was introduced more than 100 years ago in all Continental countries. Since then it has been elaborated on and improved, partly by gradual suppression of some of its inquisitorial features and by implantation of safeguards against abuse of power, and partly by creation of new procedural institutions to simplify the old, cumbersome process. Thus, several well-tested institutions and features of today's European procedural system did not evolve from the inquisitorial basis. Although some aspects of this procedure may be adjusted to the conditions of modern life better than some traditional forms on this side of the Atlantic, little, if anything, is known of them here. Introduction of some of these concepts, perhaps with modifications, into the American procedure might in fact result in its improvement.

As a prerequisite to any comparative thinking, let us first submit the briefest possible outline of the historic origin of Continental criminal procedure and then a general picture of some common and typical features of the contemporary criminal process in Europe.

I. An Outline of the Historical Origins of the Continental Criminal Procedure

A correct understanding of the modern European criminal process hinges on some comprehension of its deep-rooted inquisitorial basis. "Inquisitorial" is, of course, not a word of insult; it is a technical term, descriptive of the nonadversary form of criminal procedure, which has been developed all over continental Europe since the Middle Ages. *The basic idea in an inquisitorial process is to acquire evidence "out of the mouth" of a suspected person, that is, to extract confession through interrogation.* Two consequences are implicit in, and characteristic of, an inquisitorial procedure: First, from the time an investigator begins to suspect a person of criminal activity, a presumption of guilt begins to operate. The onus of proof falls on the suspect. He is obliged to furnish a detailed explanation of facts on which the suspicion is based (and to give any other true information wanted from him) and thus either to clear himself from suspicion, or, if guilty, to provide "the best proof" of his guilt by his confession.

Second, suspects, as a rule, do not confess a crime voluntarily, lest this may be self-destructive. Therefore, any system of justice which relies on confessions needs methods to compel interrogated persons to "give evidence against themselves." The original method, outright physical torture, was formally abolished in the Continental countries before the end of the eighteenth century. Logically and inevitably, however, the idea persists that interrogation of suspects without some kind of strong compulsion does not make sense. Various psychological means and tricks have to be used (*Inquisitionskunst* = the art of interrogating) to break the suspect mentally and thus to force him to confess.

For a better evaluation of neo-inquisitorial systems it might be useful to point out some of the characteristic features of the old inquisitorial process:

1. The procedure was a written one. The phase of *inquisitio* (investigation) consisted of detailed examinations by a judge of witnesses and interrogations of the accused. The judge also determined the kind and intensity of torture, whenever it was used, and he interrogated the accused during its administration. Every deposition was written down and filed along with all other results of the investigation. After the investigation was closed, the file was sent to a judicial body which, without any trial and only on the basis of the file, issued judgment. It may not be generally known in the United States that in the seventeenth and eighteenth centuries no oral trial existed in most parts of the Continent, including Germany and France.

2. The judge-investigator was obliged to conduct the investigation with absolute impartiality; otherwise the theoretical basis of any inquisitorial procedure, that is, the establishment of the truth, could not be reached. This duty, a cornerstone of the inquisitorial theory, was often underlined in old codes: The inquisitor-judge had to investigate "with equal care both against and on behalf of the suspect."

This was and still is pure theory; application of it through the centuries has been invariably demonstrated as psychologically impossible. An interrogating investigator cannot remain an uninvolved truth-seeker. He necessarily becomes an opponent, struggling with a suspect who keeps denying the charge.

3. In the inquisitorial procedure the accused was not a participant in the process, in the search for truth; he became an object of the investigation. He was subjected to the broad, arbitrary power of the examining authority. In fear of it, deprived of any psychological support, and held in custody, as a rule, he was to be mentally broken down to confess "the truth." Fear and uncertainty are substantial psychological elements of inquisitorial investigation.

4. Quite obviously, any inquisitorial system would be greatly impeded by contact of the suspect with a defense counsel. During the investigation phase, at least, defense had to be strictly excluded. Sometimes, as in eighteenth century France and Austria, defense counsel was excluded during the whole procedure. An uncontrolled, incommunicado interrogation of suspects was believed to be necessary to bring about confessions.

5. In the inquisitorial procedure the end was always more or less considered to justify the means. *"Non refert quomodo veritas habeatur, dummodo habeatur"* (it does not matter by which methods truth has been obtained so long as it has been obtained), says the Spanish inquisitor Eymericus in the first known manual for interrogators in the fourteenth century. The system, therefore, was strenuously opposed to any rules which might efficiently exclude the use of illegally obtained evidence as proof of guilt. Also, law enforcement officers using illegal, even clearly criminal, methods in the course of an investigation were almost never prosecuted or adequately punished.

In the German speaking part of Europe, the basic code of inquisitorial procedure was the *Constitutio Criminalis Carolina* of 1532.

The *Great Ordinance* of Louis XIV in 1670 was the culmination of the inquisitorial system in France. Its influence, at least indirectly, has outlived the French Revolution. The procedure ordained by the code was traditionally one of cruel brutality, but not until the mid-eighteenth century did public opinion in France begin to view it as a barbarous anachronism. Rather typically, this change of attitude was due not to the legal profession nor to legal scholars, but to the influence of philosophers and writers of the Enlightenment. The judiciary (the "most conservative element in the law"), French as well as German, Austrian, and others, stuck to their medieval methods of administration of justice on grounds that this was the only system capable of dealing with the crime problem.

The English adversary process along with American constitutional principles became political ideals in France on the eve of the French Revolution. After the revolutionaries abolished the inquisitorial process, they transplanted English institutions into French law through new codes. However, no time could have been less opportune for introduction of a procedural system guaranteeing rights against the state to the accused individual. Thus a compromise between both systems, the old French inquisitorial and the English adversary, evolved in 1808 with Napoleon's *Code d'Instruction Criminelle*.

By its provisions the criminal process was divided into two phases. The "preliminary investigation" was an entirely secret, written procedure conducted primarily, as before the revolution, by the investigating judge. The accused was still interrogated without counsel, being nearly always in custody, and witnesses were examined secretly. An oral, public, semi-adversary trial, held before a jury in serious cases, followed the investigation. At the trial the presiding judge, on the basis of the investigation file, interrogated the accused in a characteristically inquisitorial manner. He also examined the witnesses. At the discretion of the presiding judge, the file of investigation records, or its parts, could be read at the trial. In this mixed (or "reformed") process the revulsion against the old system of legal proofs and presumptions led to the newly formed principle that the jury—or, in nonjury cases, the court—should evaluate all evidence freely, according to their own convictions. This, of course, made it very easy for the court to evaluate also as proof of guilt the records of the investigation phase, which might contain confessions of the accused and depositions of witnesses examined in secret without any participation of the defense.

In this post-revolutionary French process the accused was not legally bound to make statements, but in practice, from the very beginning, the old inquisitorial principle fully survived, according to which a suspect had to submit to interrogation or be forced to do so. If he refused to answer questions asked either by the police, or by the investigating or trial judge, the court could infer guilt of the accused on grounds that his refusal constituted an element of free conviction. Sufficient means to enforce confessions were provided by the methods of incommunicado interrogation. The emotional shock of arrest and the influence of pretrial detention were considered important factors in disturbing the mental resistance of the accused, and this disintegration was viewed as a prerequisite for successful interrogation.

After the middle of the nineteenth century nearly all European countries adopted this French model of the "mixed" procedure. Warnings of several leading scholars who decried its clearly inquisitorial heritage, and who stressed the advisability of stronger adherence to the English process, were not heeded by the legislators. Two classic codes of criminal procedure from the late nineteenth century, which, after many amendments, are still in force, are the Austrian code of 1873 and the German code of 1877. In practice these codes have been less harshly administered in the investigation phase as was true of their French model.

In France in 1897, after French public opinion refused to tolerate any longer the abuses of the investigating judges, a profound liberalization of the phase of judicial investigation was enacted, bearing a strong resemblance to the *Miranda* rules. This revolution of the inquisitorial character of the process, however, was from the very beginning neutralized by the conservative French Supreme Court, hostile to the new legislation. It was ruled that the statements of the accused and of witnesses from the initial police phase of investigation, which had not been affected by the 1897 amendment, could be used as evidence at the trial. Later the existence of the police investigation phase, where there were no safeguards worth mentioning for interrogated suspects, was legalized by the new French Code of Criminal Procedure of 1957.

Most efforts to reform German procedure undertaken in the first decades of the twentieth century were unsuccessful; they came to a halt with the beginning of the Hitler era. It was only in 1964, nineteen years after World War II, that Western Germany adopted the "Little Amendment" to the Code of Criminal Procedure and thus brought some *Miranda-Escobedo*-like features into the early police phase of interrogation. In Italy, long-lasting reform efforts on the criminal procedure are still in progress.

Quite naturally, a separate line of development started in the USSR after 1917 and in other East European socialist countries after the Second World War. Notwithstanding some basic differences and some modifications, though, the Eastern procedural codes may still be considered as part of the Continental "mixed" system. Interesting safeguards for the accused, based on early defense by a counsel, and thus changing the inquisitorial character of preliminary procedure, have been introduced by legislative amendments in Czechoslovakia in 1965 and in Yugoslavia in 1967. Some Czechoslovak experience may demonstrate the problems as well as the practical feasibility of efficiently safeguarding the right to counsel in the earliest phase of investigation conducted by security investigators.

II. The Modern Continental Criminal Process

The course of a typical criminal process in continental Europe—a universal model, subject to many variations in different countries—might look somewhat as follows.

The early, most important, phase of "preliminary investigation" is now conducted everywhere by the same authority, that is, the police. The qualifications of police officers taking part in the investigation may differ widely, from the policeman on the beat or the plainclothes detective to the special units of the so-called judicial police, the highly qualified *Polizekommissars,* or, in the socialist countries, "investigators."

The old, classic procedural codes did not anticipate this universal trend toward a police-conducted investigation. According to their provisions, police were to take only the necessary first steps; then either an investigating judge (typically in France or in Austria) or a public prosecutor (typically in Germany) was supposed to conduct the investigation with some occasional, nonsubstantive support from the police. Within a few decades, perhaps not later than around the end of the nineteenth century, however, the actual investigation shifted to police interrogation and examination everywhere. In West Germany, the public prosecutor is nominally the leading authority during the investigation phase. He is entitled, even supposed, to conduct the investigation himself. This, naturally, can be done only rarely.

186

As a rule cases are investigated by the police alone with the prosecutor then obtaining the file which results. In France, Austria, and in other countries where there is an investigating judge, he usually begins his work only after the main outlines of the case have been established by police investigation, often, of course, after the suspect has confessed to the police. He repeats the interrogations of the accused and reexamines some witnesses. The investigating judge has nearly disappeared from German practice since the 1920s. To prevent possible misunderstanding, it should be noted that in West Germany a district judge is often requested to conduct a particular interrogation of the accused or to examine a witness during the investigation phase. In such cases, however, he does not act as an investigating judge (the authority conducting the investigation as a whole) but as a kind of judicial aide to the investigating authorities. The main reason for this kind of procedure is that records of judicial interrogations and examinations can often be read as evidence in a German trial, while confessions and depositions made before the police can, as a rule, be proved only by oral testimony from police officers present at the time they were made.

Before describing the European trial, we have to comment briefly on the character of the preliminary investigation phase, especially with regard to the position of the accused and his defense.

In the French, post-Napoleon, procedure the investigation phase was, as is generally admitted, a direct descendant of the old French inquisition. Around the middle of the nineteenth century the founding fathers of the German reformed process, Zachariae, Mittermaier, Planck, Glaser, and others, were well aware of this defect in the "reformed" French process. With the Anglo-American model in mind, they taught that the preliminary phase should be short and purely informative in character. Its main purpose was simply to enable the prosecutor to decide whether an act of accusation should be filed before the court, and if so, what the charge should be. The products of the investigation phase were not supposed to be introduced as evidence at the trial, since the only source of the decision of court was to be the evidence directly produced at the trial. Should an exceptional necessity arise in the investigation period to fix an "anticipated proof"—for example, to hear a critically ill witness—the accused and his counsel should be allowed to participate. This was the theory prevalent in Europe on the eve of the reformed process. From the very beginning, however, and perhaps without exception, judicial practice went the other way, because it was psychologically unable to dissociate itself from the deep-rooted habits of written inquisitioning. As under the old procedure, the authorities tried by lengthy and exhaustive investigation to collect all the evidence which might be relevant for the decisions of the court. Thus all over the European continent the investigation phase continued to be the most important, and in fact, remains today the usually decisive phase of the criminal process.

Unfortunately, the position of the defense in the early part of the process has always been very weak. With a few exceptions this is still the case, and it provides the main source of the recurring difficulties in the Continental criminal process. Significantly, the question of how to strengthen and safeguard the rights of a suspect in the investigating phase, together with the problem of the relationship of this phase to the trial (that is, the relevance and admissibility of written results of investigation as evidence before the court), are the focal points of nearly every major reform work on the Continent.

Throughout the nineteenth century and even in many cases up to the present, the accused remained in the preliminary phase of the criminal process more or less an object of investigation—as is natural in a neo-inquisitorial procedure. He used to be and still is interrogated again and again, by police, investigation judges, and sometimes by public prosecutors. If in custody, he usually has no legal right to speak freely with his counsel before the investigation is completed. Because of a lack of information on the file and a lack of contact with a detained accused person, the counsel's assistance in many countries can be only nominal during the "preliminary" period, which can last for months. Witnesses are examined without the cooperation of the defense. The preliminary case for the prosecution is thus completed without any real possibility of efficient defense—exactly as it was in the old inquisitorial process, where the defense counsel, if any, was allowed to start his meager work only after the investigation had been closed.

At the end of the investigation the basis for the trial is prepared. An exhaustive file has been accumulated, composed of depositions, statements of the accused, opinions written by experts, sundry official reports and documents, criminal records and other dossiers of the accused, and many other materials. The point to be stressed is that at this point the file, sometimes extremely voluminous, contains no, or very few, materials submitted by the defense.

Approximately at the end of the investigation phase, the defense (in some countries both the accused and his counsel, in others—including both German states—only the counsel) has a legal right to full prosecutorial disclosure, which means freedom to inspect and study the whole file. In most Western countries (excluding France) permission to view the file earlier may be granted only at the discretion of the investigating authority or the prosecutor.

In the socialist countries the study of the complete investigation file by the defense constitutes a characteristic and important closing act of the investigation. In view of the importance of this "preliminary" collection of evidence during the investigation, it would seem that disclosure only at the end of this phase may be belated. In a complicated case, where the materials collected in the file contain hundreds, sometimes even thousands of pages, the time for proper preparation of the defense may be short. Yet, despite this particular disadvantage to the defense in European procedure, the European defense attorney is, as a rule, spared one feature of American procedure—the surprise of unexpected evidence being produced by the prosecution during the trial. Such surprise evidence is rarely presented and can hardly be a deciding factor in the trial in Europe. Thus, the European defense attorney, once he has spent the necessary time and energy for a full study of the case, starts the trial with full knowledge of the prosecution's materials. This represents a marked contrast with American procedure.

After the investigation has been finished, the file serves first as a guide for the prosecution's decision to pursue or to drop the case. A case may be dropped during the investigative phase by police authorities, by the prosecutor, or by the investigating judge, according to the system of the country involved. If the prosecutor decides to prosecute, he files a written "act of accusation," sometimes very detailed, sometimes less so. The complete file, together with this instrument, is submitted to the court. It has to be studied minutely by the single or presiding judge and insofar as time allows, also by other career members of a panel of judges—by law judges, too, in socialist countries.

In nearly all Continental jurisdictions, at least in more serious cases, a relatively short, intermediate phase is inserted between the filing of the accusation and the trial. During this period the court is to decide, as a preliminary issue, if there are enough grounds for suspicion to try the case in court. It is interesting to note that everywhere on the Continent this admissions procedure is, and always has been, in practice, of relatively little importance although it looms larger in legal theory. In the socialist systems this judicial control over admission has still another function: The court has to check on whether the preliminary procedure was conducted according to law. No grand jury exists in the Continental systems.

Depending on the seriousness of the charge, the trials are conducted either by a single judge, or by a panel which may consist of either career judges alone or of career judges and lay assessors. The whole socialist part of Europe has a system of mixed panels including both career judges and lay judges.

Only in Western Europe do some countries still maintain a trial by jury for most serious cases. However, what at present is called *Schwurgericht* in West Germany, or *cour d'assize* in France, is not a jury in the Anglo-American sense. There are large panels of three career judges and six (in West Germany) or nine (in France) lay assessors, who jointly try the case, deliberate, and decide the questions both of guilt and punishment. No renaissance of the classic concept of jury can be expected on the Continent in the near future.

Almost no European jurisdiction knows the institution of the guilty plea as a surrogate for trial. This would be inconsistent with the ex officio character of establishing guilt which is essential to the Continental procedure. Confessions, of course—not in theory but in everyday practice—are of basic importance. When the accused has confessed, and sticks by his confession during his trial, other relevant evidence has to be introduced as a rule, but this remaining judicial procedure may be a relatively short and easy affair, if not a formality. In the absence of guilty pleas, the practice of plea bargaining is virtually unknown; such would be held to be clearly inconsistent with the duties of a public prosecutor.

As to the course of the trial, the following description may be extracted from some common features as established in most Continental countries. It is well known that the judge not only leads and conducts the general course of the trial but also he, rather than the prosecutor and the defense attorney, is responsible for producing and taking evidence. The court proceeds ex officio; it is not only entitled but obliged to procure all relevant evidence even without a motion of the parties. (By the way, a prevailing contemporary trend of German legal thinking asserts that the German process is not a process of "parties"; the prosecutor, it is sometimes maintained, cannot be degraded to a status of a party.) In practice, the prosecutor has suggested in the written act of accusation the evidence he wants to be produced, especially as he has named "his" witnesses. We have to keep in mind that—in theory—these witnesses, and other parts of evidence suggested by the prosecution, ought to be not only those which incriminate, but those which exonerate as well. Quite naturally, the practice is different. The defense, for its part, may propose additional evidence to be produced at the trial. The court is not bound by motions by any party to allow irrelevant evidence to be produced by either party.

The trial usually begins with the reading of the act of accusation. Next comes the important, often decisive, interrogation of the accused by the judge. Additional questions may be asked by other members of the panel, by the prosecutor, or by the defense counsel. This interrogation, based on former statements of the accused to the police or to other investigating authorities, is often very inquisitive—in France traditionally it has been even aggressive. The judge frequently consults the file in order to confront the accused with incongruities which may appear between his present and former statements.

It is worth mentioning that in probably no Continental country is the accused legally obliged to undergo this interrogation and to answer questions. Some codes even indicate that the judge has to caution him on his right to remain silent. Of course, according to the centuries-old tradition of inquisitorial proceedings, the accused almost never would conceive it possible not to submit to the interrogation. From time to time rare exceptions can be seen, mostly either as a form of political protest, or as a display of psychopathic personality. Should the accused refuse to make a statement, his previous statements, made during interrogations in the preliminary phase, would either be read from the file or otherwise reproduced.

Under no circumstances can an accused person be heard as a witness in a procedure against himself. What he says during his interrogation are "statements of an accused," a particular kind of evidence, different from testimony, and of course, never subject to punishment for perjury, even if knowingly false. European laws as well as European theory are completely uniform on that point. It is accepted quite generally that nobody should be placed into the antithetical position of being a witness against himself, where his very existence may depend on his statements.

The interrogation of the accused is followed by examinations of witnesses; these again are conducted by the judge, with some additional questions from other persons participating in the trial. If, as happens in most cases, the witnesses have already been heard in "preliminary" investigations, for example, by the police, they also are confronted with their previous statements when they deviate from them.

. In this connection a fundamental problem of the Continental process can be pointed out: that of the principle of direct establishment of proof by the court during the trial. In theory, this is one of the fundamental principles of the present system of European procedure. It means, chiefly, that only evidence directly produced in the court, under its direct perception, should be used as a basis for the decision. In practice, however, the impact of the investigation phase, that is, the extensive use made of the investigative file, necessarily contradicts this principle. First, as we saw, statements made to the investigating authorities may be reproduced at the trial and evaluated as part of the evidence. But there is another, no less important, factor. In practice, most of the depositions of witnesses as well as all statements of the accused have been "rehearsed" during the preliminary investigation; thus what is told before the court is to a great extent prejudiced ("precooked," as an Austrian scholar has said) by the former statements as fixed in the file. It is easy to understand (and it is a daily experience in a Continental court) that the average judge tends to influence the testimony of witnesses and even the statements of the accused so as to prevent major differences between them and the file. Such discrepancies would complicate the case and the decision. The recurring criticism of the typical Continental trial is that its outcome is so prejudiced, even predestined, by the contents of the file that the trial seems to be an "appeal from the interrogation," that is, more of a review, if not repetition, of the contents of the files of investigation than a real trial.

As is well known, the Continental rules relating to producing of evidence are substantially simpler than those governing an American trial. This may be explained partly on historic grounds, partly by the absence of a jury, and partly by the fact that the judge, not the parties, produces the evidence. Much may be said of the advantages of the relative simplicity of the European system regarding rules of evidence. It would be an error, however, to think that modern Continental procedure does not apply strict exclusionary rules to some illegally obtained evidence. This was not true even in the older reformed process of the nineteenth century. Since about 1900, the importance of exclusionary rules has been increasing; there are some strict provisions, for example, in the amended French and German codes. It can be said on this issue, as on some others, that the "inquisitorially" conservative element is the judiciary. On the other hand, many scholars seem to think that to enact, even in the clearest possible way, limitations on some undesirable methods of investigation is not worth much, unless those provisions are reinforced by strict exclusionary rules. Leaving the exclusion of illegal proof to the discretion of a judge was traditional in the old procedure. It may be felt that it is incongruous with the modern concepts of the rule of law, of *Rechtsstaat,* to leave it to the judge to decide whether a clear provision of the law needed to be followed or not.

European codes differ generally and widely from the American law on the issue of the expert witness. It is deeply felt in Europe that proof by expert opinion is basically different from proof by testimony of a witness, that, in fact, an expert is not a witness. Experts are selected by the courts. In some countries higher courts or the ministry of justice keep lists of "judicial experts." On more important issues usually two experts are appointed; should their opinions differ, another expert opinion may be asked for.

It is difficult to comment briefly on the function and activities of a European defense counsel as opposed to his American colleague. In general it can be said that, logically, an attorney in a semi-inquisitorial procedure is supposed to be considerably less active than an attorney in the adversary procedure. In the Continental process, often the most conspicuous part of the defense is the closing speech of the counsel which follows the summary of the prosecutor. In a system, however, in which the jury has been largely abolished, the closing speeches cannot be expected to have great impact on the court's decision.

The Continental trial, as a rule, is not bifurcated, that is, divided into two parts, the first concerned with the issue of guilt, the second with the penalty. Accordingly, all evidence, including parts of the file which contain the record of the accused, reports on his person, and so forth are produced before the court before it rules on both the guilt and the punishment. We expect a future trend toward bifurcation, however, especially under the influence of the so-called "social defense" movement.

Something remains to be said about appeals and various other kinds of post-conviction remedies in Europe. On the whole, the system is much simpler, and the remedies more quickly put into operation, than in the United States. There is, as a rule, a two-instance criminal procedure; only exceptionally is some sort of second appeal to a third instance allowed. Appeal procedures depend, first of all, on the system of courts existing in a particular country. Against the decisions of lower courts before which less serious cases are tried, often full appeal, both on issues of guilt and of punishment, and on matters of law as well as of fact, can be filed by the prosecution or by the defense. Sometimes the only grounds for an appeal against a decision of a higher court are legal mistakes on the part of the court, including procedural errors. Sometimes, however, as in East European countries, a full appeal even against decisions of these courts may be allowed. An appeal has to be filed in a relatively short time, typically within one or two weeks after the written copy of the judgment has been delivered to the party. In some systems the appeal court which has quashed a judgment may replace it by its own new decision; in others an incorrect judgment is only quashed and a new trial has to follow.

The accused is deemed to have some right to a review of the decision of the first court; he is not to be dissuaded from filing an appeal. In many codes, therefore, a provision can be found prohibiting the so-called *reformatio in peius:* If an appeal has been filed only on behalf of the accused (where the prosecution did not appeal against him), the punishment imposed by the first court cannot be made more harsh in the second instance.

After the decision of the last instance has been issued—or, if no appeal was filed, after the time limit for filing it has expired—the judgment becomes final. The punishment is then commonly executed in a relatively short time after the finality of the judgment.

The principle of double jeopardy, strictly respected both in law and in practice, is, in the European concept, understood to apply to final decisions only.

In exceptional cases a final decision may be reviewed by some "extraordinary" post-conviction remedies. These are mostly of two types. An "extraordinary" revision can be used to correct certain errors of law. Where it is on behalf of the accused, it cannot generally be filed by him; a prosecutor as "guardian of law" or some other authority has to do it. In cases where new and important evidence has become known, another kind of extraordinary remedy, a request for a new trial, may be filed, either by the convicted person or by the prosecutor against the accused.

III. Some Possible Lessons from Continental Procedure

We have tried thus far to summarize some characteristic features of the Continental procedure in order that they might now serve as a basis for comparative evaluation of a few selected issues.

The question which should be asked may sound like this: If the administration of criminal justice in the United States "suffers from basic ills" (as the President's Commission on Law Enforcement and Administration of Justice found in 1967) and if some of its vital problems are either not shared at all, or are believed to be far less serious in Europe, why this difference? What solutions do the Continental systems have to offer the United States?

A comparison of this kind may seem justified especially in such areas of the procedural law, where the differences between American and European procedures may not be automatically conditioned by the basic contrast between the neo-inquisitorial and the adversary systems. On such issues, a foreign model need not necessarily meet with structural difficulties.

We may point up some possibilities with a few examples:

1. Why must criminal proceedings in England and the United States still, as traditionally, *begin with the physical arrest* of the suspects? This system necessarily leads to problems: strong feelings of unnecessary personal harassment, complicated issues of pretrial release, the embarrassing practice in which the bail bondsman—in fact, a moneylender—has become an important participant in the administration of justice, and so on.

On the Continent, criminal proceedings against a person may, according to the particular code involved, start in various other ways. They may be opened, as in Germany, by the application of any act of investigation against the suspect, or, as in the socialist countries, by notification to the suspect that a decision has been made to charge him with a specified offense. From that time, the suspect becomes an accused; procedural restraints may be applied against him and he is entitled to the legal rights of the accused. An arrest, which is a purely temporary detention (usually by police, typically of between twenty-four and forty-eight hours) is allowed only in cases of necessity, where there is danger of delay, impossibility of identifying the apprehended person, et cetera. (In France, the police have considerably broader authority to detain suspects and even persons not suspected.) Only after a person becomes an accused may "regular" pretrial detention—custody—be ordered. Certain legal prerequisites for custody are provided, and they are typically of three kinds: probability that the accused will avoid proceedings by flight, that he will tamper with evidence, or that he will continue his criminal activity. (In France, similar limitations do not exist in the case of major crimes; in 1970 they were introduced as a rather half-hearted reform in cases of misdemeanors.) It must be added, however, that in whatever terms such prerequisites may be formulated in the European codes, they are always interpreted broadly enough to allow the investigating authorities, in practice, to take nearly any accused person into custody. Thus, pretrial detention is still typically used to coerce confessions. This practice is facilitated by the fact that in most countries incommunicado interrogations of an accused during custody are still allowed by law and are practiced daily. This, however, is another story; what is important for us now is a clear awareness of the fact that arrest as a typical first step in criminal proceedings is an unnecessary, and in many ways a costly, measure.

2. Some differenes in the *organization of criminal justice* on the Continent and in the United States might help to explain why Continental procedures sometimes seem to work more simply and efficiently than the American ones.

First, in European countries there are fewer jurisdictional complications arising from the federal constitutional structure. In West Germany, as well as in Austria or Yugoslavia, both substantive and procedural criminal codes are federal. This seems to carry with it no marked difficulties, despite the facts that until 1877 the German states had their own codes, and that there are still some strong regional differences between parts of Germany (not to speak of Yugoslavia). In the U.S.S.R. "Fundamental Principles" of criminal law, of court organization, and of criminal procedure were enacted as federal law in 1958. Using this as a guide, all fifteen union republics adopted their own codes. Cases from all Soviet jurisdictions, insofar as the issues bear on federal law, may be reviewed (admittedly through a lengthy and complicated process) "by way of supervision" by the federal Supreme Court of the U.S.S.R. Since much federal law is encompassed in the "Fundamental Principles," the review jurisdiction of the U.S.S.R. Supreme Court is in practice construed very broadly.

In most European countries there is a strong trend towards the centralization of the judicial police on a national level, which, of course, permits much more efficient law enforcement than in the systems of municipal, or even state, police organization. Most West European countries also have uniform, relatively simple systems of court organization, with career judges often appointed for life.

A conspicuous—and in its consequences perhaps the most important—difference between the American and Continental organizations of justice apparatus is the character and the position of the public prosecutor. His job on the Continent is not at all political; his position is never a stepping-stone in a political career. Typically he is a career official, subordinated to higher authorities in a hierarchic, centralized system. A prosecutor in Europe is therefore much more independent of local influences than his American colleague. In fact, when the procuracy (prosecutor's office) was introduced in Soviet Russia in 1922, Lenin wanted it to serve primarily as an instrument for enforcing uniform application of the new laws against local influences and pressures.

To a significant extent, the European prosecutor is supposed to be an objective "guardian of law," obliged to watch over not only the interests of the prosecuting state, but also over the interests of the accused. Theoretically, Europeans stress impartiality of the prosecutor much more than do Americans, but European practice differs strongly from theory. I can only note here that numerous problems stem from the concept where the public prosecutor is supposed to be an objective guardian of law.

3. One major difference between the duties of the prosecutor in the United States and the prosecutor in Europe is that the former has the *discretionary power to prosecute* or not to prosecute in cases where guilt may reasonably be expected to be proved before the court. The situation in Europe differs somewhat from country to country: In France the prosecutor has considerable discretion but it is to be used under strict hierarchic supervision. More typically, in West Germany, Austria, and the socialist countries, the so-called "legality principle" strictly operates. Under this principle in Germany, the prosecutor "is obliged to bring an action in all non-petty cases, wherever he is able to prove his case in court." [4] European students of

---

[4] Jescheck, "Principles of German Criminal Procedure," p. 245.

criminal procedure are simply not able to understand how far-reaching prosecutorial discretion can be practiced without constant violation of both the law and the principle of equal justice. On the other hand, it is an axiom of American legal writing that without broad prosecutorial discretion criminal law would be intolerable and justice frustrated.

I cannot resist criticizing one American practice which could not exist under the European system: plea bargaining. If a prosecutor lacks discretion as to what cases shall be prosecuted and on what charges a suspect can be brought to court, plea bargaining must, logically, disappear. It is hardly possible to imagine any system of criminal justice where plea bargaining, at least as it is presently known in this country, would not function as a malignant disease, metastatically attacking the whole organism of administration of justice. Once situations can arise where, for example, the official organization of state attorneys can openly oppose abolition of a clearly unreasonable law on grounds that its drastic penal sanctions encourage defendants to plead guilty to lesser charges,[5] or where "in many instances it is the prosecutor who, in effect, determines or heavily influences the sentence a defendant receives,"[6] or where "certain judges make an open offer to 'let the defendant off' with a suspended sentence in exchange for a guilty plea,"[7] then it seems appropriate to remove the procedural cancer of plea bargaining, whatever the cost.

It should be mentioned in passing that there is a fundamental provision in the criminal laws of East European socialist countries which can result in something not unlike a limited prosecutorial discretion. This basic provision, which originated in Soviet law and has been developed particularly in Poland and Czechoslovakia, states that in order for an act or omission to constitute a criminal offense it must include all formal elements of its legal definition, plus all general prerequisites like *mens rea,* sanity, and so on. *In addition* it must, in view of all special circumstances of the case, be *"dangerous to society,"* or "represent a more than slight social danger." If, due to all special circumstances of the case, the degree of social danger required by law was not reached, the act might become an administrative or disciplinary offense, or might not be punishable at all. This means that an otherwise criminal act, the importance of which is under given circumstances negligible, cannot be prosecuted in court as a crime. Thus a reasonable system of criminal law can be enforced without becoming intolerable, not because the prosecutor can drop the prosecution, but because he is obliged to drop it wherever the case fails

---

[5] Bruce E. Miller, "The Kansas Habitual Criminal Act," *Washburn Law Journal,* vol. 9 (1970), pp. 244, 250.

[6] *The Challenge of Crime in a Free Society,* a report by the President's Commission on Law Enforcement and the Administration of Justice (Washington, D.C.: Government Printing Office, 1967), p. 130.

[7] Stephen R. Bing and S. Stephen Rosenfeld, *The Quality of Justice in the Lower Criminal Courts of Metropolitan Boston* (Boston: Lawyers' Committee for Civil Rights under Law, 1970), p. 59.

to show the necessary degree of social danger. (This "material" concept of a criminal act carries with it, of course, many problems, but these cannot be dealt with here.) Even if any evaluation as to "social danger" is subject to personal opinion and if only a few, very broad criteria can be drawn up by law, this concept rules out the possibility that serious criminal cases will fail to be prosecuted. Thus, without a special and most exceptional pardon, a guilty "crown witness" will not escape prosecution, and nonprosecution will not be offered a suspect in exchange for information about criminal activities of other people. Moreover, pleading guilty to inappropriate lesser charges where a more serious charge could have been proved is unacceptable.

4. If, then, there is nearly no prosecutorial discretion in Europe, and if, as we have seen, there are no guilty pleas as substitutes for trials, and no plea bargaining, then this question presents itself: *How does the European system of justice dispose of the overwhelming majority of offenses,* so that the courts do not break down under their load? How do the Europeans get rid of the two-thirds to three-quarters of their docket?

Only a few possible explanations can be indicated briefly. First, my own feeling is that, on the whole, substantially fewer acts are declared punishable by European laws than by American ones, especially under the present European trend towards decriminalization. A detailed comparison of the laws of some European countries with those of some states of the United States would be an interesting and possibly rewarding project. Europeans today tend to be more skeptical of the deterrent value of criminal sanctions. Since the time of Beccaria, there has been a total disbelief in the deterrent effect of punishment in instances where the probability of detection is very small. Europeans also have a stronger belief than Americans that criminal sanctions are of little use in obtaining social goals, that is, that their function is "only supporting."

Second, at least in some countries (and this is a growing trend), many minor offenses have been shifted from judicial to administrative authorities. Administrative penal proceedings can be simple and have reasonably efficient safeguards of due process. Europeans feel that judicial procedure and judicial punishment should be reserved for more serious offenses. This not only saves money and time, but it protects many citizens from acquiring a criminal record for minor offenses and maintains the authority of the courts, which handle only serious deviations from acceptable social standards. The fact that administrative punishments, as a rule, are not included in the criminal record has proved important. If Americans should argue that, traditionally, judicial procedure in courts can be an inalienable safeguard of the citizen, a compromise solution is possible: apply administrative procedure only in cases where the person concerned does not choose judicial trial, either by simple declaration or by an appeal from the administrative decision.

Nowhere does the judicial process seem so clearly inappropriate, wasteful, and inconvenient to the citizens, as in the vast majority of traffic violation cases. For a citizen to find himself in a judicial proceeding not only when accused of theft, embezzlement, or bribe, but also for allegedly failing to obey a red light, seems highly disproportionate. To have a fine imposed for this violation included in the "criminal" record simply does not make sense. On the other hand, under the present American system, the testimony of police officers is generally the decisive factor in traffic cases. Once the case goes to court this evidence has to be obtained with a quite inappropriate expenditure of time, energy, and money. Fines imposed directly by police—or, perhaps, by some other administrative authority—seem to be a more natural and more balanced solution. In some European countries fines for minor traffic offenses, personally witnessed by traffic police, can be imposed on the spot by the officer in so-called "pad-procedure." In most cases, the motorist pays the fine at the time of the traffic violation to the officer who gives him a receipt from a pad of forms he carries with him. In some cases the fine is marked down, also on the spot, on the driver's license as sort of a driver's record. However, such procedures always require consent of the person concerned. If he does not agree with the summary "pad-fine," he can go through the regular administrative procedure with due hearing, possibility of appeal, et cetera. One possible danger of on-the-spot penalties, experience shows, is that certain police officers develop too strong a sense of their own power, and motorists, on their part, quite naturally develop a feeling of animosity towards traffic police.

In some countries, including both German states, Austria, and, beginning this year, France, many minor offenses are dealt with without trial, by a written "penal order" ("order of summary punishment") issued by the court, always on condition that the accused does not object. This summary procedure is not unlike the American "waiver" practice in some traffic violations. As an example, Articles 407-411 of the West German code provide (in part):

> In the case of petty offenses and minor crimes, punishment may be imposed by a written penal order of the judge without trial, if the prosecution so moves in writing. Under a penal order, a fine or imprisonment not exceeding three months can be imposed. The penal order shall specify the punishable act, the criminal law applied, and the evidence. If no objection is raised by the accused within a week, a penal order obtains the effect of a final judgment.

This is a simple and advantageous procedure. It can be said that in minor cases it functions as surrogate to guilty pleas without the accused having to appear before the court. Its importance in the German system is shown by the frequency with which it is used. In the sixties it was estimated that from 66 to 70 percent of all criminal cases brought before the courts were disposed of by penal orders. One criticism which might be made, however, is that the German maximum penalty of three months imprisonment is too high for summary proceedings of this kind.

5. As long as the traditional American jury trial is preserved, little simplification of trial procedure along Continental lines will be feasible. It must not be forgotten that the Continental trial, including the leading role of the judge, is preconditioned by the existence of the file of investigation (which, by the way, many outstanding scholars since the nineteenth century have felt to be an unfortunate heritage of the old inquisition). However, Continental experience would seem to support the view that the judge's role in procuring, ex officio, relevant evidence not produced by the parties is important. Likewise, a more active, but not too active, role of the judge at the examination of witnesses and expert witnesses might help to simplify the American trial.

6. The European system of receiving testimony from witnesses first as a coherent, nearly uninterrupted account by the witness of what he knows about relevant facts, followed by a closer questioning, seems to be fully supported by forensic psychology. In Europe a witness's testimony is rarely interrupted by objections to evidence on grounds that it is hearsay or irrelevant; this fact does not have an adverse effect on the procedure or its outcome. In American practice the complaint of a confused witness may seem not unjustified: "I swore to tell the truth, but every time I try to, some lawyer objects."

Legal thinking in Europe makes a great distinction between the procedural positions and the statements of, respectively, the accused, the witness, and the expert. The traditional Anglo-American practice of treating these three heterogeneous kinds of evidence as being the same—that is, the sworn testimony of a witness—leads to at least two unfortunate consequences. First, wherever the very existence of the accused depends on his "testimony," he will nearly always try to commit at least some amount of perjury, which hardly seems to be too reprehensible. Second, an expert's opinion can be reliable evidence only if he is absolutely impartial. In many cases expert opinion is the decisive basis of a verdict. In an American procedure, unfortunately, an expert is selected, consulted (sometimes even briefed?), produced at the trial, examined, and worst of all, paid by either the prosecution or the accused. Selection of experts by the court, as in Europe, after hearing of motions of both parties, would seem to be a useful and excusable deviance from a strictly adversary form of proceedings.

Repeatedly the attention of comparative legal thinking in the United States and in Great Britain is drawn to other, inherently inquisitorial, aspects of the European criminal process. A profound knowledge of European practice and of its evaluation by Continental scholars may demonstrate, however, that a particular concept or institution necessarily risks the destruction of basic due process values, or that it may not carry the advantages expected. Any legislative transplantation of a particular Continental institution to the United States should therefore be based on an understanding of the history and character of that institution, of how it functions in practice and under what conditions, and of what favorable and unfavorable consequences stem from it.

Perhaps I may be allowed a cautionary note on at least two issues. First, reformers of the adversary procedure have long been attracted by the concept of an investigating magistrate. Actually, the institution of the European investigating judge, so far as it still is in existence, is no more than a survival of the old inquisitorial system, maintained in parts of Europe chiefly from strong tradition. The activities of such a judge are a needless and costly procedural phase inserted between the police investigation and the revision of its results at trial. The investigating judge has proved inefficient as a safeguard against abuses in police investigation practices; on the contrary, the fact that judicial impartiality is mystically presumed to provide a safeguard in itself stands in the way of the establishment of really efficient safeguards in the investigating phase. A leading French treatise on criminal procedure says: "As to the safeguards ensured to the accused during judicial investigation, they are useless, where police perform the investigation and tender to the magistrate a case already completed; what à mockery, if the accused is then cautioned that he has the right not to be interrogated without his counsel being present."[8]

The fact that the investigating judge is nearly extinct in the West German process illustrates the dispensability of this institution in modern procedure. In Austria, a country where the tradition of investigating judge is nearly as strong as in France, the practice was pictured in 1933 by Professor Ferdinand Kadečka as follows:

> All who have already been heard by the police are called before the investigating judge; here they are once more examined with as much detail as possible on matters already put into the file. Eventually, with every witness a deposition is written where he states that he has nothing to add to his statement already made before the police.

Kadečka's final evaluation is that "judicial investigation fits into our modern criminal process about as well as a stagecoach into a garage. Let us store it in a museum and learn to drive a car."[9]

Second, as a conclusion, I would point out that much current opinion in the United States favors some weakening, if not abolition, of certain safeguards against investigatory abuses. There is support for measures to allow more latitude to secret police interrogation of suspects; to abolish the caution, and especially the aid of defense counsel, in the first, often decisive phase of police questioning; to induce suspects to make statements by implying that silence will lead to a presumption of guilt at the trial; and to abolish strict, therefore efficient, rules excluding illegally

---

[8] Roger Merle and André Vitu, *Traité de droit criminel* (Paris: Editions Cujas, 1967), p. 841.

[9] Ferdinand Kadečka, "Reform oder Abschaffung der Voruntersuchung?" *Juristische Blätter,* vol. 11 (1933), pp. 225, 228.

obtained evidence from the trial, and instead to allow such evidence to be admitted at judicial discretion.

For a proper evaluation of these and similar suggestions, a profound study of modern European practice and literature is useful—in fact, necessary. Continental experience over the last 150 years would probably surprise supporters of the suggestions listed above, however, with the evidence that abolition of the present safeguards would shift the American criminal process to an inquisitorial one—a process where the decision usually is formed in the inquisitorial phase of secret police investigation. The results of this all-important investigative phase would—in the United States—be submitted to judicial review in an adversary form only in that 10 percent of cases where truth is supposed to be established by trial instead of by guilty pleas and plea bargaining.

ENGLISH CRIMINAL PROCEDURE AND THE SCALES OF JUSTICE

John Ll. J. Edwards

When I was invited to prepare a paper for this conference outlining some of the principal features of English criminal procedure, I recalled an earlier occasion when I had addressed the National District Attorneys' Association here in Washington in 1966 on a somewhat similar subject. At that time there were still to be heard the reverberations from the notable decisions in *Miranda* and *Escobedo* by the United States Supreme Court regarding pretrial procedural standards. As an interested observer, I was struck by the frequent reference of commentators in the United States to the intrinsic lessons that could be drawn from the Judges' Rules in England and their central place in the law enforcement procedures followed by the British police.

Ironically, at the same time that these views were being aired on this continent, a substantial revision of the selfsame charter was being undertaken by the English Criminal Law Revision Committee, a standing body consisting of judges of the Court of Appeal and the High Court, the Director of Public Prosecutions, the Metropolitan Magistrate of London and senior academic lawyers. The English committee can be compared with the American Law Institute, with the added distinction that the former has witnessed the translation of practically all of its recommendations, contained in the 10 reports that it has produced since its establishment in 1959, into law. Its latest report, entitled quite simply, *Evidence (General),*[1] was published a few weeks ago as I was preparing this paper, and the public debate in England on the committee's controversial recommendations is already in full swing.

In this debate, the careful reasoning of the committee's prelude to its various proposals for change is almost certain to be lost in the welter of public interpretations of the committee's work. Before I proceed to examine some of the more significant of the reform measures, I should emphasize, as the committee itself does at the outset of its report, that the essential features of English criminal trials will remain much the same as at present, namely:

1. The English "adversary" system will not be replaced by the Continental "inquisitorial" system.

---

[1] Cmnd. 4991 (London: Her Majesty's Stationery Office, 1972).

2. Trial by jury will remain, and the judge will not retire with the jury when they consider their verdict.

3. Magistrates will continue to try the great majority of criminal cases, and of these a very high proportion will be tried by lay justices.

To convey an understanding of the fundamental characteristics of a foreign system, albeit one which has so much in common with United States law and practice, it will be wise to concentrate on a few topics. This I propose to do and in my choice of subjects I have understandably paid special attention to the recommendations for reform issued by the Criminal Law Revision Committee.

I. The Machinery of Criminal Prosecutions

There exists in the criminal justice system of England and Wales an office that is the subject of much misunderstanding. I refer to the Director of Public Prosecutions (DPP). This office, which is less than 100 years old, by its very title conveys an impression of overall control in the field of prosecuting crime in England. In actual fact, there are considerable limitations on the powers exercisable by the director and his staff of lawyers. The director is responsible in the exercise of his functions to the attorney general who, in turn, must discharge his public accountability on the floor of the House of Commons. Like all other ministers of the Crown, the attorney general is a political minister in the sense that he is elected like any other member of Parliament. It is important, however, to recognize the fundamental character of the system of prosecutions that obtains in England whereby the attorney general, as the chief law officer of the Crown in charge of prosecutions for all indictable offenses, make his decisions from a position of total independence vis-à-vis his colleagues in the government. My study of the administration of justice in England and Wales, published in 1963 under the title *The Law Officers of the Crown,*[2] develops at some length the historical and political reasons for this state of affairs. Suffice it to emphasize at this point that whereas the DPP on occasion seeks directions from the attorney general, in normal circumstances there is no contact between the DPP and the principal law officers of the Crown.

The principle of independence is no shallow doctrine in the day-to-day administration of the criminal law. To discover the range of responsibilities of the DPP, reference must be made to the Prosecution of Offences Acts of 1879-1908 and the regulations made thereunder. For our present purposes it will be enough to indicate the three principal areas in which the director is empowered to intervene or to take over criminal prosecutions and also to tender advice to chiefs of police throughout the entire country. First, it is the duty of the DPP to institute or undertake criminal proceedings: (1) in the case of any offense punishable by death (this is no longer applicable since the almost total abolition of the death

---

[2] London: Sweet and Maxwell, 1963.

penalty in Britain earlier this year), (2) in any case referred to him by a government department in which he considers that criminal proceedings should be instituted, and (3) in any case which appears to him to be of importance or difficulty or which for any other reason requires his intervention. Secondly, the same legislation sets out in detail those cases which the police must report to the Director of Public Prosecutions with a view to his possibly undertaking a prosecution. These include every offense in respect of which the prosecution has by statute to be undertaken by the DPP, every indictable case in which the prosecution is wholly withdrawn or is not proceeded with within a reasonable time, every case in which a request for information is made by the DPP, and every case in which it appears to the chief officer of police that the advice or assistance of the director is desirable. There is also a list of specific offenses that have to be reported by the chief officer of police in every district, the total range of which makes the opportunity for intervention by the director considerable.

Superimposed on these obligations there is a further provision, the significance of which is perhaps best understood by the chiefs of police themselves. It permits the director to give advice, whether on application or on his own initiative, to chiefs of police in any criminal matter which the director views as important or difficult; such advice may be given at his discretion either orally or in writing. When one realizes that in England and Wales there exists, as in so many countries, a multiplicity of police forces, the opportunity provided by the above legislation for developing proper standards of investigative practices is one that has been recognized by successive holders of the office of DPP. Advice is freely sought and freely given, and the independent nature of the DPP, together with the remarkable personalities of the holders of this office, have each contributed to the present position whereby advice that is tendered from the director's office is generally accepted without question.

From what I have said, it should not be understood that the director assumes the responsibility for the direct investigation of crime in the manner that appears to be an integral part of the office of the district attorney in the United States. Normally it is the police who inquire into the circumstances of an alleged crime, who obtain information from potential witnesses, and who accumulate evidence sufficient not only to identify the accused but to approve the bringing of a charge. The duties of the staff of the Department of Public Prosecutions are to prepare the case for presentation in court, and either to conduct the case in court personally or to prepare instructions for a solicitor or counsel who will then appear as the lawyer acting on behalf of the director.

It may be pertinent at this juncture to recall the evidence given in 1929 by Sir Archibald Bodkin, then DPP, before the Royal Commission on Police Powers and Procedure. Bodkin stressed the importance of keeping distinct, on the one hand, the duty which lies upon the police of preventing and detecting crime, and on the other hand, the duty of bringing to justice persons who have broken the law. In Bodkin's view, which I share, it is undesirable that investigators into crime should also act as advocates who present to the court the circumstances of the crime. This basic philosophy can be said to permeate the entire system of criminal prosecutions in England. Although in 1929 the same Royal Commission visualized exceptional circumstances in which statements by potential witnesses would be taken by the DPP's staff—for example, when a case was particularly intricate or complex—it is significant that the former DPP, Sir Theobald Matthew, developed a policy which excluded officers of his department from taking statements from witnesses in any circumstances whatsoever. To the best of my knowledge this policy continues to be applied.

In identifying the factors and influences which control investigative practices and interrogation procedures in England, we must pay proper regard to the indigenous character of the machinery of criminal prosecutions in England and Wales. Perhaps I should emphasize that the situation in Scotland is also distinctive, but my remarks, unless otherwise stated, do not refer to Scottish criminal procedure. Apart from the special position occupied by Treasury Counsel at the Old Bailey in London and by solicitors employed by municipal authorities, and except for the occasional intervention by the staff of the DPP, it is entirely correct to say that England has not recognized the principle of public prosecutors. I have described at length attempts to transform the system during the nineteenth century in my study, *The Law Officers of the Crown*. More recently, in a report published by *Justice* the case was strongly argued for the adoption in England and Wales of the Scottish system of prosecutions.[3] In my judgment, it would be surprising if such a transformation was to be seen as imminent. In this respect, the English system also differs markedly from that which obtains in Canada, where the Crown attorney is a central figure in the conduct of criminal prosecutions at all levels of the criminal courts.

It is true that in the summary courts of jurisdiction presided over by lay magistrates, the police in England and Wales handle a large number of straightforward cases, particularly those involving traffic infractions, and there is a growing tendency for municipalities to appoint full-time prosecutors to conduct cases involving violations of municipal bylaws. The important feature to be recognized is that in England and Wales the ordinary citizen has a right to launch a private prosecution. There are obvious limitations to the unrestricted exercise of this right, but there are a number of notable instances in which prosecutions have been maintained in circumstances where, for reasons of expediency or otherwise, the DPP has seen fit not to embark on the particular prosecution. If I were to venture an opinion in this field it would be to assert that the private prosecution as an

---

[3] *The Prosecution Process in England and Wales* (London: Justice Educational and Research Trust, 1970).

institution is likely to expand in popularity and significance. I would regard this as a healthy development, provided there are the necessary restraints against litigious individuals whose ulterior purpose is more concerned with embarrassing the harassed defendant than in upholding the criminal law.

Before leaving the handling of criminal prosecutions in serious cases, I want to stress the importance of the standards of fairness epitomized by the English bar. As I pointed out earlier, most prosecutions in serious crime are left in the hands of counsel appointed for individual cases. With the divided profession that exists in England and Wales, this means that the overall supervision of the conduct of criminal prosecutions is handled by the relatively small body of 2,800 practicing barristers, only a small proportion of whom undertake criminal law as their exclusive field of practice. As stated by Lord Devlin in his book *The Criminal Prosecution in England:*

> The policeman, like any other litigant, is to a large extent in the hands of his counsel, and to try to advance one's case by means of some unfair practice is not much good if one's counsel is not going to aid and abet. The barrister who appears as often for the defence as for the prosecution acquires no special sympathy for either.[4]

The same jurist has rightly drawn attention to the special community of thought and the common adherence to traditional standards of fairness that exist between the bench and bar in England. "What the judge disapproves of the Bar is unlikely to do; and if the Bar would not do it the police must conform."[5] In addition, there is the unique situation that commonly obtains wherein the duties of a recorder, a sort of part-time judge, are discharged by the same lawyer who will be appearing the next day in a different court as counsel on behalf of the accused, or for the Crown as its prosecutor. It is difficult to describe adequately the channels of understanding whereby judicial standards of what is deemed to be right and wrong are communicated to the barristers involved in criminal cases. But those who have had the opportunity to observe the atmosphere of the Inns of Court in London and the Bar Messes on circuit, will have gained some appreciation of the universal and firm adherence to fundamental standards that are a part of the English legal tradition.

II. Major Reforms in the English Criminal Court Structure

Since the Middle Ages the court structure for dealing with criminal cases in England and Wales has remained relatively unchanged, with the justices of the High Court traveling around the country on assize, bringing the Queen's justice to the people with that adherence to pomp and ceremony that seems so normal and

---

[4] London: Oxford University Press, 1960, p. 21.

[5] Ibid., p. 22.

appropriate in Britain, but so incongruous when exported. Between the High Court of Justice and the Magistrates' Courts were the Courts of Quarter Sessions, with intermediate jurisdiction and presided over by a practicing barrister.

With the volume of criminal cases spiraling during the postwar period, the court structure, as I have described it, creaked and groaned to such an extent that a Royal Commission on Assizes and Quarter Sessions was established. By a masterful stroke of political judgment, the last Labor government appointed as its chairman and driving force an industrialist in the person of Lord Beeching who, some years earlier, had reformed the British railways. One day the story will be told of how Beeching brought the English judges around to accepting major changes in England's criminal justice system and to the institution of a modern court administrative structure. In 1971, Parliament enacted the Courts Act, and as of January 1, 1972, the ancient and venerable Courts of Assize and Courts of Quarter Sessions were relegated to the history books. In their place, England and Wales now have Crown Courts, which are superior courts of record. Together with the Court of Appeal and the High Court of Justice, they form the Supreme Court of Judicature. Replacing the old system of itinerant justices traveling to numerous cities and towns throughout the country, the Crown Court is based on a more centralized set of locations. There are to be first, second, and third-tier centers, with the first-tier centers dealing with both civil and criminal cases, and presided over by High Court and circuit judges. Second-tier centers, covering less populated areas, will deal with criminal cases only, and will also be presided over by both High Court and circuit judges. Third-tier centers will deal with criminal cases only, and will be served and presided over by circuit judges only. The latter occupy a position somewhat inferior in status to that of a High Court judge. The classification of offenses triable by the respective tiers of Crown Courts reflect corresponding levels of crime according to their seriousness. I think it inevitable that the movement will continue and we shall see the delegation to lower courts of jurisdiction to hear criminal cases that formerly were thought to require the exclusive attention of a High Court judge. My experience of the criminal courts in Canada has fortified me in the belief that the criminal law can be administered successfully by legally trained judges without too much regard for their position in the judicial hierarchy.

At the lowest end of the scale, minor offenses have been left to the jurisdiction of lay justices of the peace, sitting in what are known as courts of summary jurisdiction. Not long ago serious questions were being raised as to the desirability of abolishing lay magistrates and transfering their responsibilities to full-time professionals, as is the case in some cities with the appointment of stipendiary magistrates. With the resort to a wider diversity of backgrounds and talents in the making of new appointments, and a great deal of attention to sentencing seminars, however, few voices are presently to be heard calling for large-scale reform in the magistrates' courts.

III. The Concept of Fairness and the Privilege against Self-incrimination

It has long been regarded as one of the basic tenets of the English law of evidence that an accused person should not be required to incriminate himself out of his own mouth. This privilege rests on the concept of what is fair and just, but it is noteworthy that in its latest report the Criminal Law Revision Committee makes the important point that it must be clear what fairness means in this connection. In the committee's words:

> It means, or ought to mean, that the law should be such as will secure as far as possible that the result of the trial is the right one. That is to say, the accused should be convicted if the evidence proves beyond reasonable doubt that he is guilty, but otherwise not. We stress this, although it may seem obvious, because fairness seems often to be thought of as something which is due to the defence only. At least there seems to be an idea that the defence have a sacred right to the benefit of anything in the law which may give them a chance of acquittal, even on a technicality, however strong the case is against them. We disagree entirely with this idea. It seems to derive from an unwarranted extension of the principle that, in order that the accused should be convicted, the prosecution must prove their case and perhaps also the convention that those appearing for the prosecution are not concerned to secure a conviction but only to present the case. As a result the habit has grown up of looking at a criminal trial as a kind of game to be played, according to fixed rules, between the prosecution and the defence; and since the defence are naturally likely to be the weaker (and the accused may very likely seem stupid and helpless), it seems to be expected that the prosecution will refrain from using all their strength and that the judge will take any opportunity to make the contest more even.[6]

There may be those amongst you who, by inclination or persuasion, will frown on the disturbing of the balance reflected in the old rules of English criminal procedure. For my part, I share the general philosophy expressed by the Criminal Law Revision Committee that fairness must be viewed in the general circumstances of the administration of justice, and that "it is as much in the public interest that a guilty person should be convicted as it is that an innocent person should be acquitted."[7]

Inherent in the traditional rights enjoyed by an accused person under English law is the requirement that it is for the prosecution to prove the guilt of the accused, and that where the accused refrains from giving evidence the prosecution may not comment on his omission to enter the witness box and give evidence on his own behalf. The so-called "right of silence" also means that if the suspect, when being interrogated, omits to mention some facts which would tend to exculpate him and keeps this information back until the trial, it is not permissible

---

[6] Cmnd. 4991, p. 15.

[7] Ibid., p. 16.

for the court or the jury to infer that his evidence on such an issue at the trial is untrue by virtue of his having remained silent during the period of interrogation.

The Criminal Law Revision Committee makes the strong recommendation that it should be permissible to draw such an inference if the circumstances justify it. The suspect will continue to enjoy the right of silence to the extent that it will be no offense to refuse to answer questions or to refuse to tell his story when interrogated; if, however, he chooses to exercise his right of remaining silent, he will run the risk of having an adverse inference drawn against him at the trial. The arguments that will undoubtedly be advanced against the proposed change will probably rest upon the unfairness of a system that puts pressure upon a suspect during the period of interrogation. To this the English committee rejoins by citing Jeremy Bentham's famous comment: "If all criminals of every class had assembled and framed the system after their own wishes, is not this rule [the right of silence] the very first which they would have established for their security? Innocence never takes advantage of it, innocence claims the right of speaking as guilt invokes the privilege of silence." [8]

IV. The Police Caution and the Judges' Rules

Clearly, if the recommendations of the Criminal Law Revision Committee are adopted in principle, there must be drastic changes in the system of administering cautions to those who are being interrogated by the police. The traditional caution has been contained in the statement, "You are not obliged to say anything unless you wish to do so, but if you do, anything you say may be given in evidence." Under the present Judges' Rules, such a caution must be given (1) when the police officer has reasonable grounds for suspecting that the person in question has committed an offense, and (2) when the suspect is charged with, or informed that he may be prosecuted for, an offense. The question is whether the arguments in favor of removing the familiar police caution are convincing, and what alternative safeguards are needed to protect the innocent.

It is claimed that practiced criminals have little respect, anyway, for the caution. The committee points to the illogic of imposing upon the police a duty to question persons for the purposes of discovering whether and by whom an offense has been committed, and at the same time imposing on the police a parallel duty to tell the person being questioned that he need not answer. What the new proposals envisage is that a person being interrogated with regard to alleged criminal activity should have his attention drawn specifically to the fact that adverse inferences may be made from his refusal to mention any fact upon which he is going to rely at the trial. The burden of choosing between silence and explaining suspicious conduct is thereby dramatically changed and, if the change is implemented, British citizens

---

[8] Ibid., p. 18.

will become familiar with a caution couched in the following terms: "You have been charged with (informed that you may be prosecuted for) such and such an offence. If there is any fact on which you intend to rely in your defence in court, you are advised to mention it now. If you hold it back till you go to court, your evidence may be less likely to be believed and this may have a bad effect on your case in general. If you wish to mention any fact now, and you would like it written down, this will be done." The standing committee suggests that the notice be given in writing to the accused, thereby insuring that a record exists that it was in fact given. Significantly, it is not recommended that there be a general requirement to warn suspects at an earlier stage of the interrogation because this might have the disadvantage of interrupting a natural course of interrogation and unduly hampering the police in their investigations.

What does this do to the Judges' Rules? It has long been the practice of the English judges to offer guidance to the police in the field of criminal investigation and interrogation. The original rules were formulated in 1912 as a result of conflicting judicial advice during the early part of this century regarding the administering of a caution to persons suspected of crime. Originally there were four rules. In 1918 another five were added to the original quartet, and in 1930 a further statement was prepared to clarify certain points of ambiguity in the original set of rules. Difficulties in setting down exact rules for the interrogation of suspects was further reflected by the distribution to chiefs of police in 1947, and again in 1948, of circulars prepared by the Home Office after consultation with the Lord Chief Justice of England.

Doubts continued to plague the application of the original Judges' Rules. It came as no surprise when in January 1964 a revised edition of the rules was announced by the Court of Criminal Appeal. Lord Parker, Chief Judge, in introducing the new judges' rules, described the criticisms that had been leveled against the original guidelines as falling into two main categories. Thus, on the one hand, it was claimed that the rules suffered from lack of clarity or efficacy in protecting persons who are questioned by police officers; on the other hand, it was maintained that their application unduly hampered the detection and punishment of crime. If one reads the latest report of the Criminal Law Revision Committee it is clear that this latter argument has prevailed. What we are now witnessing is a fundamental shift in the balance between the divergent principles of fairness to the accused and of not hampering the police.

What remains unresolved is the place to be accorded to the principle enunciated in the preface to the original Judges' Rules which declares: "Every person at any stage of an investigation should be able to communicate and consult privately with a solicitor." Strict adherence to this right of the citizen very naturally occasions concern on the part of law enforcement officers in England, no less than in the United States and Canada, where the limits of the principle have recently been the subject of judicial decisions in the supreme courts of both countries. In an attempt to reconcile the two extreme positions that can be taken on this vital question, the English judges in 1964 stated that the right of a suspect or an accused person to the availability of legal counsel was subject to the important proviso that "in such cases no unreasonable delay or hindrance is caused to the processes of investigation or to the administration of justice by his doing so." Here is revealed once again the English penchant for developing a principle that permits flexibility in its application. No absolute right to legal counsel is conferred at every stage of the process of criminal interrogation; instead, an attempt is made to permit a balancing of considerations of effective investigation with due regard to the relative helplessness of the citizen when he finds himself in a police station subject to interrogation by one or more police officers.

It is at least arguable that insufficient regard has been paid by the Criminal Law Revision Committee to the fallibility of even the most experienced individual when confronted with police interrogators in the unfamiliar surroundings of a police station. In their concern to insure adequate protection for ordinary citizens who encounter criminal interrogations the committee did consider recommending the use of tape recorders so as to insure reliable accounts of the interrogation. For a number of reasons, however, a majority of the members refrained from recommending that tape recorders be brought into general use in interrogations because of the technical difficulties of insuring total accuracy as to what happened. As to the argument that the use of recorders would cause offenders to refuse to answer questions, I find fairly convincing the view that, in practice, the existence of a recorder would soon be forgotten by the person under interrogation, particularly when it comes to be realized that the proposed new law would provide a powerful sanction for the answering of questions by the police. At present the Judges' Rules provide that all statements made by a person in custody must be written down at the time; the proponents of the use of electronic recording maintain that it would be hardly more inhibiting for an offender than the sight of a police officer writing down what he is saying. In essence, it is argued that even if some suspects refuse to answer when they know that their replies are being recorded on tape, the loss of this evidence must be accepted as the price to be paid for an essential safeguard.

V. The Inquisitorial System and its Rejection by the Criminal Law Revision Committee

Many claims have been made in favor of the system of interrogating suspects in line with the mode adopted in the Continental "inquisitorial" system, the essential feature being that at a certain stage in the criminal investigation, the suspect is compelled to appear before a judicial officer and is obliged to listen to questions. The questions, and the suspected person's answers, if any, would then be admissible at the subsequent trial. Under the Indian Evidence Act of 1872, which is often quoted in this connection, evidence of anything said during an interrogation by the police before the suspect was taken before a magistrate would be inadmissible. The underlying argument in favor of a system of inquisitorial interrogation by judicial officers is that this procedure would insure beyond doubt the fairness of the interrogation and thus would avoid the disputes that generally accompany claims to admit answers made by the accused in the course of police interrogation.

In the view of the English Criminal Law Revision Committee there is no substance to the claim that the alternative system would make it more likely that the person interrogated would tell the truth. Instead, the committee maintains that the formality of the procedure would often defeat its own purposes. Furthermore, if there is a dispute as to what was said during the interrogation or how it was conducted, it is reasonable to suppose that the magistrate would need to be called as a witness and to be cross-examined. In the opinion of the committee it would be undesirable for magistrates to be subjected to this inconvenience and possible embarrassment. I think that the problem of relating the theoretical advantages or disadvantages of the inquisitorial procedure to the practical exigencies is no different when set against the English background from that which applies in Canada or in the United States. And the issue is a lively one at present in Canada where the National Law Reform Commission is charged with examining the entire criminal process and making recommendations for any reforms that are thought to be necessary. Wedded as I am to the well-tried supervision of police interrogation practices by the courts, I will be interested to hear the response of members of this group to this particular question.

VI. Confessions Resulting from Threats, Inducements or Oppressive Measures

Evidence of an accused's confession, or of an admission which tends to prove that he committed the offense charged, are admissible under English law as exceptions to the general rule against hearsay. Although the statements are said to be hearsay, they are nevertheless admissible on the grounds that what a person says against himself is likely to be true. English courts, however, have always treated confessions by accused persons with a healthy degree of suspicion, and for any confession to be admissible it must be shown that it was made voluntarily. Voluntary, in this context, means that the statement shall not have been obtained from him by fear of prejudice, or hope of advantage exercised or held out by a person in authority, or by oppression. This principle has been upheld to the extent of rendering a confession inadmissible, no matter how mild or slight the threat or inducement happened to be.

Describing the historical origins of the rule and its modern application, Lord Justice Winn declared in a recent decision of the Court of Appeal:

> In these days it really does seem that the undoubtedly well-established
> doctrine of our law that persons who are minded to make a confession or

admission to the police or other authorities must be very strictly safe-guarded against any persuasion or inducement to make any such confession or admission is in some respects somewhat out of date. In these days the criminal classes are only too well aware of their position of virtual immunity in the hands of the police. It does seem that some of the present doctrines and principles have come down in our law from earlier times when the police of this country were not to be trusted, as they are now to be trusted in almost every single case, to behave with complete fairness towards those who come into their hands or from whom they are seeking information. It was then thought right, and no doubt then was right, to take an extremely strict position with regard to any favours or inducements which might be said to have been offered.[9]

The English Criminal Law Revision Committee has now recommended a change from the existing position, though not without some dissenting voices among its members. In the view of the majority, the rule as to the general inadmissibility of confessions should be limited to threats or inducements of a kind likely to produce an unreliable confession. All the committee members adhere to the view that confessions procured as a result of oppression should continue to remain inadmissible. After considering several possible variants, the committee concluded that the rule should be that a threat or inducement, whether made by a person in authority or not, should render a resulting confession inadmissible only if the threat or inducement was of a sort likely "in the circumstances existing at the time to render unreliable any confession which might be made by the accused in consequence thereof."[10] Under the proposed change, the trial judge, in exercising his powers of admitting or rejecting the alleged confession, should imagine that he was present at the interrogation and heard the threat or inducement. The confession should be rejected only if, in the light of all the evidence given, the judge considers that at the point when the threat was uttered or the inducement offered, the accused's confession should be treated as unreliable. It will be necessary for the trial judge to consider evidence of the whole course of the interrogation, including the terms of the confession itself, in order to gauge the likely effect of the nullifying threat or inducement.

The proposed new test, it should be emphasized again, will not apply when it is shown that the confession was obtained as a result of oppressive measures. No exceptional circumstances will condone oppression. Interestingly, the concept of oppression is a fairly recent development in the English law, and derives originally from a statement made by Lord Parker, the Chief Justice, in the case of *Callis* v. *Gunn* in 1964. For a fuller analysis of oppression as a ground for invalidating a confession, I would refer you to the judgment of Mr. Justice Sachs in 1965 (later adopted by the Court of Appeal) when he declared:

---

[9] R. v. Northam (1967), 52 Cr.App.R.97 at p. 102.
[10] Cmnd. 4991, pp. 43 and 45.

... to my mind, this word in the context of the principles under consideration imports something which tends to sap, and has sapped, that free will
which must exist before a confession is voluntary. . . . Whether or not
there is oppression in an individual case depends upon many elements.
I am not going into all of them. They include such things as the length of
time of any individual period of questioning, the length of time intervening
between periods of questioning, whether the accused person had been
given proper refreshment or not, and the characteristics of the person
who makes the statement. What may be oppressive as regards a child,
an invalid or an old man or somebody inexperienced in the ways of this
world, may turn out not to be oppressive when one finds that the accused
person is of a tough character and an experienced man of the world.[11]

The standing committee has more to say on some of the other controversial aspects
of the law relating to confessions, all of which will repay study. In all these questions, logic must take second place to considerations of policy, and the public
debate in this area will wax eloquent for months to come. Of that I have no doubt.

VII. Should the Accused Be Required To Enter the Witness Box?

Under the existing English law an accused person may choose between giving
evidence on oath (or making an affirmation) and making an unsworn statement
from the dock. In the latter case his evidence is not subject to cross-examination.
The Criminal Law Revision Committee has argued strongly that the time has come
to abolish the right of the accused not to give evidence and to make an unsworn
statement. To understand this highly sensitive problem it is once more necessary
to have regard to something of the history behind the existing law.

Until the enactment of the Criminal Evidence Act in 1898, an accused person
was not allowed to give evidence on oath. Before 1898, whether he was legally
represented or not, the accused had a choice between making an unsworn statement
and entering the witness box. When the 1898 Criminal Evidence Act allowed him
to give evidence on oath in all cases, Parliament saw fit expressly to preserve the
accused person's right to make an unsworn statement instead of giving evidence
under oath. This was in keeping with the policy of the act that pressures should not
be put on accused persons to take advantage of their new right to give evidence under
oath; the preference was to accord the accused the option of taking shelter in an
unsworn statement which precluded any possibility of his being cross-examined.
Furthermore, the 1898 statute expressly denied to the prosecution the right to
make any adverse comment on the failure of the accused to enter the witness box.
This right was permitted to the trial judge, but it would be correct to say that the
right to comment has been used very sparingly. Adverse judicial comment has
never been permitted to go so far as to suggest that failure to give evidence is
enough to lead to an inference of guilt.

---

[11] R. v. Priestley (1965), 51 Cr.App.R.1.

In line with its other recommendations, the Criminal Law Revision Committee has concluded that the present law and practice are much too favorable to the defense. They recommend that when a prima facie case has been made out against the accused, it should be regarded as incumbent on him to give evidence in all ordinary cases. Furthermore, the committee proposes that the prosecution, like the judge, should be allowed to comment in a situation where the accused fails to enter the witness box. The stronger the prima facie case against the accused, the more significant will be the interpretation to be placed on his failure to give evidence. In view of this, the committee concludes that if and when the court decides that there is a case for the defense to answer, the accused should be expressly informed by the trial judge that at the appropriate time he will be called upon to enter the witness box and to give evidence in his own defense. The accused should also be informed as to the effects of his refusing to do so, thereby insuring that he is under no mistake as to his obligations and the consequences that will flow from his decision.

VIII. Majority Verdicts

As is probably well known, Scottish criminal procedure has long recognized the legitimacy of settling differences of opinion within the jury room by permitting majority verdicts. A series of "hung" juries in several recent notable trials of professional criminals at the Old Bailey eventually tipped the scales in favor of yet another reform in English criminal law which, not more than a decade ago, would have been thought impossible. Now, by virtue of section 13 of the Criminal Justice Act of 1967, the verdict of a jury in an English criminal trial no longer has to be unanimous. Where there are ten jurors it is sufficient if nine of them agree on the verdict; likewise, if there are at least 11 jurors, it suffices if 10 of the members agree upon the verdict. The trial judge is not allowed to accept a majority verdict of guilty unless the foreman of the jury has stated in open court the number of jurors who agree to and the number who dissent from such a verdict. Moreover, the judge is precluded from accepting a majority verdict if it appears that the jury has had not less than two hours of deliberation or such longer period as the court thinks reasonable having regard to the nature and complexity of the case. The general impression that I have gained during the few years that this new law has been in operation is that the change has been welcomed and that, though one more of the hallowed traditions has been disturbed, the foundations of English criminal law remain as stable as ever.

IX. Preliminary Investigations of Indictable Crimes by Examining Magistrates

Until the reforms embodied in a statute of 1968, the English law governing preliminary hearings was contained in the Indictable Offences Act of 1848, itself a

216

measure notable for its reforming spirit. Thus, for the first time it entitled the accused person to be present at the examination of witnesses against him. By emphasizing that the room or building in which the local justice of the peace conducted the preliminary hearing was not to be deemed an open court for that purpose, the act recognized the discretionary power of the justice of the peace to sit *in camera*. The same act explains the true character of the preliminary hearing, which is not a trial in the true sense of that word. The magistrate is not to decide whether the accused is guilty or not guilty, but simply to satisfy himself whether a prima facie case has been made out by the prosecution and, if so, to commit the accused person for trial before a judge and jury in a higher court.

As I understand it, the grand jury remains a venerable institution in the eyes of most Americans. In England and Wales during the nineteenth century and the early part of this century, the powers of the grand jury to determine whether a "true bill" or "no bill" should be returned in indictable cases duplicated the procedure of a preliminary hearing before examining justices. In this situation the inevitable was not long delayed. With the passing of the Administration of Justice (Miscellaneous Provisions) Act of 1933, the English model of the grand jury was relegated to the limbo of ancient procedures that have been discarded and well nigh completely forgotten by the average layman.

In a memorandum that I prepared for the U.S. Senate Subcommittee on Improvements in Judicial Machinery in July 1966, I drew attention to the considerable dissatisfaction that had become evident in England with the preliminary hearing procedure. The reasons were not difficult to discover. First, there was the undoubted fact that committal proceedings before the examining magistrates rarely gave rise to any serious contest as to the evidence relating to the particular charge. Secondly, the accused was often not legally represented at all, and even if he was, there was little inclination to put before the magistrate evidence disclosing the line upon which the defense would be based at the subsequent trial. In view of the tedious and time-consuming nature of the recording in writing of all the statements tendered at the preliminary hearing, it had become increasingly apparent that the proceedings were rarely more than a formality.

Calls for reforms have not gone unheeded and, as with so many changes in the criminal law that have been instituted in recent years, England has looked to Scotland for its new models. Scottish criminal procedure has never known a system of preliminary hearings before examining magistrates and has relied instead upon its public prosecutors, called procurators fiscal, to ascertain the evidence which the Crown's witnesses will give when called upon at the subsequent trial. The accused is neither present nor legally represented at the time when these statements, called precognitions, are taken from the prospective witnesses. Before the trial, however, the defense is supplied with copies of the indictment, a full list of the prosecution witnesses and their statements of evidence. The decision to proceed to trial is taken not by a court but by the public prosecutor; this requires action by either the procurator fiscal or the Crown Office, which acts on the directions of the Scottish law officers or the Advocates Depute, counsel instructed by the Crown Office.

The reforms instituted under the Criminal Justice Act of 1967 have not abolished preliminary hearings, but their significance in criminal cases has been drastically diminished. A full-scale hearing is now undertaken only at the instance of the accused or where the accused is not legally represented. Otherwise, the written statements tendered to the court are made available to the prosecution and defense, as the case may be, in advance of the hearing. The written statements are admissible to the same extent as if the evidence had been given orally. As expected, the new procedure has considerably speeded up the processing of cases, and no voices have been heard to complain that the old protections to the accused have been sacrificed.

Another important change effected by the Criminal Justice Act of 1967, heralding some of the Criminal Law Revision Committee's latest recommendations, is the requirement that an accused may not, without leave of the court, call evidence in support of an alibi, unless he has given advance notice to the prosecution of the particulars upon which he intends to rely for his alibi defense. This, too, has been imported from Scottish criminal procedure and, I think, makes good sense.

X. News Media Publicity of Preliminary Hearings

Another important assimilation of English and Scottish law, which has been effected only after much heart searching and bewailing of violations of the freedom of the press, concerns the reporting of preliminary hearings. Let me begin by summarizing the Scottish position as described in 1961 by Professor T. B. Smith in his Hamlyn Lectures. He wrote:

> In Scotland as in England, once an accused has been apprehended, the function of the Press in commenting upon the guilt of a suspected person or the nature of the charge against him is suspended under severe sanction of law. This in Scotland is not a right solely of the accused, nor is infringement necessarily an aspect of contempt of court; interference with the administration of justice can take many forms. Thus no comment is permitted which might influence the mind of the public in favour of an accused awaiting trial—as by attacking the merits of the prosecution. Scottish protection against injurious publicity goes further. Publication of statements by witnesses before they testify at the trial is absolutely forbidden, as is publication of photographs of persons under suspicion, especially after arrest, since this might influence the reliability of evidence of identification. The overriding purpose is that the accused should be tried by a jury which comes to its duty without any preconceptions whatsoever regarding guilt or innocence. After arrest—in one view, as soon as the official investigation has started—and before trial of an accused, the Press in Scotland is permitted to publish only the bare facts that a

named person has appeared before the Sheriff, charged with a particular crime and that he has been committed for trial. This contrasts sharply with the situation in other parts of the United Kingdom.[12]

This is no longer so, but it has taken a long time to see the law changed. One of the turning points was undoubtedly the 1957 Old Bailey trial and acquittal of John Bodkin Adams, M.D., charged with murdering one of his patients. At the preliminary hearing the prosecution laid evidence of the circumstances in which two other patients of Dr. Adams had died in highly suspicious circumstances. At the trial this evidence was not admitted, and in his summing up to the jury Mr. Justice Devlin expressed the opinion that it would have been wiser if the committal proceedings had been held in private "because when you have a case of this character it arouses widespread discussion, and it is inevitable that reports appear in the press and that it will be read by people who subsequently have to serve on the jury." In the following year the government appointed a departmental committee to examine the whole subject of pretrial publicity under the chairmanship of Lord Tucker. The crux of the debate surrounding this question is well expressed by the Tucker committee in the passage that reads:

> We realise that any restriction on the reporting of what occurs in court was believed by the representatives of the press who gave evidence before us to infringe that freedom of reporting which they regard as essential to the proper administration of justice. We agree that freedom of report trials is essential, and we re-affirm the right of the press to report proceedings which result in the discharge or conviction of the accused; but we draw a clear distinction between reporting the trial itself and reporting preliminary proceedings. It is, in our opinion, illogical and wrong to permit such latitude in the reporting of preliminary proceedings that confidence in the fairness of trial is undermined.[13]

In 1965 the Wilson government declared its intention to give effect to the recommendations of the Tucker committee. It was not until two years later that the necessary legislation was introduced and finally enacted.

Under section 3 of the Criminal Justice Act of 1967, unless the accused applies to have the statutory restrictions lifted, it is forbidden to report or broadcast an account of committal proceedings except for certain items of information. These include the names of the examining justices, the identity of the court, particulars of the defendant and witnesses, the names of counsel and solicitors engaged in the proceedings, the charges that are involved and the decision of the court, as well as particulars regarding bail and legal aid. The statutory restrictions are lifted once the examining justices decide not to commit the accused for trial or, if there is a committal, at the conclusion of the subsequent trial.

---

[12] *British Justice: The Scottish Contribution* (London: Stevens, 1961), pp. 123-24.

[13] Cmnd. 479 (London: Her Majesty's Stationery Office, 1958), paragraph 71.

It may be of interest to note that Canadian criminal law adopted a similar policy in 1959 by amending its Criminal Code to provide that:

> Everyone who publishes in any newspaper or broadcasts a report that any admission or confession was tendered in evidence at the preliminary enquiry, or a report of the nature of such admission or confession so tendered in evidence, unless (a) the accused has been discharged, or (b) that the accused is being committed to trial, or (c) the trial has ended, is guilty of an offence punishable by summary conviction.[14]

This law was repealed in 1968 and new provisions instituted to regulate the publication of evidence taken at a preliminary inquiry. The present legislation states:

> (1) Prior to the commencement of the taking of evidence at a preliminary inquiry, the justice holding the inquiry shall, if application therefore is made by the accused or, where there is more than one accused, by any one of them, make an order directing that the evidence taken at the inquiry shall not be published in any newspaper or broadcast before such time as
>
> *(a)* the accused who made the application is discharged, or
>
> *(b)* if the accused who made the application is committed for trial or ordered to stand trial, the trial is ended.
>
> (2) Where an accused is not represented by counsel at a preliminary inquiry, the justice holding the inquiry shall, prior to the commencement of the taking of evidence at the inquiry, inform the accused of his right to make application under subsection (1).
>
> (3) Every one who fails to comply with an order made pursuant to subsection (1) is guilty of an offence punishable on summary conviction.[15]

Having been actively involved in the successful 1953 campaign to introduce in Northern Ireland similar restraints against pretrial publicity, I take pardonable satisfaction in seeing the reforms embodied in legislation in England and Canada and I wonder how long it will be before the United States follows suit.

---

[14] S. 455 (2).

[15] Criminal Code, R.S.C. 1970, Chapter C.34, S. 467.

COMMENTS ON THE
PAPERS IN SEMINAR

J. Patrick Gunning

I should begin by saying that I know very little about continental European and British criminal procedures. The two papers are, to me, sources of information. There is no way that I could proceed to evaluate them except to say that neither of the authors ventured an opinion about how the contents of his paper could be used in conjunction with this conference. In particular, the question should be asked: How can descriptions of foreign criminal procedures be of help to those who would like to evaluate American criminal procedure?

It does not seem difficult to develop historical or theoretical explanations about why criminal procedures in different countries differ. It is a different matter, however, to use some criterion to argue that one procedure is better than another.

Since this conference is concerned specifically with the use of economic criteria for evaluation, it might be useful to explain generally how an economist would go about the task of evaluation. An economist may be constrained in two very different ways and his analysis will depend crucially upon his constraints. In the first, he is constrained by the task which is defined for him. For example, a politician may ask the economist to determine the effects of certain changes in criminal procedure. In this case, the economist has a straightforward job. He uses his assumption that higher benefits and lower costs encourage certain behavior and that lower benefits and higher costs discourage it. His problem is to find out the extent to which the behavior is influenced by changes in benefits and costs. In the terminology of economics, he seeks to determine the elasticity of supply of the identifiable behavior. Besides determining the elasticity of supply, he must also attempt to account for *all* of the resulting behavior. That is to say, he tries to identify all of the individuals whose behavior would be affected by the proposed change in criminal procedure. As a rule, of course, the economist faces some budgetary limitation. Consequently, he cannot investigate all of the possible behavioral effects. He must make choices concerning which behavior he should investigate and to what extent he should investigate the chosen behavior.

At another level, the economist is asked to evaluate a certain action, say, a change in criminal procedure, and to recommend changes in it on the basis of his evaluation. This is quite a different ballgame, for the economist is now confronted with the task of developing evaluation criteria. He has more responsibility and a wider range of choice. He must not only determine the effects of procedural changes, but he must also choose a criterion to evaluate those effects. Some of the more popular criteria are "the greatest happiness for the greatest number," the largest benefits after the parties who gain from the change compensate, possibly financially, those who lose, and the greatest number of votes on a referendum.

Having provided a brief explanation of what economists do, let me now turn to the two papers and suggest some of the items which might be evaluated. I have listed several questions, the answers to which might be a useful objective of future research:

1. Should a change in procedure be made which raises the extent to which the legal system allows the ends to justify the means? For example, should we permit illegally obtained information to be used as evidence in a court case?

2. To what extent should a judge be a director of proceedings as opposed to a referee in a game between lawyers?

3. What would be the effects of raising or reducing the penalties to the accused of lying in the courtroom?

4. What would be the effects of requiring the judge to select so-called "expert witnesses," instead of allowing such witnesses to be selected by the defense and prosecution?

5. Should courts be centralized or decentralized?

6. What would be the effects of requiring (under legal sanction) the accused to give evidence which may incriminate him?

I shall conclude by saying that it appears that the information available to those who are in a position to change criminal procedures is sparse and frequently incorrect. One who wishes to make changes in criminal procedures ought to have unbiased, reliable information upon which to base his recommendations for change. I believe that the economist is well suited to provide that information. This is not a call for more research money. I am merely saying that *if* one desires to change procedures, he should be willing to pay the price to obtain reliable information upon which to base his recommendations. And the tools of the economist have been developed sufficiently to warrant their use.

Simon Rottenberg

The papers by Messrs. Štěpán and Edwards develop an international comparison of criminal justice systems. They discuss the distribution of authority among police, prosecutors and judges, and differences among countries with respect to rules of procedure, the admissibility of evidence, the right of accused persons to counsel, whether the process has adversary or nonadversary properties, whether charged persons are informed of their rights, the form in which that information is given, and the stage at which the information is given. There are, of course, differences among countries with respect to the whole complex of criminal justice procedures.

Mr. Landes, in his discussion, raised positivist questions. He asked, what consequences can be expected, given the differences among countries in the organization of the system and its processes. I would like to raise normative questions.

How do we know which is the better rule, the better set of procedures or the better system for the organization of the system for the administration of criminal justice, and which are worse?

In order to respond to that question rationally, it seems to me that it is necessary to construct an objective function. One must first define what the social maximand is. Lawyers, judges and presidential candidates tend to talk of the principle of choice among alternative rule systems and organizational systems in terms of "fairness" and "justice," and at least Mr. Edwards's paper refers to things as being more fair and just than others.

I do not know operationally how to define what is fair and just nor can I operationally distinguish what is more fair from less, and what is more just from less. We might poll a random sample of the population and ask, among alternatives, which is thought by them to be more fair but this is no way to settle questions of that kind in honest scholarly discourse. So I should like to suggest another kind of maximand. Suppose what we seek to do is to maximize good behavior or minimize its residual—bad behavior—subject to some cost constraint. What we would then want is to establish some appropriate set of rewards and punishments that would have marginal behavioral effects. It would be a set that would encourage good behavior by rewarding, or at the least refraining from punishing good behavers, and would discourage bad behavior by punishing its perpetrators.

If this is the purpose to be served by the criminal justice system, what is wanted is a set of rules and the systemic organization of arrangements that would tend to maximize the probability that guilty and innocent individuals—bad and good behavers—are correctly distinguished and identified, per unit of cost of administration of the system. We would then have a standard for knowing which rules are better, and which worse, and which organizational systems are better, and which worse. The preference test would be whether, for given cost, a change in the rules would more correctly distinguish the guilty from the innocent.

The correct slotting of individuals into the guilty and innocent sets is, of course, essential to the efficient operation of a rewards-punishments system. We need only think of the alternatives to perceive the consequences. Suppose individuals were chosen from the population at random in the distribution of punishment. Or suppose the process of choice were perverse so that the guilty were systematically rewarded and the innocent were systematically punished. Clearly, the outcomes in both cases would be to enlarge the quantity of bad behavior occurring in society. The random distribution of punishment among individuals would not produce disincentives for bad behavior; whether or not an individual behaved well, he would have an equal chance with all others of having punishment inflicted upon him. The systematically perverse distribution of punishment would give even worse results; individuals would be given an incentive to behave badly because only in this way could they increase the probability that they would escape punishment or be rewarded.

If the social purpose is defined as the maximization of good behavior, it would be ill-served by either of these alternatives. Therefore, any rule of the criminal justice process that tends to bring either of these alternatives into being also ill-serves that purpose. If a rule does not assist in distinguishing the guilty from the innocent and is neutral with respect to the drawing of that distinction, it will tend to cause punishment to be randomly distributed. If a rule has perverse effects and tends to cause the guilty to be classified as innocent and the innocent to be classified as guilty, it will cause punishment to be perversely distributed. Such rules will, in both cases, cause the production of a greater quantum of bad behavior than would some alternative rule which possessed more efficient classifying power.

Thus, a test is suggested for the rational response to such questions as whether the accused should have the right to representation by counsel, whether evidence of a particular kind should be admissible, whether charged persons should be warned of their rights, whether processes should be adversary in form, et cetera. The test is whether the procedure or arrangement will or will not distinguish the guilty from the innocent more efficiently than would some alternative procedure, since such a distinction is the essential first step to the appropriate allocation of punishment among individuals, and that allocation is essential to the achievement of a cost-constrained maximization of good behavior.

It might be objected that some procedures are objectionable per se, even if they *are* efficient taxonomic instruments for the slotting of guilty and innocent. For example, it might be said that the extraction of information by the application of hot irons to bare flesh is not tolerable whatever its efficiency, and that, if the burning of flesh is not to be permitted, this implies that other less intense and graphic procedures may also be implicitly proscribed and that some other criterion than efficiency must also govern in the contrivance of the procedural arrangement.

This may well be. Perhaps it does not suffice to define the social maximand as the maximization of good behavior, subject to a cost constraint, but rather that it is subject to a cost *and some other* constraint. It then would become necessary for protagonists of this view to define the additional constraint and indeed, to value it, in some units of measure that would permit a trade-off calculus to be computed between it and increments of good behavior that would be foregone as a consequence of the application of the new constraint.

But it may not be necessary to go this route. The burning of flesh may not be consistent with efficiency. Innocent persons may soon learn that they can keep hot irons at bay by pleading guilt. Hot irons, then, would not be efficient instruments for correctly distinguishing the innocent from the guilty, but precisely their opposite; they cause both innocent and guilty to confess guilt.

Similarly with respect to the whole gamut of procedural rules that are sometimes said to inhibit the police and prosecutors: police and prosecutors, as agents of the state, have the legal capacity to administer violence and coercive constraint. Like others, they have their foibles. If they had completely free hands, some of them would employ their power to punish the innocent for reasons of personal animus that have no relevance to the systemic control of socially and legally defined bad behavior. Therefore, to assure that the innocent and guilty are correctly identified, police and prosecutors must have less than perfect power; their hands must be somewhat tied.

It may be that I have not correctly defined the object that is sought to be served in the design of the criminal justice system. If I have not, some other object must be sought. In the absence of defining the object, however, it is not possible to rank-order procedural criminal justice system rules. It does not suffice to say that we seek fair and just procedures unless the words "fair" and "just" can be made operational.

William M. Landes

The purpose of a session on foreign criminal procedure is not simply to acquaint persons with alternative legal systems but to stimulate an analysis of the possible effects and the desirability of incorporating particular elements of foreign procedure into the American criminal justice system. To make judgments of this kind, one requires knowledge of both foreign criminal procedure and the effects these procedures have on behavior. The papers by Professor Edwards and Dr. Štěpán provide information of the first sort, and the authors are to be commended for their clear and concise descriptions of criminal procedures in Great Britain and Europe. Unfortunately, neither of these papers goes beyond the descriptive stage. We are left unenlightened as to whether the differences between American and foreign procedures result in significant differences in actual behavior. Nor are we given, in the absence of empirical analysis, any attempt by the authors to develop the implications or to make predictions about the likely effects on behavior of procedural differences. The authors are lawyers and not economists and this may explain their reluctance to pursue this type of analysis. The questions I have posed require one to utilize the theoretical and quantitative techniques of economics rather than the traditional methods of legal scholarship. In this paper I illustrate the economic approach to legal studies by examining three important differences between foreign and American criminal procedure which are described by Professor Edwards and Dr. Štěpán: the use of private prosecutors in Great Britain, the absence of plea bargaining and guilty pleas in Europe, and the weaker exclusionary rules for evidence in Europe. I attempt to formulate hypotheses on the behavioral effects of these procedural differences, and to suggest empirical tests of these hypotheses.

Private Prosecutors

The system of public prosecutors does not exist in England. For serious crimes, prosecution is left in the hands of private counsels appointed for individual cases. The investigation of the crime and the accumulation of evidence are the responsibilities of the police, while the presentation of the case in court is the responsibility of the prosecutor. These arrangements contrast with the American system where public prosecutors (that is, district attorneys) are the rule, and both the accumulation of evidence and prosecution are the primary responsibilities of the public prosecutor. In evaluating these differences two questions must be answered. Are the differences more apparent than real? What are their actual effects on behavior? The two questions are related since an indirect method of answering the first is to determine if the predicted effects on behavior of utilizing private instead of public prosecutors are empirically significant.

In examining the difference between private and public prosecutors, the relationship between the structure of incentives and performance by a prosecutor should be analyzed. Do barristers who act as prosecutors in England tend to specialize in prosecuting cases and derive a substantial fraction of their earnings from this activity? Are barristers who have a greater rate of successful prosecutions appointed as prosecutors more frequently than the less successful ones in criminal prosecutions? Is the advancement of district attorneys in the United States dependent on successful prosecutions and convictions? If the answers to these questions based on empirical evidence are affirmative, then in both England and the United States we have a class of prosecutors whose wealth will tend to be maximized by demonstrating their ability to convict defendants, and hence the distinction between private and public prosecutors will have little effect on the incentives to convict defendants.

A number of implications and testable hypotheses can be derived from the difference between separating or combining the functions of investigation and prosecution.[1] When these activities are combined, one might expect a greater reluctance on the part of the prosecutor to dismiss a case, particularly when large sums have been spent on investigation. Dismissal is an acknowledgment of error on the part of the prosecutor and his staff. The cost of this error is positively related to the expenditures on the investigation. Dismissal may also produce adverse effects on the morale of the district attorney's staff in charge of investigating and accumulating evidence. In contrast, when investigation is not the responsibility of the prosecution, there is less reason for the prosecution to concern itself with expenditures already undertaken for investigation or with the morale of investigators. Hence, we would predict higher dismissal rates when investigation and prosecution are separated than when they are combined, and the difference in dismissal rates would be more significant in cases involving large expenditures on investigation.[2] As a corollary, when investigation and prosecution are combined we might expect a greater use of settlements (and possibly the development of methods of settling) that avoid the acknowledgment of error when it appears that the evidence is insufficient to convict the defendant in a trial. I have in mind a plea of guilty to a minor offense together with a negligible penalty, such as probation or a small fine.

The predicted differences between the English and American systems would not show up if the formal separation of investigation from prosecution were not an actual separation as well. To the extent that prosecutors and investigators collude so that each internalizes the interests of the other, the English and American systems would be operationally equivalent. The empirical tests described above would present indirect evidence on this point. For example, a finding of no significant difference in the dismissal rates between the two systems, when other relevant factors are held constant, would be consistent with the collusion hypothesis.

Plea Bargaining and Guilty Pleas

The near absence in Europe of both plea bargaining and guilty pleas is cited by Dr. Štěpán as an important difference between American and Continental criminal procedure. In Europe the typical procedure consists of an investigation or inquisitorial stage, during which evidence is acquired in part from the suspect himself, followed by an oral judicial trial. In the United States most criminal cases are disposed of before trial (in the range of 90 percent for felonies and an even higher percent for misdemeanors) by either a guilty plea or a dismissal of the charges.

---

[1] These implications are based on an analysis by Richard Posner of the effects of combining investigation, prosecution, and adjudication in an administrative agency. See his "The Behavior of Administrative Agencies," *The Journal of Legal Studies,* vol. 1 (June 1972).

[2] In practice it may be difficult to test this hypothesis because of numerous other factors that also affect the dismissal rate (for example, the prosecution's budget, the volume of cases to be prosecuted, the amount of discretion prosecutors have in dismissing cases, and court delay).

In a recent paper, I worked out in detail the conditions under which either a pretrial settlement or a trial will take place.[3] In brief, a necessary condition for a voluntary settlement is that both the prosecutor and defendant gain more from a settlement in comparison to the expected outcome of a trial (that is, the utility is higher from a settlement than a trial). It followed from this condition that a large proportion of cases would be settled, given that the costs of conducting a trial exceeded the costs of settling, the prosecutor and the defense were in general agreement on the expected outcome of the trial, and neither party had a strong preference for risk. From the defendant's viewpoint, a guilty plea saves him legal and other costs, avoids the uncertainty of a trial, and results in a lower sentence (often through a plea to a lesser charge than the original) than he would have received if convicted by trial.

Although American and Continental procedures for disposing of criminal cases appear to be different (that is, settlements predominate in the former and trials in the latter), one can argue that in actuality they are nearly equivalent. This is because the investigation phase of Continental procedure that is directed toward extracting a confession from the suspect is analogous to the bargaining that produces guilty pleas in the United States. According to Dr. Štěpán, confessions are extracted by some form of psychological pressure aimed at breaking down the suspect. I would offer another alternative. As an inducement to confess, the defendant receives a lighter penalty than he would receive if he does not confess and is convicted in a trial. There does not have to be an explicit bargain between the prosecutor and the defendant. It is sufficient that the courts operate in a manner to reward defendants who have confessed with lighter sentences, and that this fact be known to defendants. We would predict that European trials in which a confession has been made in the investigation stage would take little time, since the defendant's guilt has already been established. Trials for these defendants would be similar to the formal proceedings before a judge in the United States for defendants who plead guilty. If my hypothesis is correct, then confessions in European criminal procedure serve the same purpose as guilty pleas in American procedure. The distinction between the two would be primarily one of terminology and not substance. This is not surprising since the forces I cited as producing guilty pleas (for example, savings in resources, avoidance of risk, and agreement on the expected trial outcome) would operate on the Continent to produce confessions.

A recent paper by Casper and Zeisel on German criminal procedure presents some empirical evidence on confessions that is consistent with my hypothesis.[4] Of the 1200 cases in their sample, there were full or partial confessions in nearly 70 percent of the cases. Ninety percent of the confessions were made before the

[3] See William M. Landes, "An Economic Analysis of the Courts," *The Journal of Law and Economics,* vol. 14 (April 1971).

[4] See Gerhard Casper and Hans Zeisel, "Lay Judges in the German Criminal Courts," *The Journal of Legal Studies,* vol. 1 (January 1972).

trial, and in only one case was the confession not upheld in the subsequent trial. Moreover, the trials were relatively short when the defendant had confessed prior to the trial. This evidence, though limited, suggests that confessions are quantitatively important and play a role similar to that of guilty pleas in the disposition of cases.

Additional empirical research is necessary to establish the equivalence or near equivalence between confessions and guilty pleas. I would propose the following testable hypotheses. First, for comparable crimes, defendants who confess will receive lighter sentences than those who are found guilty but do not confess. Second, the likelihood of going to trial in Europe without a confession would be positively related (1) to the extent of disagreement over the expected trial outcome (disagreement can be measured by the clarity and consistency of previous decisions on similar cases), (2) the severity of the crime as measured by the potential sentence, and (3) the degree of subsidization of the defendant's legal fees. Last, the likelihood of going to trial in Europe would be inversely related to the length and unpleasantness of pretrial detention.[5]

Rules of Evidence

Let us consider differences in rules of evidence for our final example. It is well known that there are weaker exclusionary rules for producing evidence in European trials than American trials. Other things being constant, the weaker the exclusionary rules the higher, on average, is the probability of convicting a defendant. Two hypotheses can be derived from this inverse relation, and both are amenable to empirical analysis. First, the greater the probability of conviction, the smaller the reduction in sentence for those who plead guilty or confess compared to the sentence (if found guilty) in the absence of a plea or confession.[6] Therefore, the sentence received by persons who settle (that is, confess or plead guilty) relative to the sentence received by persons who do not settle but are found guilty of similar offenses would be higher in Europe than in the United States. The magnitude of the predicted difference between European and American sentencing will depend directly on the extent of the differences in exclusionary rules. Second, assuming that the prosecutor requires a minimum value of the probability of conviction in order to prosecute, we would expect that the difference in exclusionary rules would lead to a higher rate of dismissals in the United States than in European countries.[7]

---

[5] In my "Economic Analysis of the Courts," I develop these hypotheses in more detail.

[6] Ibid., pp. 64-67.

[7] The above empirical tests require more sophistication than indicated because other factors must be held constant. In particular, the resources available to the prosecutor will affect the probability of conviction, and it may be that stricter exclusionary rules are offset by greater budgetary allocations to prosecutors in the United States.

Concluding Remarks

I have outlined a number of testable hypotheses to determine the actual effects of differences between American and foreign criminal procedure. My own research on American criminal procedure indicates that data are generally available to test hypotheses on the legal system although the data are limited in quantity and less systematically collected than most economic data. The obvious social importance of criminal procedure and the scarcity of empirical research in this area suggest that the returns from empirical research will be substantial.

LIST OF
CONFERENCE PARTICIPANTS

Allen, Harry E., *Professor, Ohio State University*

Anderson, Mrs. Annelise, *The Hoover Institution on War, Revolution and Peace*

Bailey, William C., *Professor, The Cleveland State University*

Brito, Dagobert L., *Professor, University of Wisconsin at Madison*

Broussalian, Vartkes, *National Bureau of Standards*

Buchanan, James M., *Professor, Virginia Polytechnic Institute and State University*

Burnett, Arthur L., *U.S. Magistrate for the District of Columbia*

Butts, Joseph G., *American Enterprise Institute*

Canes, Michael, *Center for Naval Analyses*

Cobb, William E., *West Virginia Tax Department*

Cohen, Albert, *Professor, University of Connecticut*

Dwyer, Jean F., *U.S. Magistrate for the District of Columbia*

Edwards, John Ll. J., *Professor, University of Toronto*

Erickson, Edward W., *Professor, North Carolina State University*

Erickson, Maynard, *Professor, University of Arizona*

Feldman, Paul, *The Public Research Institute*

Flowers, Marilyn R., *Virginia Polytechnic Institute and State University*

Fuqua, Paul, *Police Science Services*

Gasper, Louis C., *Professor, University of Arizona*

Gibbs, Jack P., *Professor, University of Texas at Austin*

Gordon, Richard, *Treasury Department*

Gunning, J. Patrick, Jr., *Professor, Virginia Polytechnic Institute and State University*

Hines, Howard, *National Science Foundation*

Horton, Paul B., *Professor, Western Michigan University*

Huszagh, Frederick, *National Science Foundation*

Ianni, Francis A. J., *Professor, Columbia University*

Ireland, Thomas R., *Professor, University of Wisconsin at Milwaukee*

Jeffrey, C. R., *Professor, Florida State University*

Johnson, David B., *Professor, Louisiana State University*

Johnson, Thomas F., *American Enterprise Institute*

Klein, Benjamin, *National Bureau of Economic Research*

Krohm, Gregory, *Professor, Virginia Polytechnic Institute and State University*

Landes, William, *National Bureau of Economic Research*

Larkins, Dan, *American Enterprise Institute*

Lejins, Peter P., *Professor, University of Maryland*

Leyden, Dennis R., *Professor, West Virginia University*

Logan, Charles H., *Professor, University of Connecticut*

Margolis, Lawrence S., *U.S. Magistrate for the District of Columbia*

Meiselman, David, *Professor, Virginia Polytechnic Institute and State University*

Moskowitz, Dan B., *McGraw-Hill Publications*

McKenzie, Richard B., *Professor, Radford College*

McKnew, Charles R., *Professor, West Virginia University*

Nelms, Henning, *The Pioneer Foundation*

Niskanen, William A., *Professor, University of California at Berkeley*

Phillips, Llad, *Professor, University of California at Santa Barbara*

Rottenberg, Simon, *Dean, University of Massachusetts*

Rubin, Paul H., *Professor, University of Georgia*

Santarelli, Donald E., *Associate Deputy Attorney General of the United States*

Slott, Irving, *Department of Justice*

Solomon, Henry, *Professor, The George Washington University*

Štěpán, Jan, *Research Librarian, Harvard Law School Library*

Stringer, Thomas C., Jr., *State Board of Corrections (Georgia)*

Sullivan, Richard F., *Professor, Carleton University, Ottawa*

Thaler, Richard, *Professor, University of Rochester*

Tittle, Charles R., *Professor, Florida Atlantic University*

Tullock, Gordon, *Professor, Virginia Polytechnic Institute and State University*

Voorhees, Theodore, *Attorney, Washington, D. C.*

Votey, Harold L., *Professor, University of California*

Zalba, Serapio R., *Professor, The Cleveland State University*